LEARNING THE RULES

THE GUILFORD SERIES ON PERSONAL RELATIONSHIPS

Steve Duck, Series Editor
Department of Communication Studies,
The University of Iowa

LEARNING THE RULES

The Anatomy
of Children's Relationships

BRIAN J. BIGELOW
GEOFFREY TESSON
JOHN H. LEWKO

THE GUILFORD PRESS
New York London

© 1996 The Guilford Press
A Division of Guilford Publications, Inc.
72 Spring Street, New York, NY 10012

Printed in the United States of America

This book is printed on acid-free paper.

Last digit is print number: 9   8   7   6   5   4   3   2   1

Library of Congress Cataloging-in-Publication Data
Bigelow, Brian J.
    Learning the rules : the anatomy of children's relationships /
Brian J. Bigelow, Geoffrey Tesson, John H. Lewko.
        p.   cm. — (The Guilford series on personal relationships)
    Includes bibliographical references and index.
    ISBN 1–57230–084–1
    1. Friendship in children.   2. Social interaction in children.
3. Interpersonal relations in children.   4. Children—Family
relationships.   I. Tesson, Geoffrey.   II. Lewko, John H.
III. Title.   IV. Series.
HQ784.F7B54   1996
302.3′4′083—dc20   96-15609
                                                                        CIP

Acknowledgments

No one is an island unto oneself, and this is particularly true with this book. We are especially indebted to James Youniss, whose intellectual and personal guidance to "the boys from Canada" was (and is) indispensable, and to Steve Duck, whose encouraging editorial guidance gave us the necessary energy and insight to complete our task. We are also grateful to John La Gaipa, whose supervisory influence on the first author has for two decades been like expanding ripples in a pond. To be sure, we are also thankful to the Sudbury Board of Education and their students for their generous cooperation. Also worthy of appreciation are Kate Pautler and Phyllis Davison for their dedicated interviewing, Rhonda Sandberg for her painstaking help with the manuscript; Claudette Larcher, Rejeanne Prpic, and Shirley Fletcher for their patience with seemingly endless revisions, and certainly Valerie Bigelow, who made her husband write things that could actually be read.

The research on which this publication is based was supported by a grant to John Lewko, Brian Bigelow, and Geoffrey Tesson from the Social Sciences and Humanities Research Council of Canada, Family and Socialization, of the Child Strategic Grant Program.

The first author would also like to acknowledge the energy and dedication of his coauthors, without whom this creative synergy would not have come to pass.

Preface

We only know ourselves and others through our relationships. This is a book about children's relationships, what they mean, and how children manage them. We share the position expressed by Duck (e.g., 1991a, 1994) that the world is in need of interpretation and that people actually construct their own personal versions of events principally by sharing these meanings through talk. This is especially true of relationships. By talking with children about their relationships, we learned a lot about how they conceptualize and govern those relationships.

A meaningful social relationship, then, consists in large measure of mutually constructed attempts to order the relationship, which Youniss (1978) termed "social rules." For example, Youniss (1980) characterized children's peer relationships as "co-constructed," whereby the checks and balances of freely expressed opinions are validated through cooperation (Piaget, 1932/1965) and mutual consensus (Sullivan, 1953). Social rules are the "grammar" of social relationships (Haste, 1987). By examining social rules across several relationships, we were in a privileged position from which to examine the interplay between the overarching structures of authority and cooperation, on the one hand, and the supportive features of a relationship that transcend these structures, on the other.

We also viewed children's personal and social relationships as prototypic of adult ones: adults "create meaning from chaos" (Duck, 1991a), and even infants struggle to order their world (see Fogel, 1993). After all, an advantage in addressing issues from a developmental perspective is that more mature and complex adolescent (Tesson, Lewko, & Bigelow, 1990) and adult phenomena can then be seen in their earlier nascent forms, bringing into sharper focus the elemental processes that govern them. It is for this reason that a work such as this is important for our understanding of relationships in general and should not then be dismissed by students of adult relationships as simply a book "about children."

Because we argue that children's social rules are relationally embedded (Chapter 1), sensitive to the prevailing social order (Chapter 2), and derived from children's personal constructions of relationships (Chapter 3), it is essential for us to present our argument in reference to this sequence of issues. The origins and meanings of the social rules reported in Chapters 4, 5, and 6 will then be properly understood.

As we explain in Chapter 1, we were also quite aware that the literature on children's social relationships has been effectively dominated, if not somewhat distracted, by behavioral social skills approaches to peer relationships that, while contributing enormously to our understanding of peer social competence, have left vacant a considerable landscape of social meaning, namely, the child's conceptual representation of *relationships* with peers and other significant persons and of how those relationships work. Children's conceptual representations of relationships are important in their own right and are large segments of children's meaningful social experiences. Any externally observed behavior can be socially understood only in light of the child's construction of the relationship out of which the behavior springs. Given the prominence of peer relationships in the literature on child development, we felt that it was fitting to begin here by illustrating the need for a reexamination of interpersonal relationships, using friendship as a prototype.

Social scientists, and more particularly students of personal and social relationships, must inevitably come to terms with the need to examine the fuller social context within which interpersonal events occur. We argue that social rules are implicitly shared models of dealing with relationships within the context of a wider social order (Bronfenbrenner, 1979). The meaning of each social relationship is then only properly revealed by examining its content in light of the other relationships or domains (e.g., family, peers, nonfamily adults) within which the relationship is embedded. A sociology of childhood is sensitive to the social and community contexts that are represented in a child's construction of face-to-face encounters (see, e.g., Corsaro & Rizzo, 1988). Only by taking this contextualistic "high road," can we claim to have captured any of the real meaning of interpersonal events.

As we illustrate in Chapter 3, the sense of a social world as one which is structured and rule governed is nothing new and appears with a certain regularity in the literature on phenomenology. Both Youniss (1980) and Fogel (1993) have described social relating in "coregulated" terms. Fogel has claimed that cognition itself is relational and that coregulation is a product of the blending of joint actions that mutually creates a set of social actions. Thus, social rules are discovered patterns of acting and thinking about how we relate to other people; in Fogel's terms, social rules are ways in which children "frame" their experiences with others and with the world at large: "Cultural activity will emerge via the child's own creative solutions to everyday problems" (p. 14). Thus, our notion of a social rule is not a static, codified one; rather, it is reflective of the dynamic process of social understanding.

At one juncture, one of us quipped that we were in search of the periodic table of social development. While fanciful, this comment contained a kernel of truth. We chose social rules as our unifying unit of analysis because those rules address how children develop conceptual schemes to manage their personal and social relationships, since these are the principal contextual conditions that drive children's construction of social reality. Our essential frustration in dealing with the science of relationships was that developmental psychology, social psychology, and sociology, unlike our sister disciplines in the life sciences, have not yet discovered their elementary units of analysis. In investigating children's interpersonal relationships, there is no such "periodic table," anatomy, or other form of classification that is universally used. There have been genuine attempts at such compendiums for adults (e.g., Argyle & Henderson, 1985) but not for children. A first step in our research, therefore, was to empirically identify the rules in children's relationships. Attempts to scientifically characterize children's social lives without first addressing the rule-and-relationship matrix are misleading.

Social rules were extracted through presentation of our recursive interviewing technique, which was adapted from the work of George Kiss (1972), without whom this endeavor would not have been possible. Recursive concept analysis is a "theory-neutral" information-processing approach that we adapted to unearth children's social rules. To our knowledge, there has been no other method that is as rigorous or as exhaustive and that provides a viable technology for examining how children manage their social and personal relationships. A cornerstone of our approach is that such in-depth interviewing is indispensable if we are to probe the deep structure of children's social rules and relationships.

Our social rule repertoire contains a set of alternative "macro-themes" designed to achieve some personal aim, such as "*compliance*" and "*autonomy*": "following rules," showing deference," "pleasing others," "avoiding and ignoring others," and "being assertive"; "*self-control*" and "*conflict management*": "not upsetting others," "controlling feelings," "expressing feelings," "figuring others out," and "repairing relational damage"; as well as "*mutual activities*" and "*obligation*": "being sociable," "helping others," "talking," "reciprocating," and "being loyal and trustworthy." These themes are also addressed "microscopically," as particular rules and sample rule strategies, in order to grasp the finer, subtler senses in which a particular personal or social relationship is governed and what that given relationship means.

Since the childhood literature that addresses the above themes generally speaks to either specific relationships (e.g., peers, parents, friends) or specific issues (e.g., conflict, intimacy) and seldom uses social rule content that is constructed by the participants themselves, our data provide a scope and perspective that is currently lacking in the relationship literature. By inspecting the broad differences and more subtle nuances in children's usage of social rules within and between types of relationships, our findings provide a characterization of parents, friends, and siblings that comes to terms with relationships as living systems, with all their boundaries and built-in redundancies. In so doing, we were entertained by a host of "relationship talk" that revealed children as keen "relationship philosophers" in their own right. Children are fully aware that different relationships have different goals and that knowledge of the self is only possible through interaction with others (Sullivan, 1953). Through children's social rules and rationales, we discover how children's personal and social relationships are structured in practice.

Contents

List of Figures and Tables

FIGURES

TABLES

CHAPTER 1

Social Competency and Friendships in Middle Childhood

"LORD OF THE FLIES" REVISITED

This book is about relationships and how children manage them. It also presents a method, a phenomenology of social rules, that permits meaningful comparisons among different kinds of relationships. Unless researchers producing literature in children's peer relations devote more time and energy to examining what children's relationships consist of and how they work, we will not be in a position to address the normative order of childhood relationships (see Chapter 2). Duck (1990) has identified this as *the* key question for the field of personal relationships in general. Meaningful comparisons of relationships must address the ways in which they are actually constructed and represented by their participants. The social rules approach that we advocate in this book accomplishes this goal.

It is fitting that we begin by asserting our philosophical position, which is that much, if not most, of what constitutes a *relationship* lies in the meaning that its members accord to it (Bigelow, 1977; Duck, 1994). The constructions of participants contain within them the constituent parts or rules that are, in our view, the building blocks of meaningful social life. An examination and analysis of children's social rules is by definition a task sensitive to relationships, revealing children as participants in the wider social order. And they have to actively construct their role in that social order. By demonstrating the value of children's constructions and rules and viewing them as an integral part of their relational phenomenologies, we may then find ourselves in a favorable

1

position from which to understand how children govern their social behavior within and between the nominal types of relationships (e.g., with parent, siblings, friend, teacher) that figure so prominently in their social lives. Our academic approach is, therefore, not a common one because (as we explain in the next chapter) attempts to integrate both psychological and sociological perspectives on children's relationships and social rules (Youniss, 1978) are not common; but our approach holds, we believe, great promise.

A contextual approach that locates a given relationship in the context of others is necessary even if all one wishes to understand are the key features of a single relationship, such as friendship. Newcomb and Bagwell (1995) claim that the study of friendship, which many would regard as a "flagship" of relationships, would significantly benefit from such a comparative exercise. And although we are interested in social rule distributions across various relationships, because friendship can be viewed in many ways as an archetypal relationship, an examination of its salient features is an excellent starting point for an examination of personal relationships in general.

As we will reveal in Chapters 4, 5, and 6, our examinations of children's friendships can be broadly compared to studies of children's conceptions of friendship and peer relationships, since the rules of friendship are often embedded, at least implicitly, within such descriptions. Indeed, at times, particular social rules (e.g., loyalty) were actually first thought to be mere friendship expectations (Bigelow & La Gaipa, 1975); in this volume we unveil friendship expectations in their fullness of form and function as organized sets of social rules.

FRIENDSHIP

Children's friendships provide an excellent focus for reintroducing the importance of relationships in general. We assert that conceptualizations of relationships have considerable validity as a basis for analysis. However, research on children's social *behavior*, whether of peer relationships and "friendship" (e.g., Newcomb & Bagwell, 1995) or of social status (see, e.g., Asher & Coie, 1990), has virtually dominated the field of peer relationships. By research on behavior, we mean either direct observations, self-reports, or reports of the behavior of others, rather than reports of relational properties by participants (see Newcomb & Bagwell, 1995). When "friendship" is investigated behaviorally, it is, in our view, popularity in disguise, since the conceptually meaningful features of the relationship are not sufficiently addressed. As Bukowski and Hoza (1989) have cogently argued, popularity is not friendship.

The prominence of children's peer *relationships* has therefore been overshadowed, often missing the very conceptual material out of which relationships are formed. An appreciation of children's relationships and how children represent those relationships is indispensable if we are to lay a proper foundation for capturing the *meaning* of children's social behavior in relation to the social order. The importance of meaning is reflected in sensitivity to developmental change. When children and adolescents represent their friendship *relations,* there is a greater sensitivity to age change that is lower when contrasted with friendship *behaviors* in isolation (Newcomb & Bagwell, 1995).

As we show in the following chapters, children's representations of their relationships often show a sensitivity to the broader social order. The meaning of a social relationship is grounded in the context in which it is located (Duck, 1994). Consequently, to grasp the meaningful character of children's social relationships we must see those relationships as elements of an interlinked matrix of different relationships that, together with the context furnished by particular situations, defines the rules that govern the relationships. This chapter's task is to illustrate the importance of children's relationships by examining the properties of friendship.

As a useful metaphor, Golding's (1954) novel *Lord of the Flies*, without benefit of the modern social science literature, was in our view prescient of two current themes in the peer relationships literature: sociometry (i.e., social status, social skills, social acceptance) and friendship (i.e., close friends, chumships), each of which addresses different aspects of social competency. The distinctions between these various aspects of peer experience in the character developments of this novel, particularly the crosscurrents of popularity and peer acceptance, as well as friendships, set the stage for a fresh look at the peer literature, especially in reference to relationships and how children manage them.

As the reader may recall, the main characters in Golding's novel (Piggy, Ralph, Simon, and Jack), together with their schoolmates, are shipwrecked on a deserted island without adult supervision. The boys, who differ in age and personality, set about to organize their lives as prospects of rescue grow dim. They develop relationships with one another that are often at variance with their acceptance by the larger group. The plot progressively thickens as the main characters assume their various positions in the pecking order of the island. Mirroring the divisions mentioned above that appear in the literature on children's peer relationships, the boys are partitioned interpersonally and intrapsychically in regard to group acceptance and popularity, on the one hand, and emergent friendships, on the other.

Piggy mirrors the profile of the submissive, unassertive and chronically victimized boy (Schwartz, Dodge, & Coie, 1993). Nearsighted and overweight, Piggy is the most nurturant and responsible child, who develops a mutually supportive friendship with Ralph, who is unlike Piggy in every outward way, including initial acceptance by the wider group. Ralph is like the popular child, helpful and appropriate (Coie & Kupersmidt, 1983; Dodge & Coie, 1982). However, Piggy is eventually treated as an outcast by the aggressive and dominant Jack (see Coie, Dodge, Terry, & Wright, 1991; Pettit, Bakshi, Dodge, & Coie, 1990) and his band of followers, who ultimately orchestrate Piggy's violent death. Jack's hostile manner escalates and leads him and his gang to reject Ralph and his mild-mannered followers. As time unfolds, and in spite of his insensitivity and lack of meaningful dyadic relationships, Jack eventually takes over the island.

Golding's (1954) novel was written over 40 years ago, at about the same time that the first serious attempts (see, e.g., Sullivan, 1953) were being made to identify the features of children's friendships. While interest in children's friendship relations has surfaced from time to time since then (see, e.g., Bigelow & La Gaipa, 1975; Furman & Bierman, 1984; Reisman & Shorr, 1978), the larger focus has been on social skills and sociometrically measured group acceptance (see, e.g., Oden & Asher, 1977), not friendships per se (on friendship formation, see Gottman, 1983).

Social status research, as modern sociometry is now called, defines children variously by their acceptance within the larger peer group (see Gresham, 1981), as shown, for example, by ratings of desirability as playmates, of "likability," and of mutual likability (see, e.g., Howes, 1990; Peery, 1979; King & Young, 1981), as well as by ratings as best friends and by nominations for favorable roles in a class play (Bower, 1969; King & Young, 1985; Pellegrini, 1985). Levels of acceptance are generally used to partition children into popular, accepted, rejected, isolate, and controversial categories. Levels of group acceptance are often also linked to behavioral manifestations of social skills (see, e.g., Pellegrini, 1985), and for this reason social acceptance is taken as a measure of peer competency.

Social acceptance is unarguably a vital aspect of social competency. Being a social outcast has its share of problems, especially for a child during the formative peer-oriented times of middle childhood. Valuable social interactions are missed, skills are not exchanged, and the self is left unexamined. On the other hand, while it may be an asset to be popular, it is erroneous to claim that popular children are necessarily better able to function within a friendship or that lack of peer acceptance necessarily results from social incompetency. One need only study the characteristics of "Piggy"—who, we must acknowledge, has many real-world counterparts—to appreciate the possibility that social ostracism may be based on factors quite distinct from social sensitivity and maturity. Even though Piggy had a meaningful relationship with Ralph, which allowed them both to understand each other and to make sense of their existence, Piggy was socially inept within the context of Jack's gang, since his maturity offered him no effective defense against hostility. But are we to define social competency purely as acceptance by the group? Was Jack an example of a socially successful boy?

Unlike our imaginary castaways, can we comfort ourselves with the fact that most real children are not stranded on a deserted island where they have to fend entirely for themselves without adult supervision? We think not, because real children may be isolated from adult authority to some extent by the social island of peer relationships. As children get older, their peer relationships do become progressively more independent of adults (Ellis, Rogoff, & Cromer, 1981) and of adults' authority (Piaget & Inhelder, 1956; Sullivan, 1953; Youniss, 1980) and exist largely on their own terms (Berndt & Hoyle, 1985; Tisak, 1986). So, perhaps the lessons of Piggy may not be so far-fetched after all and may have some bearing on real-life peer relationships.

Even though friendship is largely independent of popularity, much of the child development literature still equates popularity skills with social competency, as if social competency were simply a collection of prosocial actions. Relationships are often ignored in the bargain. Moreover, some perceptive researchers have found it difficult to avoid the topic of relationships even when researchers are attempting to deal exclusively with group acceptance. Parker and Asher (1993) and Bukowski and Hoza (1989) have indicated that commonly used sociometric measures of acceptance are confounded with friendship. By having children limit their liking or friendship nominations to a few other children (e.g., "Name your three best friends"), we don't know if the liked peer, or even one nominated as a friend, is really a person with whom the child has a functional relationship or is simply someone who is nice to the child and who has attractive mannerisms and valued social skills.

To sharpen the point, children may have real friends (as opposed to those whom they simply nominate as being liked a lot) who possess some undesirable attributes (Parker & Asher, 1993). It may also come as a surprise to learn that some popular children don't have close friendships and that some unpopular children do (see, e.g., Parker & Asher, 1993). We also think that whether or not they are part of a sociometric study, friendship nomination procedures are formatted in such a way as to take for granted that all children have a coherent notion of what a friendship is before the children make their choices. We argue later on in this chapter that this is a risky assumption indeed. It is simply not sufficient to have a reciprocal mutual nomination as a measure of friendship (see, e.g.,

Bukowski & Hoza, 1989), one also needs to examine its conceptual content—its meaning.

If friendship were simply a collection of social skills, then its normative basis could be inferred by examining aspects of acceptance and rejection as extreme instances of the normative relational order. With few exceptions (e.g., antisocial behavior), such is not generally the case. In principle, a child's position on the peer acceptance and rejection scale ranges all the way from being very popular, positively radiating social grace and charm, to being an outright antisocial outcast, deficient in the most rudimentary of social skills (see, e.g., Asher & Gottman, 1981). One is tempted to conclude, with some justification, that children with better social skills development are more accepted by their peers.

It might also be said that, by virtue of their greater interactional skills, socially fluent popular children should have a more differentiated sense of friendships than their less well accepted counterparts have. As logical as this linear premise may appear, recent investigations (see, e.g., Bichard, Alden, Walker, & McMahon, 1988; Parker, & Asher, 1993; Pellarin, 1988) have found little or no linkage between peer nominations (i.e., popular, accepted, rejected, neglected) and the maturity or overall quality of children's conceptions of friendship. While Parker and Asher (1993) found selected differences in the rated qualities (e.g., validation and caring) of low-accepted children's friendships, this finding sheds little light on how much low-accepted children understand friendship or how much they value their friendships. Perhaps the criteria for these two aspects are different. For example, Dodge, Price, and Coie (1990) have observed that boys in mutually aggressive relationships tend to dislike each other to a higher degree than children in other kinds of relationships, but form friendships with each other anyway.

Taken at face value, then, these findings paint what some may feel to be a disconcerting picture, since the findings suggest that conceptual understanding of friendship and satisfaction with friendship as a mode of relating do not have a necessarily causal relationship to social acceptance and social skills development and are therefore not really important discriminators of individual social competency. Such *conclusions*, however, *ignore the fact* that friendship in its own right is a vital component of social development and that not all children have satisfying friendships (see, e.g., Berndt, 1981; McGuire & Weisz, 1982; Parker & Asher, 1993), no matter how skilled or popular they may be.

One can argue then that friendship knowledge and the rules that constitute friendship and other relationships may result from separate and unique sets of relational experiences that have given rise to them independently of other forms of social competency. Until now, precious little has been known about relationship rules in their own right; they are the conceptual skills that one needs in order to effectively manage a personal relationship. The contents of this book show that the fuller landscape of children's personal and social relationships, including their friendships, is in fact a rich one that much of the literature to date has not yet examined in sufficient detail.

Why then is it so difficult to connect sociometric status and friendship knowledge? As mentioned in the next chapter, the literature has only recently shown a clearer awareness of the value of relationships per se in children's social lives. For example, Schneider, Wiener, and Murphy (1994) have claimed that it is now time for peer relationship researchers to "go beyond" social status research to examine dyadic friendship processes. Armed with this distinction, and the recognition that friendships are relationships with properties of their own, we can see the academic "fault lines" emerging within the peer literature between behavioral or skill indices of "friendship," on the one hand, and conceptually based friendships, on the other (Newcomb & Bagwell, 1995).

For example, Foster, DeLawyer, and Guevremont (1986) have claimed that much of the substance of friendship, its defining features, is not directly accessible to the outside observer, whereas Gottman (1983) and Price and Ladd (1986) have argued that children's friendships need to be observed directly. As we try to reveal below, various investigators from these two research traditions have very different assumptions about social competency and its meaning. Our position in this volume is that friendship, as well as other types of personal relationships, is constructively processed by its participants, which reduces the value of strictly behavioral or "objective" approaches to its investigation. This is particularly true for middle childhood and adolescence where conceptualization and meaning are paramount concerns.

SOCIAL SKILLS AND RELATING

By design, the emphasis of sociometric research is more clinical than normative (Sroufe & Rutter, 1984). Nevertheless, social skills and group acceptance are deemed essential for normal life outcomes. In the child psychology literature, the degree to which children are accepted by their peers is used as a way of assessing their level of social adjustment (Hartup, 1978), which in turn has long-term implications for their subsequent success in the adult world as far as academic achievement, job and marital stability, and mental health are concerned (see, e.g., Bower, 1969; Cowen, Pederson, Babigian, Izzo, & Trost, 1973; Ginsberg, Gottman, & Parker, 1986; Laucht, & Schmidt, 1987; Morrison & Masten, 1991; Putallaz & Gottman, 1981a; Rolf, 1976; Wentzel, 1991). Sociometric ratings are designed to tease apart the social skill deficiencies of a minority of children (i.e., the isolates and rejecteds) in relation to either an ideal (i.e., the populars) or the norm (i.e., the accepteds) and accordingly minimize the issue of how most children get along with other children with whom they have a close relationship.

To illustrate, children who are least liked by their peers more often have problems with self-esteem (Duck, 1991b), have trouble handling peer conflict (Asarnow, 1983; Gottman & Parkhurst, 1980; Hartup, 1979; Renshaw & Asher, 1982, 1983) and tend to interpret ambiguous social situations in more aggressive terms (Dodge & Frame, 1982). They are also less knowledgeable about how to make friends (see, e.g., Gottman, Gonso, & Rasmussen, 1975) and tend to interrupt others and draw excessive attention to themselves (Asher & Renshaw, 1981). Asher and Renshaw have indicated that children who are not nominated as "friends" also lack social skills normally acquired by having access to peers, such as the ability to engage in complex forms of play, management of aggression and cross-sex relationships, and a sense of security in various social situations. About 5 to 10% of children lack friends in school. While some of the reasons for this social isolation stem from factors out of children's control, such as looks, gender, race, opportunities for peer involvement, or even names (McDavid & Harari, 1966), children's lack of social skills figures prominently in the equation.

On a normative basis, however, Renshaw and Asher (1983) found that third graders through sixth graders, regardless of their peer status, share the same goals in attempting peer contact, play entry, dealing with friendship jealousy, and handling peer conflict. These goals resemble social rules in many respects (Bigelow, Tesson, & Lewko, 1992). Even low-status children recognize the need to be positive and outgoing, accommodating, rule oriented, conflict avoiding, and appropriately hostile in response to such peer contexts. Only after in-depth interviewing were populars more likely to spontaneously verbalize competent social strategies for achieving social goals.

Chalmers and Townsend (1990) also found no connection between contextually trained, social, perspective-taking skills and referential communication ability in socially maladjusted girls. As with Renshaw and Asher (1983), it seems that low-status children are broadly equivalent to their popular counterparts in their comprehension of the social goals or expectations of peer interaction and friendship; but, as suggested by Pope, Bierman, and Mumma (1991) and King and Young (1981), low-status children are less knowledgeable in applying specific social strategies appropriate to changing situations.

At this point, the literature is silent on the types of social strategy deficiencies that interfere with establishing and maintaining a close mutual friendship. Naturally, close personal relationships do not occur in a behavioral vacuum (Zarabatany, Hartmann, & Rankin, 1990); and as we report in the following chapters, children's social rules incorporate many of the behaviors associated with friendship (Newcomb & Bagwell, 1995). Because mutual sensitivity is an essential ingredient for close friendship (see, e.g., Mannarino, 1980) and since low-status children generally have competent perspective-taking skills (Dodge & Feldman, 1990), then, as we reveal below, children's social status and its behavioral correlates do not inform us very well about how they conceptualize the components of their personal relationships.

The literature also cautions us about generalizing from broad aggregate categories of social status, however they are measured, to successful friendships. Among preschoolers, Masters and Furman (1981) found that being classified as popular was associated with "overall rates of receiving and dispensing reinforcing and neutral acts" (p. 344). The defining feature of populars was that they were more likely to say pleasant things to their peers than average children were. On the other hand, friendship choice was not related to overall social behavior but rather to specific interactions between individuals and those whom they chose as best liked. These findings highlighted the relational importance of examining the meaning of a particular child's interactions with a selected partner.

Consistent with this approach, several earlier studies have avoided placing children in broad social status categories and instead have focused on children's conceptualizations of a particular peer whom they designated as liked or disliked. Scarlett, Press, and Crockett (1971) found that males in middle childhood used significantly more constructs to describe liked than disliked boys and that older children were more likely to use abstract, psychological constructs than concrete ones to describe the liked peer. Peevers and Secord (1973) found essentially the same results, with older children using more differentiated statements to describe a liked than a disliked peer; and, regardless of age, the disliked peer was described with fewer, more egocentric terms than the liked peer was. Livesley and Bromley (1973) extended this finding to the early adolescent period. Notice that these are not social status studies; the disliked child for one respondent could well be a liked child for another respondent.

Seldom have studies on social status attempted to identify the kind of information that children process when they are asked to rate a peer as liked or preferred as a "friend." Logically speaking, if the class of behaviors and personal characteristics that describe popular children is used to predict a totally different class of behaviors—those that pertain to friendship—then it is not so surprising that the result should be insignificant. Essentially this is just what we found. Pellarin (1988) (see also Bigelow & Pellarin, 1989) addressed the issue of popularity and friendship by having children from grades 3, 5, and 7 write descriptions of popular children in their class. Popular children were defined as those kids in the class that a lot of other kids liked. They also wrote a story about what makes a person a best friend. Content analysis of responses showed that only four constructs—evaluation (e.g., "kind, sweet, nice," etc.), receiving help, receiving sharing, and considerateness—were common to both of these peer domains. The other 33 constructs were unique to each domain.

Friendship embodied familiar concepts (e.g., Bigelow & La Gaipa, 1975) such as friend as teacher, similarity of attitudes and values, demographic similarity, mutual liking, helping and sharing with the friend, common activities, general and organized play, proximity, character admiration, history of interaction, loyalty, acceptance, genuineness, intimacy potential, and common interests. Popularity, on the other hand, dealt with variables routinely connected with peer status cited above and reviewed in Hartup (1983) as popularity and attraction. These included (1) physical characteristics, such as being older or athletic or having artistic and academic abilities, an unusual hobby or talent; a sense of humor, similar socioeconomic status; and (2) the effect of social status itself, such as having many friends, being well liked by others, and being involved in the social network. Ironically, populars were at times also described in unflattering terms, such as inconsiderate, snobby, antisocial, envious, and conceited. With the possible exception of a sense of humor, these popularity variables failed to address social skills, which suggests to us that social skills (e.g., saying nice things, not interrupting others, waiting your turn) are essentially processed out of conscious awareness. We take the view that relationships are very conscious entities.

Gottman (1983), Howes (1990), and Mannarino (1980) have also cautioned us to not view liking as a reliable index of friendship. For Howes, popularity essentially defines an individual child's place within a social group, not relationships with particular persons. As with Masters and Furman (1981), friendship is a dyadic relationship based on *mutual* liking. For Mannarino, a true friend is one who is stably involved with the child and who reciprocates positive feelings. Mannarino (1976, 1980) and McGuire and Weisz (1982) have concluded that reciprocity and mutuality are the cornerstones of friendship; they are not measures of social status.

FRIENDSHIP AND SOCIAL COMPETENCY

Can we equate social status with social competency without considering how children conceptualize their friendships? We think not. Social competency must surely incorporate how we govern ourselves within relationships. Relationship competency is just as salient a feature of social competency as being socially skilled is in the wider sense, a point recently made also by Parker and Asher (1993), echoing similar distinctions made by Mannarino (1980) and McGuire and Weisz (1982). Bigelow et al. (1992) have underscored the fact that children's knowledge of friendships has considerable significance for their ability to manage relationships in general. Understandably then, we have argued for a redress of this imbalance.

Investigators have only just begun to identify the defining social features of friendship, and have shown that these features contain important social competencies of their own. Children with friends are more prosocial (McGuire & Weisz, 1982) as well as more compromising and accommodating (Berndt, 1981). Newcomb and Brady (1982) found that friends are better able than acquaintances to solve problems together. There is also a greater probability that conflicts will be resolved with friends rather than with nonfriends (Gottman & Parkhurst, 1980; Hartup, Laursen, Stewart, & Eastensen, 1988; Nelson & Aboud, 1985). This is a very important manifestation of social competency since conflict is a very large aspect of normal peer relationships (Shantz, 1987) that extends to other types of relationships, with parents, siblings, and teachers (Bigelow et al., 1992), suggesting that a core corpus of relational skills (i.e., social rules) may eclipse those of friendship in many respects.

Dodge (1986) has proposed that social cognition conforms to an information-processing sequence, with accurate encoding and interpretation, generation and evaluation of responses to particular dilemmas, such as observing a neutral act that may be potentially threatening. Rather than view the low-status child as having a general cognitive deficit, Dodge and Feldman (1990) have concluded that low-status children's social cognitions are highly variable and sensitive to particular situations. The salient goals or norms of the group at the time are more germane, as our experiences of "Piggy" would support.

While we are not interested in social status per se, we do take from these observations the view that even rejected children actively construct their peer relationships, which then form, albeit maladaptively in some instances, the social rules that govern present and future relationships. The tendency, for example, for some children to perceive the world in hostile terms is likely to perpetuate the world as a product of their own creation (Dodge, 1980). This reciprocal constructive process, so clearly illustrated by Piaget (1932/1965), Sullivan (1953), and Youniss (1980), applies to the way in which all children create a meaningful social existence, principally with their friends.

Friendships foster a number of other social competencies, such as stability, honesty, reciprocity, and sensitivity. Of course, valid definitions of friendship must include mutuality, referring to either the real or inferred reciprocal preferences that children have for each other as friends or, preferably, referring to the qualities of provisions that the relationship affords. A number of investigations have made considerable progress in operationally defining friendship.

Mannarino (1980) employed the stability of preadolescent males' mutual friendship nominations over a 2-week period, together with a high score on the Chumship Checklist, which was fashioned to reflect Sullivan's (1953) theory of consensual validation in preadolescents' notions of friendship, such as honest communication and sensitivity to the chum's needs (e.g., "Tell each other things we wouldn't tell anyone else"; "Sit together on the school bus"). On both self-report and behavioral measures, children with chums were significantly higher in altruism and were also higher on a measure of self-concept. For a group of preadolescents, McGuire and Weisz (1982) also found that involvement in a stable, mutual relationship, as measured by Mannarino's (1976) Chumship Checklist, predicted high levels of observed altruism and affective perspective taking. In contrast, popularity ratings as indexed by mere "friendship" (i.e., likability) nominations did not predict either of these two measures. One's choice of a friend does not guarantee that that person will reciprocate the feeling of friendship. When both people regard each other as friends, it is then a mutual friendship. Consistent with Sullivan's theory, McGuire and Weisz concluded that children with *mutual* friends who are sensitive to each other are more able to coordinate their own behavior with the behavior of others and thereby contribute to their well-being.

Mutuality of friendship selection is not necessarily more common for popular children. In a longitudinal study spanning grades 1 through 3, Howes (1990) investigated mutual friendships and social status, finding some relationship between these variables by the third grade. Although children in all status groups had mutual friends, by the third grade, the populars did not have friendships with rejected children, although most rejecteds were friends with someone. It must be kept in mind, however, that Howes's criteria for mutuality—reciprocal nominations and ratings— were more lenient than those used by Mannarino (1980) and McGuire and Weisz (1982). McGuire and Weisz used mutual nominations, behavioral involvement indexed by the Chumship Checklist, and friendship stability over 3 weeks. As a result, in Howes's study, 88% of participants had mutual friends, compared to 47% for McGuire and Weisz, who found that mutuality operationally defined by these stricter criteria was unrelated to popularity.

We have not yet considered the descriptors of unfriendliness, but other work (Bigelow & La Gaipa, 1980) on friendship growth and decay in older children and adolescents suggests that disloyalty, lack of admiration (i.e., a negative moral judgment about the person), and saying hurtful things contribute to friendship breakdown. The loyalty features of these data support Mannarino's (1980) Chumship Checklist items that reflect the need for loyalty, such as " 'Stick up' for each other if an older boy is picking on one of you." Aggressiveness issues, such as calling people names, also show that friendship as well as acceptance by the wider peer group (Olweus, 1978; Pope et al., 1991) are undermined by these sorts of actions. Aside from this exception, because popularity and friendship, popularity and rejection, and friendship growth and decay are not usually governed by the same set of variables, it is very difficult to predict friendship conceptions from peer ratings of social status, as Bichard et al. (1988) attempted to do, since different classes of behavior are addressed (see also Parker & Asher, 1993).

REFLECTIONS

From the preceding findings, we reached an important conclusion about the reasons contributing to the lack of connectedness between social status and concepts of friendship. Friendship as a highly differentiated relationship, with a coherent and elaborately constructed meaning system, has not been sufficiently appreciated. General social skills cannot simply be equated with the social interactions characteristic of friendships. Nevertheless, Bichard et al. (1988) concluded that peer nominations "provide a reliable and valid index of current peer relations for preschool and elementary school children" (p. 34). We could not disagree more. Popularity ratings and friendship are not identical; they therefore may well require different conceptual and operational descriptors (Mannarino, 1980). As children become acquainted with an increasing number of other children, they develop special relationships with one or more specific peers with whom they enjoy a mutually satisfying relationship—friendship (Perry & Bussey, 1984). But the social skills called for in this relationship are not identical with those needed to deal with the broader social network.

As we found in our investigations (Bigelow et al., 1992), friendships are specific forms of attachment, and the conceptual rules that govern them are different from those governing other social relationships (see also Hartup, 1978). Dweck (1981) also stressed this point in proposing that some of the most socially skilled children might well find themselves amongst the isolates because of developmental mismatches in social-cognitive needs. Admittedly, part of the difficulty with child ratings may also stem from the fact that peer ratings are less predictive and reliable measures of social competency than teacher ratings are (Connolly &

Doyle, 1981). Shuart and Lewko (1988) found that it was not until about 12 years of age that children become reliable coders of social data, compared with teenagers and university students. Presumably, accurate coding skills are a precondition for reliable and valid peer ratings that reflect social competency. However, by age 12, friendship begins to acquire its fuller, more differentiated character (Bigelow 1977; Bigelow & La Gaipa, 1975; Selman, 1980; Sullivan, 1953; Youniss, 1980), thus further enhancing its distinctiveness from popularity and group acceptance, which, taken as a whole, are based on younger subject samples with more concrete needs (Gottman, 1983).

The connection between thought and behavior is neither necessary nor direct. This is particularly so with respect to the level of development of friendship conceptions and actual social skills. While most people with long-term social adjustment problems were socially rejected or neglected as children (see, e.g., Coie & Dodge, 1983; Cowen et al., 1973; Kohn & Clausen, 1955; Gresham, 1981; Liddle, 1962; Roff, Sells, & Golden, 1972; Roff, 1961), it does not necessarily follow that socially rejected or neglected children will develop long-term social adjustment problems. Simply because children are unpopular does not automatically mean that they have no friends and cannot conceptualize what it is like to function within a friendship or know what it takes to be liked by other children (McGuire & Weisz, 1982; Bichard et al., 1988; Renshaw & Asher, 1983). As noted before, Renshaw and Asher found that high- and low-status children typically share the same goals. As well, it does not mean that popular children necessarily have closer friendship ties than their less popular age-mates do. Indeed, as indicated previously in this chapter, hyperactive, skill-deficient children are not typically shunned by their peers (King & Young, 1981; Pope et al., 1991), and chumship ratings are independent of popularity ratings (McGuire & Weisz, 1982).

Admittedly, the threshold of social skill knowledge required for entry into a friendship relation has yet to be determined. Pope et al. (1991) pointed out that children with significantly undercontrolled behavior who have no peer relationship difficulties are still potentially a high-risk sample since they may experience subjective distress and "lack of fit to environmental demands despite adequate peer acceptance" (p. 670). We extend this logic further to claim that social skill deficiencies pertinent to the accomplishment and maintenance of a friendship also place the child at serious developmental risk.

However, peer nominations have not bridged specific deficiencies in friendship knowledge (Bichard et al., 1988; McGuire & Weisz, 1982). Teacher-observed behavior problems such as social immaturity, withdrawal, and aggression interfere with popularity (Pope et al., 1991) as well as impair friendship involvement (Bigelow & La Gaipa, 1980; La Gaipa &

Wood, 1985; Pellegrini, 1985), but the specific behaviors observed in the wider peer group have not yet been connected to those used within the specific context of the friendship (Masters & Furman, 1981).

We stress, though, that our emphasis on the child's active construction of relationships through the development of social rules is not at all at odds with all thinking in current social status research (Coie, 1990). Variations in the skills of group acceptance, as well as the rules of relationship formulation, stem from a child's history of interactions with parents, siblings, and peers. Coie (1990) summed it up nicely: "Children's groups have norms for what is acceptable and appropriate and these norms may involve distinctions that, at first glance, seem subtle and complex to adult observers" (p. 371). This normative process, as we argue in the next chapter, links psychological and sociological approaches to relational theory.

However, Coie (1990) has equated a successful friendship with trust, similarity, goal compatibility, feeling good about oneself, and skillful mutual influence (Asher & Williams, 1987). While these are important features of friendship that overlap with social status, we show in our volume that the social rule landscape for friendship is much more complex than this and is a field of inquiry in its own right. Coie (1990) and Rubin, Lemare, and Lollis (1990) seem to be arriving at this point in their appreciation of the influence of early maternal–child *relationships*, which creates in the child "a particular way of relating to other people that is more comprehensive than behavioral acts or skills" (Coie, p. 393). While we agree, the same can be said for friendship, for it too is a comprehensive way of relating. The current work launches from this position with respect to parent–child, child–child and teacher–child relationships.

MEASUREMENT CONCERNS

Research on social cognitive development has not been as concerned with measurement problems as mathematical cognitive development has (see, e.g., Brainerd, 1973a, 1973b). Perhaps this has been due to a pervasive belief that social knowledge is verbally constructed (see, e.g., Sullivan, 1953) and therefore must be accessed verbally. However, there are several different ways to present verbal information: for example, by means of questionnaires (La Gaipa & Wood, 1985; Furman & Bierman, 1984) or with nonverbal (i.e., unlabeled) picture sequence tasks (see, e.g., Bigelow, 1983) that covertly address the linguistic syntax of social events. Bigelow found that children with less well developed concepts of friendship did relatively better on the interview but that those children with more abstract concepts did better on the picture sequence task. It is precisely during the beginning of this preadolescent period that friendship takes on its fuller meaning (Mannarino, 1980; Sullivan, 1953) and is therefore more sensitive to measurement error.

Normally, this method issue would be a separate, perhaps esoteric, topic; but the data clearly show that use of judgments (Brainerd, 1973a, 1973b), questionnaires (Furman & Bierman, 1984), and picture sequence tasks (Bigelow, 1983) can result in substantially more measured competency than traditional open-ended interviews or questionnaires alone. These findings contrast sharply with the greater sensitivity of in-depth interviews used by Renshaw and Asher (1982) in predicting children's social behavior.

Whether social competency is more validly detectable by means of judgmental tasks, such as questionnaire ratings, or by means of in-depth interviews is obviously a hotly contested issue (Furman, personal communication). These observations are important because peer nominations and desirability ratings are judgment tasks. To classify children on the basis of their peer ratings and to then ask those children to describe how they should behave in selected friendship situations (Bichard et al., 1988; Selman, 1976), or to write a story about what makes someone your best friend (Bigelow, 1977; Pellarin, 1988), is the methodological equivalent of overestimating who children's friends are and of underestimating children's understanding of friendships.

As we illustrate in Chapter 3, we approached this measurement problem by asking children to verbally construct the features of their relationships and then compared relationships by using both these verbal descriptions and the rating scales derived from them. In this way, the theoretical advantages of phenomenology, which capture the constructed meaning of a relationship, are combined with the common metric provided by a questionnaire, the items of which have been crafted on the basis of the children's own comments.

IMPLICATIONS FOR SOCIAL RULES

The meaning of a personal or social relationship is more fully illuminated by accessing its rules, which reveal the relevant content of the relationship. We know so little about relationships; and by examining how children actively construct their relational rules, we are in a far better position from which to learn about the constituents of relationships and how they work. The strategies that children access in dealing with others within structured relationships are not simply extensions of those strategies used in managing their behavior outside of these relationships.

As we illustrate in Chapters 4, 5, and 6, friendships are very differentiated in the rules that children use to construct them. For example, the friendship expectation of intimacy potential (see, e.g., Bigelow & La Gaipa, 1975) differentiates into several rules of "information management" (e.g., "You shouldn't tell them some things"). For this reason, it would be very useful to examine the social rule knowledge of children in various social status groups. Since, as we explain in Chapter 3, social rules are transformed versions of actual social experience, perhaps children who are deficient in social skills show subtle differences in the way they define the rules of relating because of deficiencies in the way they process or attend to social information that gives rise to their social rule knowledge. However, this remains an intriguing avenue for further research since our present undertaking is to learn about relationships and how children structure the regulation of those relationships.

As we show in the following chapters, our investigation of children's social rules is an instance of a more general concern in the field of social relationships that the elements within a relationship (i.e., the rules) are as complex and necessary to the understanding of social behavior as the publicly observable behaviors outside of it. Each set of rules within each type of relationship at each developmental and gender location provides us with an "implicate order" (Shotter & Newson, 1982) that governs the understanding of relating. It is to this social order that we shall now turn.

CHAPTER 2

Social Rules
and the Implicate Order
TOWARD A SOCIOLOGY
OF CHILDHOOD

Children's interactions with each other are highly structured and reflect the need not only for social acceptance in a general sense but also for the particular skills necessary to manage friendships independent of the wider peer culture. However, children's friendships represent only one of a broader range of relationships, with their parents, siblings, other kids, and other adults. Through these relationships, children structure their social interactions with the various people in their lives, each of whom is integral to their socialization. In this chapter, we maintain that the meaning of children's social and personal relationships can be examined through children's construction of this social structure—the rules of relating—which places us squarely within the realm of a sociology of childhood. Social rules are the strategies that children say they use in relating to other people with whom they have a personal or social relationship.

INTERDISCIPLINARY BOUNDARIES
AND SOCIAL RULE FENCE MENDING

Without an appreciation of the interdisciplinary significance of social rules, students of sociology or psychology may well extract from our endeavors an incomplete view of them. As we explain below, the fields of children's relationships and communication are unique in that they are located essentially at the boundary between sociology and psychology, and our efforts were to help integrate these two worldviews through the eyes of children by asking them to explicate the strategies they understand and use in dealing with other persons in their lives. Social pressures are manifest in children's face-to-face interactions with others and this context provides an ideal meeting ground for sociology and psychology.

THE SOCIOLOGICAL QUANDARY

Important in this interdisciplinary development is the recognition that it is not possible to represent the impact of society on the child as a single set of circumstances, nor is it claimed here that all that is germane in the "big picture" of social influence is inevitably filtered down to the relatively microscopic world of personal relationships. Indeed, sociologists (Goffman, 1983) have become increasingly aware that everyday face-to-face interactions cannot simply be seen as a microcosm of the macrosocial environment. Thus, some investigators (Dannefer & Perlmutter, 1990; Elder, 1984; Featherman & Lerner, 1985) have concentrated on the impact of the broader society upon the developing child, trying to address the developmental experiences of different age cohorts within a changing set of economic and social circumstances. Others (e.g., Corsaro & Rizzo, 1988; Corsaro, 1981; Youniss, 1980) have focused their efforts on the detailed character of children's microsocial relationships. Programmatic attempts to incorporate these different levels within one all-encompassing framework (see, e.g., Bronfenbrenner, 1979) have met with only limited success and been criticized (see, e.g., Dowd, 1990) for according only a passive role to children in response to external circumstances and for neglecting any serious consideration of children as important agents in the socialization equation. Hence, the need to examine how children actively construct their social lives.

A subjective orientation to social relationships, such as ours, is not new to sociology. It is a central precept of Weber's (1968) theory of social action that has been recast in various forms by other social theorists (such as Parsons, 1937), by symbolic interactionists (Mead, 1934), and by phenomenological sociologists (Berger & Luckman, 1966; Garfinkel, 1967). With the exception of Denzin (1977), however, this approach has not been systematically applied to children. Moreover, in general, sociologists have not extended their investigations very far into the world of childhood.

To be quite fair, sociologists have not had any reason to be interested in children's social rules. After all, children's social rules can be conveniently, if perhaps inaccurately, viewed as imperfect versions of those that adults use. And, with the exception of Corsaro's (1981) and Corsaro and Rizzo's (1988) careful work, sociologists have not been all that interested in how children manage to learn these rules; therefore, it is no wonder that interest in the development of social rules is so lacking. To make matters more confusing, we know that children are not simply miniature adults; they learn in significantly different ways as they develop, often transforming information in the process. This has prompted much of sociology to abdicate the field of children's social relations to developmental psychologists, who are quite naturally more concerned with internal methodology and mentalistic constructs than with external validity (Furstenberg, 1985). Nonetheless, any investigation of social rules must take into account the effect of developmental limitations on the levels of cognitive complexity that are called for by different configurations of social relationships. However, as Hinde (1979) and Youniss (1978) have pointed out, it is impossible to tease these two components apart, since they do not exist in isolation from their interaction in the course of development. Hence, we may learn more about the processes of social development by closely examining its component parts or rules, which are the active ingredients of socialization.

Notwithstanding sociology's lack of interest, the microworld of face-to-face relationships is very much a socially structured one. We embraced the old sociological maxim that normative behavior with another person is often determined by the social role that person assumes. Collins (1988) reminded us that classic American sociological theorists such as Cooley (1902) and Mead (1934) asserted that the self would not exist if it were not for the role expectations of society. The social structure is made up of a variety of selves in the form of these roles, which must, eventually, be coordinated with each other and which include their applicable frictions. Indeed, Collins proposes that the self is actually a myth—a notion that often shocks psychologists—and that the person is more properly defined in terms of Goffman's (1967) "interaction rituals."

The significance of Goffman's (1983) work is that it acknowledges the importance of everyday social routines as key constituents of the broader social structure. Traditional social theories have viewed the forms of individual behavior as largely derivative of macrosocial structure. The primary model of the impact of society on the child has reflected this view by considering socialization as essentially a unidirectional process in which society's norms and values are transmitted to the child through the agency of parents. But once we grasp that the everyday interactions of the child are not simply knee-jerk reactions to external social pressure, but that they also express the agency of the child, then documenting the social character of these interactions becomes an important task. The way in which children negotiate their social interactions, not as puppets but as agents, becomes the very expression of children's sociality.

Social theorists have increasingly defined their task as reformulating the linkages between face-to-face interactions and the more general construction of society (Bourdieu, 1990; Collins, 1985; Giddens, 1984). Social structures do not exist independently of the multiple actions of the individuals that inhabit them: such structures are "reproduced" or embodied in the everyday routines that characterize people's social lives. People do not learn these social patterns in strict compliance to some external standard or code but actively enact them in the "social marketplace" (Goffman, 1983). According to Giddens (1984), human beings as social creatures have a "practical consciousness"; that is, people will normally be able to explain most of what they do in the daily "flow of intentional action" (p. 8). Human beings are purposive agents, able to describe discursively the reasons for many of their social actions. Social competency is evaluated by others on the basis of one's ability to rationalize and monitor one's actions within the prevailing social context. Giddens explains that social structures do not dominate because people are " 'docile bodies' who behave like automata" (p. 16) but achieve their effectiveness through a "dialectic of control" of dominant over weaker human beings. Prescient of the current investigation, Giddens claimed that awareness of social rules is "at the very core" (p. 21) of human social agency. Accordingly, these social patterns are not merely the result of external pressure, the imprint of society on the individual; they are also the willful enactment of society's forms (Giddens, 1984; Tesson & Youniss, 1995).

Corsaro and his associates (Corsaro & Rizzo, 1988) have adopted this view as a new source of insight into children's social patterns. Through their play behavior and their social routines, children not only reflect but also actively reproduce the culture they inhabit. The relation between external culture and the social world of children is seen, thus, as a two-way street; and viewed in this way, children's social behavior takes on a new contextual significance. It is for this reason that the social rules that children adopt to organize their interactions with others represent a particularly important datum.

Children's social rules lie at the interface between the microsocial world of immediate face-to-face interactions and the more general culture of children's macrosocial environment. When children do chores to please their parents, when they give in to their peers' initiatives just to avoid conflict, or when they laugh at others' jokes that they have not understood, they are in each case responding to the immediacy of particular situations, but they are also expressing in their own ways forms

that are common to the more general culture: forms of helping, deference, and politeness. Detailing the nature of these rules is therefore to
develop a special window on culture as it is understood and enacted by
children.

For reasons elaborated on in Chapter 3, knowledge of social rule
content is also vital if we are to embrace the fuller meaning of social roles
(i.e., father, teacher, etc.) and their development. Sociologists are interested in the defining features of the prevailing social order but have not
until recently been keenly interested in using socialization trends in social
rule attainment to examine the origins and function of social roles. We
wish to stress that our examination of children's social understanding
through an explication of their rules and relationships is but an instance
of a more complete and generalized understanding of social functioning.
We look forward to companion pieces that address rules and relationships
throughout the adolescent and adult lifespans. We also invite investigations that examine how sensitive children's social rules are to the influence of wider social structural features (e.g., social class, school) that
filters down to them.

THE PSYCHOLOGICAL QUANDARY

As Furstenberg (1985) aptly indicated, sociologists and psychologists
seldom cover the same terrain, echoing the view of Bronfenbrenner
(1979), who observed that developmentalists commonly acknowledge an
interactionist view in principle but not in practice. In the legitimate
preoccupation with developmental stages and social behaviors (see, e.g.,
Kohlberg, 1969), the point is often missed that what children learn is
based on a complex social context. As products of this complexity, the
need to establish a set of children's social rules with which to compare
social relationships is also prompted by what Corsaro and Rizzo (1988)
refer to as the absence of sociological theoretical approaches to the social
development of young children, compared to the increasing acceptance
of the Piagetian constructivist approach to development (Damon, 1977;
Shantz, 1987). While few developmentalists (cf. Brainerd, 1978) uncriti-
cally embrace Piagetian theory, the psychological focus is still on the
cognitive "engine" (Shotter & Newson, 1982). As Flavell (1981) amply
illustrated, the surge in neo- or even non-Piagetian research reflects a
hotly contested debate about the existence of stages (see Brainerd, 1973a,
1978). However, whether the quest is to package children's thinking in
cognitive-developmental stages, skills, or memory store, the goal is to
understand how children think.

Hence, the constructivist/ontogenetic model of development

(whether Piagetian, neo-Piagetian, or componential), so commonplace in developmental psychology (Furstenberg, 1985), has been portrayed as antithetical to sociological analysis on account of its relative focus on the individual (Corsaro & Rizzo, 1988) at the expense of sensitivity to social influences. Indeed, earlier work on children's friendship expectations (Bigelow, 1977), which, together with Youniss (1978, 1980), helped to set the paradigmatic stage for the current social rules investigations, is cited more in relation to its Piagetian-like stages of development of children's friendships than to the conceptual components that govern them. In addition, in Harré's (1977) view, children's interpersonal interactions are not simply internal individual accomplishments but a reflection of the cultural and social systems of which such interactions are a part. Any examination of one type of relationship without simultaneously comparing it with other relationships risks mischaracterization. However, this is precisely the error that is so often made in child development research. Reports are classified as parent–child relationships, mother–child relationships, friendships, sibling relationships, peer relationships, and so forth, without considering how the particular relationship compares and contrasts with other types and how all relationships are framed by the child within the context of broadly held cultural assumptions. As we explain in more detail in the next chapter, social-contextual approaches to constructivism have not been sufficiently appreciated in this light.

Thus, while contextualism is acknowledged (see, e.g., Lerner, 1992) as the dominant model of developmental psychology for the last two decades, it is seldom fully integrated into investigations of children's actual social relationships. At a metatheoretic level, it is consistent with our view and Youniss's (1978) that the organismic characteristics of the individual (e.g., puberty, cognitive stage) interact with social conditions (e.g., family and peer relationships), producing diversity and change in outcomes (e.g., well-being). In this way, as Lerner (1992) explains, contextualism retains a key integrative feature of Piagetian constructivism while being sensitive to the embeddedness of relationships within the culture. At a procedural level though, our approach, like that of Corsaro and Rizzo (1988), represents a radical departure, since it views context as an active conceptually constructive process. Rather than be preoccupied with the child's general information processing capacity, social rules reveal how the child processes social relationships in relational context.

Emde (1994) clearly understands the virtual inevitability of the need for this social constructivism. Emde posits, as we do, that people *impose* meaning on an otherwise very complex and unwieldy set of personal relationships. For example, for a family of four, there are no less than 15 different dyadic permutations within the family system. If one includes the child's peers, including different levels of friendship, as well as relationships with teachers—as we did in our own research on social rules—not to mention selecting from among several dozen different courses of action, the social complexity facing the child is considerable. To create any meaning at all, the child must literally impose it or be overwhelmed. It is just this sort of constructive contextualism that allows us to bridge theory and practice. As we indicated in Chapter 1, some developmental psychologists (e.g., Asher, 1978; Coie & Kupersmidt, 1983; Dodge, 1983; Ladd, 1983; Putallaz & Gottman, 1981a, 1981b) have dwelt on social competency purely in relation to social skills, thus giving the impression that social competency is simply the execution of a collection of correct actions (e.g., not hitting, waiting your turn, etc.).

We cannot claim to be the first to discover the need to examine children's relationships as well as their behaviors, since the tensions between these two approaches have naturally given rise to corresponding divisions in the child literature. Students of children's interpersonal behavior have tended to focus on one of two working models: one is primarily psychological and individual (see, e.g., Renshaw & Asher, 1982, 1983; Strayhorn, 1988), and the other is social and relational (Hinde, 1979; Mannarino, 1980; McGuire & Weisz, 1982; Youniss, 1978, 1980). Psychological approaches to social competency focus on the skill repertoires of socially competent children that contribute to children's mental health (see, e.g., Strayhorn, 1988). Even though it is recognized that social skills are learned by relating to others, the thrust is to make the skills an aspect of an individual's personal characteristics. This is an indispensable approach when dealing with individual problems, such as the inability to deal with separation, intolerance of frustration, or social rejection. However, this approach reveals only part of an intricate puzzle and leaves open the question of how children conceptualize the social order that governs their existence. Moreover, much that is meaningful in interpersonal life is inherently covert, symbolic, and subjective, that is, it exists in large part "in our heads" (Duck, 1990).

SOCIAL RULES AND RELATIONSHIPS

Our fundamental contention is that social rules are embedded in children's descriptions of their personal and social relationships and the situations in which those relationships occur. Social rules and the relational knowledge that they embody constitute one's understanding of social and personal relationships. Social rules are condition–action sequences (e.g., the condition is "How do you deal with your mother?" and the action is "When she gets moody I keep my feelings to myself"). Social rules may also have goals or rationales (e.g., "So that she won't get mad at me"). According to Youniss (1978), children selectively attend to their social environments and code or internally represent some features of behavior. As the children mature, they integrate and rearrange new features with previous ones, generating new appropriate behaviors by accessing memories of past events.

A social rule is not a social skill in that it does not refer simply to a specific appropriate behavior elicited toward a particular person at a particular time. In addition, social rules as we define them are not externally imposed with rigid codes but are conceptual "framing" devices (Fogel, 1993). A social rule is a linguistically represented element of experience that describes how to behave with the person who occupies the given social relationship within which the rule was learned. An example of a social skill may be not hitting others, since this is appropriate behavior with virtually anyone and may not necessarily enter into a child's conception of a relationship. A social skill does not necessarily convey information about the relationship the child is in. On the other hand, the child's explicit statement "Do what they ask you to do" is a social rule since it implicitly assigns meaning to the other person's and the self's behavior by defining the child's own behavior (i.e., compliance) with respect to specific persons in authority, such as parents or teachers.

Social rules are learned through interactions with others and are transformed by developing cognitive abilities for verbal representation (see, e.g., Bandura, 1977) and role taking (see, e.g., Selman & Byrne, 1974). According to Youniss (1978), "Getting out of oneself and into another is an essential developmental advance in the general task of understanding persons" (p. 207). Youniss (1980) elaborated his conception of the social rule by integrating Sullivan's (1953) and Piaget's (1932/1965) theories of social development into the now well-known Sullivan–Piaget hypothesis. According to Sullivan, preadolescence is a precious time for children because it represents an occasion for genuine friendship (i.e., "chumship"), in which children become very involved with one another as equals. They also learn the meaning of trust and intimacy, which continue to be valuable aspects of close relationships throughout life. Through this intense exchange, children learn about themselves, each other, and the world.

According to Piaget (1932/1965), children's essential task is to order their social interactions by constructing relational rule systems that define how they relate to others and that order their behavior across a wide assortment of social networks. At about the same age that Sullivan (1953) identified as the time for chumship, or close mutual friendship, Piaget observed that children in the preadolescent years change from an egocentric morality, where rules are immutable—representing parental authority—to a cooperative morality, where rules of conduct, such as those involved in playing a game of marbles, are modifiable and can be negotiated between themselves and other children perceived as equal participants. Youniss (1980) described this developmental change from unilateral authority and compliance to cooperation and negotiation in reference to the Sullivan–Piaget hypothesis. For our present purposes, Youniss's primary contribution refers to the notion of the social rule-relationship. Youniss (1978) explained that social rules are developed through social interactions between persons and, as a result, are not directly observed but are accessible chiefly through the child's description of the relationship with that person.

Newman (1986) identified the parallel notion of mutual knowledge in social development. As in the social rule, which is co-constructed (Youniss, 1978), children attempt to establish a correlation between their own behavior and the behavior of the social object (i.e., the other person) with whom they are interacting. While the social rule embraces the structure of the personal relationship, mutual knowledge represents a growing understanding of a world held in common with others and stems from and extends research on perspective taking (see, e.g., Selman & Byrne, 1974; Chandler & Greenspan, 1972). However, with social rules there is no necessary appeal to an objective or impartial criterion for the establishment of the truth value of those rules, even though it would be interesting to examine this. We are of the view that people take from their shared experiences their own versions of events, which then become part of their construction of their relationships. Parenthetically, Vygotsky (1978) also held this view, believing that knowledge itself is socially cultivated by the interactions that children have with their parents, peers, and caretakers and that convey the culture's accumulated knowledge. Butterworth (1982) argues that the individual's cognitive processes are dependent on language that is essentially shared between the child and another person. Hence, the meaning of language resides within the social relationship and its context. Duck (1994) provides a captivating example of this event:

> Ben, my son, was 15 months old. . . . I had been pointing hopefully to the lights in our kitchen and saying "light." . . . As I pointed upwards, he resolutely stared at the end of my finger, grinning gleefully and proudly at his understanding—but from my perspective he really didn't get the point (as it were). Apart from being the only child who will grow up thinking that he has two thumbs and eight lights on his hands, he did not take my pointing as a sign saying, "Go beyond here and look further." (p. 1)

In the same vein, children attempt to learn the scripts (Nelson & Gruendel, 1981; Schank & Abelson, 1977) that inform them of the regularities and expectations of acceptable social behavior. Social rules are the representation of this social knowledge within the contexts of specific relationships.

Social rules are the marriage of social learning theory and Vygotskyian contextualism: they are the conceptual building blocks of social thought. A theory and its methods are very intimately related. While we don't pretend to offer a new theory as such, we do suggest a new constructivistic method for the examination of personal relationships that has implications for theory. Social rules have been directly or implicitly referred to by several prominent authors who appreciate an active cognitive ingredient in developmental theory. For example, Bandura (1978) reasons that the self is a system that cannot be effectively understood by behavioral technologies that are essentially unidirectional. Rather, "People create and activate environments as well as rebut them" (p. 344). For Bandura, the environment is not an "autonomous force" in governing behavior; rather, reality is reciprocally determined. Similar to Youniss's (1978, 1980) notion of a rule-relationship as a constructed event, Bandura found it necessary to invoke the person as an essential moderator between the reciprocal forces of environment and behavior. The core of this reciprocal determinism is symbolic: "The extraordinary capacity of humans to use symbols enables them to engage in reflective thought, to create and to plan foresightful courses of action in thought rather than having to perform possible options and suffer the consequences of thoughtless action" (p. 345).

Bandura's (1977, 1978) cognitive element is primarily a means of governing competent behavior. The transformation of activities into images and symbols serving as behavioral guides is in principle quite consistent with our own view of social rule construction. Bandura's (1978) theory of reciprocal determinism of the self is also relevant to our own view in that he recognized, quite like Vygotsky (1978), that people "actively process and transform" (pp. 39–40) situational influences. However, his theory is silent regarding personal relationships, even though he (Bandura & Walters, 1963) acknowledged the powerful role of "social norms" in the child's observational and symbolic learning. His theory stops short of examining social-relational thought (e.g., rules), even though the mechanisms of observational learning often leave their mark within children's verbalized social rules (e.g., "Do your chores and behave, so they'll let you stay up late").

Social cognition is an interactive process between children and the other persons with whom they relate. An interactionist, contextual view of social relationships is not simply another exercise in examining the "cognitive engine" (Shotter & Newson, 1982) but reflects what Youniss (1978), Glick (1978), and Bandura and Walters (1963) might commonly refer to as the "particularities" or details of social behavior. As Youniss explains it, "Actual experiences with objects, persons and events are mere occasions for organizing the world" (p. 208). As all three of these authors have noted, in one form or another, there has been in cognitive-developmental theory (see, e.g., Kohlberg, 1969; Piaget, 1970; Selman, 1980) too great an emphasis on stages and sequences that overshadows what Tesson and Youniss (1995) and Wozniak (1993) stress as the key feature of cognitive co-construction that undergirds all other aspects of cognitive-developmental theory.

In a social vein, Youniss (1980) refreshed our reading of Piaget (1932/1965), drawing our attention to the interpersonal network within the child's life, which the child then must continually order. Through the creation of this order, the child constructs "rule systems, or *relations*" (p. 211). Piaget as well as Light (1979) make the interpersonal relationship basic to knowledge. Fogel (1993) extends this process of relational co-construction to a general process of knowing. Whether this "co-constructive," rule-generating process is inherently social or not is a hotly debated issue (see, e.g., Glick, 1978) but should not distract us from the main argument that social rules reflect a common constructive learning process. Unfortunately, most investigators have ignored constructive content. Perhaps Bronfenbrenner (1979) says it best:

> To assert that human development is a product of interaction between the growing human organism and its environment is to state what is almost commonplace in behavioral science. It is a proposition that all students of behavior would find familiar, with which none would take issue, and that few would regard as in any way remarkable, let alone revolutionary, in its scientific implications. I am one of those few. I regard the statement as remarkable because of the striking contrast between the universally approved twofold emphasis that it mandates and the conspicuously one-sided implementation the principle has received in the development of scientific theory and empirical work. (p. 16)

Voyat (1978) carefully examines from a Piagetian perspective how the child constructs social cognition, but Voyat takes the view that individual social development as an "intraindividual" event occurs in a parallel cooperative fashion with the child's knowledge of the physical world. In this model, the egocentric child is incapable of truly cooperative relationships, which are unilaterally governed by the family. While this appears superficially quite like Youniss's (1980) Sullivan–Piaget hypothesis, by focusing on the child's cognitive engine, Voyat misses the constructive process and the regulation that unfolds from it. Culture and social context are not treated as interactive with the child from the beginning.

Vygotsky (1934/1962) is more consistent with our position (and that of Piaget!) in his description of Tolstoy's failed attempt to teach peasant children literary language. Vygotsky found that children learn such things much better within the general linguistic context. In like fashion, social rules, even in young childhood, are constructed out of a linguistic and cultural context (see Corsaro & Rizzo, 1988; Gaskins, Miller, & Corsaro, 1992) that gives those rules substance.

Bronfenbrenner (1979), like Vygotsky (1978) and Piaget (1932/1965), clearly recognized the constructive nature of the child's imposition of meaning. Consistent with our rules approach, Bronfenbrenner claimed that social understanding derives mainly from face-to-face (e.g., mother–child) interactions, which in turn are affected by the "role demands, stresses, and supports emanating from other settings" (p. 7). Moreover, like Bronfenbrenner, our emphasis is not on learning processes (although one can often infer those from social rules content) but on content and how it varies as a function of relationships. Since our approach encompasses eight personal and social relationships, we may have begun to satisfy what Bronfenbrenner termed "ecological validity," which requires the encompassing of the child's phenomenological field.

SPECIFIC RELATIONSHIPS
AND HOW THEY ARE CURRENTLY PORTRAYED

A perusal of the child development literature on interpersonal relationships, which is largely psychological in its emphasis, quickly points out the inherent deficiencies of studies that do not integrate social context with children's personal constructions of their relationships. Studies that, for example, try to describe friendship by examining it in isolation from other relationships, risk premature generalities as to the characteristics of a relationship; and relationship comparisons accomplished through contrived questionnaires are of doubtful validity since they risk loss of the very contextual meaning that is sought.

The Peer Domain

Friends

Friendship has been variously described as cooperation (Youniss, 1980), helpfulness (Mannarino, 1980; Sullivan, 1953), genuineness, loyalty, and intimacy (Bigelow, 1977; Selman & Jacquette, 1978). The implicit message here is that friendships, particularly close or "best" friendships, are rather exclusive arrangements compared to less intimate encounters with peers. Even though children and adolescents readily designate peers as either friends or nonfriends and even though older children and adolescents distinguish between an ideal versus an actual friend (Bigelow & La Gaipa, 1980), the features distinguishing close friendships from mere acquaintances in middle childhood are not well understood (Hartup, 1979; Oden, Herzberger, Mangione, & Wheeler, 1984). As a case in point, Oden et al. found that up to one-half of children's peer encounters are dictated by circumstance, such as school routines, opportunities to play, and so forth, rather than by the nominal level of intimacy or closeness of the relationship as designated by the child. Without examining social functions (e.g., intimacy, trust, obligation) within their relational contexts, nominal distinctions between levels of peer relationships are difficult to support. By the same token, the "obvious" major differences that occur between parent and friend relationships, such as unilateral authority and mutual cooperation (see, e.g., Youniss, 1980), are difficult to support without examining them in the contexts of various relational issues. For example, are close friends always more disclosive than acquaintances, or do they also withhold information as well? Are children always more compliant with their parents, or are they also compliant with friends on selected issues?

The Family Domain

Parents

Given the fact that children's experiences within the family are probably the most prepotent that the child will ever have, we were particularly interested in examining how children represent these most fundamental of social relationships. While we appear to know a great deal about the conceptual terrain of children's friendships and peer relationships, such as the need for trust, loyalty and intimacy (see, e.g., Bigelow, 1977), we know comparatively less about the conceptual features of the parent–child relationship. This is a pity, because the parent–child relationship is more central to early socialization. At least one study (Reid, Landesman, Treder, & Jaccard, 1989) found that children perceive their mothers as the best "multipurpose social provider available" (p. 907). Understanding the parent–child relationship is further complicated by the fact that parents and preadolescents do not seem to share a common view of each other. Preadolescents are relatively unaware of their parents' beliefs about them (Alessandri & Wozniak, 1987), and the converse is also likely true. It is then particularly important to record the child's own account of the parent–child relationship instead of simply relying on what the parents say. The importance of this imbalance in the literature is more than trivial because there is the disturbing possibility that parents may not be very good sources of information about their children (see, e.g., Robbins, 1982) compared to the children themselves (see, e.g., Sheingold & Tenney, 1982). To borrow an analogy (Bronfenbrenner, 1979), if you want to know how a prison is run, don't ask the guards, ask the inmates!

There is a wealth of literature on the parent–child relationship, and most of it, quite naturally, stresses the role and nature of authority and control on the part of the parent. Maccoby and Martin (1983) summed this up well: "Any parent who is functioning in any degree in the parental role exercises some control over children" (p. 44). However, many of the key ingredients of a positive, supportive parent–child relationship are contained within the authoritative parenting model (Baumrind, 1967, 1971; Maccoby & Martin, 1983; Maccoby, 1984a; Peterson & Rollins, 1987), where the parent explains limits and encourages discussion. Thus, psychological nurturance, such as listening and talking things over, commonly associated with close friendships, is seemingly a large feature of the parent–child bond (see, e.g., Furman & Buhrmester, 1985a; Reid et al., 1989; Weisz, 1980). Informational and instrumental help is also a shared feature of peer (e.g., Mannarino, 1980; McGuire & Weisz, 1982) and parent–child relationships (Reid et al., 1989; Furman & Buhrmester, 1985a). Evidently, in addition to imposing authority and demanding compliance, the parent functions somewhat like a companion or friend. Moreover, virtually all of these comparisons were accomplished through rating scales; what is missing are children's own constructions of how they function differently between specific kinds of social relationships.

Siblings

Sibling relationships are special because they appear to mirror peer relationships; however, the terms of the relationships are not voluntary, but are dictated by family membership. Sibling relationships are both compulsory and enduring (Bank & Kahn, 1982); in comparison, peer relationships are voluntary and are more similar in age and sex (Hartup, 1983). These differences aside, siblings look just like peers, and they learn a lot from each other. For example, Dunn and Kendrick (1982) found that younger children quickly learn how to deal with their more aggressive older brothers and sisters by seeing how they are treated relative to themselves. Not surprisingly, relationships with siblings have been de-scribed in rather harsh, controlling terms (see, e.g., Stoneman, Brody, & MacKinnon, 1984) compared with relationships with peers with whom children readily cooperate in play. Furman and Buhrmester (1985a,

1985b) also found that during middle childhood "sibships" are more ambivalent and conflictual than are peer relationships. Interestingly, Shantz (1987) found that conflict is a central aspect of children's *peer* relationships, although peer relationships were not compared to sibling relationships. However, phenomenological examinations of sibling relationships are rare: we did not know how, as far as children's social rules are concerned, children viewed their relationships with their siblings compared with their friends. This set the stage for our current work, which, among other relationships, addressed this problem directly.

Nonfamily Adults

The child's adult world is increasingly occupied by people other than the parents and extended family (Furth, 1980). Beginning in kindergarten and primary school, the teacher plays a more central part in the child's life. During adolescence, the appearance of an employer or a coach introduces the child to the formal world beyond the family and school. In principle, these nonfamily adults essentially govern the child's attention to specific tasks of learning, work, or play and are only secondarily, if at all, supportive. Yet, this type of relationship has received scant attention in social relationship literature. Because of its formally prescribed and universally relevant role in the child's life, this type of relationship is also a control against confusing parents with nonfamily adult authority, a provision that has heretofore been missed by contextless ventures into the world of adult–child relationships.

TOWARD A RECONCILIATION

From the above considerations, it is no wonder then that the intercourse between psychology and sociology regarding the treatment of children and the process of socialization has often been a dialogue of the deaf. Almost without exception (see Corsaro, 1981), psychological theories of development have failed to take sufficient account of the constructivistic social context in which development takes place. Sociological theories of development have been "top-down," assuming that development can simply be equated with socialization understood as the internalization of externally codified and imposed social "rules" and values that, by some little understood and mysterious process, are internalized by the child.

Fortunately, there has been a bridging of this gap, as developmental research (see, e.g., Emde, 1994; Tesson & Youniss, 1995; Youniss, 1978, 1980) has become more oriented to social concerns and, specifically, has focused more systematically on the relational context of developmental processes. More important, there has also been an effort directed at trying to understand the child's social world as children themselves see it (Corsaro & Rizzo, 1988; Corsaro, 1981; Youniss, 1980). We were particularly inspired by theoretical advances (see, e.g., Youniss, 1978) pertaining to children's use of social rules. Up to that time, we had been all but resigned to the fact that it was going to be impossible to examine children's relationships as a meaningful vehicle for discovering the boundaries of their social domains and relationships. After all, if social relationships are ordered events, then this order should be evident.

It became clear to us that if we were going to properly characterize children's personal and social relationships, we needed to have a complete accounting of the social rules that children use within those relationships. Attempts to characterize children's social lives without addressing this rule-by-relationship matrix are potentially misleading because when one describes one type of relationship, such as friendship, one implies that its qualities are unique to it alone, when empirically we do not know if this is true. As we explain in the next chapter, the interdisciplinary glue needed to integrate psychological and microsociological perspectives was through the phenomenology of relationships, which is sensitive to the child's construction of the wider social order.

We suspected then that the literature was ripe for an investigation of children's social rules and relationships since the past decade has witnessed a burgeoning of research on children's social conduct. It is worth noting, however, that others (e.g., Bigelow, 1977; Chandler, 1982; Selman, 1980; Youniss, 1978, 1980) have helped to clear this empirical trail by creating a new tradition of social-cognitive developmental research that is sufficiently interactive in character to have begun to satisfy some of this large need for relational content, expressing the view that the child's social reality reflects both internal (cognitive) and external (social) processes (Shotter & Newson, 1982). In so doing, these investigators have shifted focus from disciplinary dogma to the actual social relationships in which the child is involved.

By examining children's representation of social rules, the social structure that impinges on their lives should be in evidence since social relationships exist within a cultural context. The individual's cognitive accounting of social relationships should then reflect the culture at large, at least to the extent that children are cognizant of the forces that govern their behavior. This shift permits an examination of the developmental sociology of children. A sociology of children must, therefore, describe how children understand the different social domains and relationships in which they are involved (Youniss, 1980).

Relational approaches identify the interpersonal behaviors and regulatory concepts of children involved in diverse relationships, such as friendships (see, e.g., Mannarino, 1980; McGuire & Weisz, 1982; Youniss, 1980) or more complementary parent–child relationships (see, e.g., Hinde, 1987; Youniss, 1980). Hinde (1987) expresses the contextual problem of behavior as "dialectical relations" (or more accurately, the "interconnectedness") "between individual behaviour and the successive levels of social complexity" (p. viii) (see also Hinde, 1992). The same statement can be made about relationships. Social complexity ranges from individual characteristics to dyadic interpersonal relationships, contextual influences of the family and peer network, and the influence of the culture at large. Moreover, Hinde (1992) argues that we cannot properly understand the causes of particular behaviors that children exhibit without examining the origins and meaning of these behaviors with respect to the child's relationships. In his words, "Children are not fish" (p. 1021). This obviously makes a strong case for describing relationships rather than dwelling solely on the discrete behaviors of children, which serve more to classify children into types (e.g., populars, rejecteds, etc.) than to describe the normative order and children's place within it.

As we argued in Chapter 1, a purely behavioral–psychological approach to social behavior is not all that fruitful in helping us to understand relationships. While a strictly behavioral approach is unquestionably useful in assisting our understanding of the quality of children's social lives and the benefits that accrue from such lives, inputs from behavior must be tempered by a recognition of the limits of a behavioral approach in illuminating the process of interpersonal understanding. Certainly, to round out the argument, conceptually derived social rules do not occur in an experiential vacuum, and the observable social skills that typify normative exchanges between persons are but one side of the very complex puzzle that constitutes social experience. Social relationships, in our view, are at least as complicated at their conceptual level as they are at their behavioral level, perhaps even more so. Moreover, as we elaborate in considerable detail in the next chapter, much of the content that is transacted between persons is in itself symbolic in nature and does not readily lend itself to direct observation. Instead, one must account for these events by communicating with the participants themselves.

As we also showed in Chapter 1, socially underskilled children are not necessarily friendless, and children who are skilled in dealing with their wider peer group are not necessarily identified as having a mutually satisfying peer relationship (i.e., a friendship) with an age-mate (Mannarino, 1980; McGuire & Weisz, 1982). On the other hand, individual skills are not irrelevant to relationships. Children identified on the basis of their behaviors as being isolates or aggressives tend to be less trusting or more alienated from their peers (La Gaipa & Wood, 1985), which presumably spills over to some extent into their individual friendships since trust and altruism form the bedrock of a chumship (Strayhorn, 1988; Sullivan, 1953). After all, betrayals and hurtful comments undermine successful friendships (Bigelow & La Gaipa, 1980). Thus, while there are two schools of thought (i.e., psychological and relational) as to how children's social competency should be pursued, the membrane separating them is recognized as being semipermeable. We argue that a more complete examination of social competency must perforce embrace a relational perspective if it is at all to succeed, since children's successes or failures within the social domain are in the main measured by their adaptive behavior across a wide span of personal relationships, beginning with the mother and extending to the sibling and peer groups and fanning out to relationships with teachers, the opposite sex, and eventually, employers. In answer to Denzin's (1977) plea, this could be the foundation of a genuinely useful sociology of childhood.

Social rules are different from social skills in that they are linguistic representations of the relationship between persons that serve to enhance or maintain the relationship. As such, social rules are not derived from observing what particular children do in interacting with other children or with their parents (cf. Gresham, 1986) but rather by obtaining children's commentaries about how they say they manage their personal relationships. In contrast, social skills do not necessarily address the need to preserve a mutual relationship (see Chapter 1). Data dealing with social rules are only just beginning to be compiled. The social rules and relationship matrix, presented in Chapters 4, 5, and 6, is an opportunity to bridge this gap.

It is essential though for the reader to understand that our phenomenological and descriptive enterprise is not a substitute for a rigorous scientific approach: it is a necessary preliminary to it (Wohlwill, 1973). Thus, in our work, we are not testing any specific overarching hypothesis but rather are illustrating the contextual patterns of rules and relationships that then permit us to shed light on the more specific issues (e.g., compliance and autonomy) that have governed research on children's and adolescents' social relationships. Our descriptive and phenomenological approach places children's social relationships in sufficient context from which to validly address such issues. As such, our work is consistent with a new trend in developmental science expressed by Wozniak and Fischer (1993): "Instead of expecting explanations of behavior to take the form of a few simple universal principles similar to those in Newtonian physics, researchers and theorists have moved toward approaches that are rich in description" (p. xi).

SOCIAL RULES AND THE IMPLICATE ORDER

Why is it so important to know the content of children's social rules? As Youniss (1978) indicated, there is no obvious way to determine the nature of the processes of socialization other than to inspect the content of the social rules that children express. That is, it is necessary to know the fuller depth and breadth of social rules in order to grasp the way in which this information is constructed and, therefore, in order to appreciate the meaning of social relationships to children and adolescents. For example, when a child is told; "Don't play now, get ready for bed, you need your sleep," it is implicitly clear that the social relationship giving rise to this statement is both authoritative and nurturant. In a friendship, a child might say, "Keep things to yourself, you might hurt her feelings otherwise." Here, it is obvious not only that personal restraint of information exchange is important in order to preserve the feelings of the friend but also that feelings are important in a friendship. Because they are not relationship embedded, social skills (e.g., "Ask her to play") don't readily convey the social-relational contexts within which they occur; however, social rules do. This is not to say that social skills are not important for socially competent behavior; nothing could be further from the truth. However, social skills do not normally convey the verbal codes of managing relationships.

Extending from Shotter and Newson's (1982) argument, each social rule reflects the prevailing culture's "implicate order" (Bohm, 1973, 1980) and contains "social affordances" that reflect the wider moral order. Since a child exists only in interaction with the environment, a child's unique environment is reciprocally defined by active immersion in it. Using the metaphor of Gibson's (1979) "ambient optic array," each part of our social experience is to some extent a "perceptual invariant" of the wider ecology that is contained on a smaller scale within this experience. Accordingly, Shotter and Newson (1982) continue to say that children do not build up their knowledge of people "piece by piece" in an additive manner but essentially remake that world out of current experiences. This singular point, that the organization and understanding of social relationships can only be understood through examining social rule content (Youniss, 1978, 1980), makes rules an ideal medium through which to examine specific social-relational issues.

Earlier studies supported the thesis that social rule knowledge varies in part as a function of type of personal relationship. For example, Youniss (1980) observed that children expect adults to have unilateral authority over them, whilst relationships with peers are based more on reciprocity and cooperation. The distinction made between family and nonfamily adults (e.g., teachers) is less clear, nor is it evident what additional themes compose a fuller descriptive account of social-relational conduct. Since much, if not most, normative social interaction in middle childhood and after is reflective and verbal, where social information is consciously reviewed and scripted (see, e.g., Kassin & Pryor, 1985; Ladd & Crick, 1989; Rubin & Krasnor, 1986), we needed to compare verbalized social knowledge within and between relationships.

Corsaro (1981) helped to pioneer an understanding of the role that social structure plays in governing children's social lives—in particular, their peer relationships. Using a microlinguistic analysis of preschoolers' playground behavior, Corsaro was able to tease out social knowledge that is reminiscent of Golding's *Lord of the Flies*. While Corsaro's participants were not stranded on a deserted island, they nonetheless demonstrated many of the intricate crosshatchings of social relationships (i.e., friendship) and group acceptance that permeate Golding's book. Corsaro argued that before children make friends, their social bonds are with their parents and teachers. But within the family, as with teachers, children have few opportunities to negotiate; they must "recognize, accept, and adapt" to their family members. Corsaro found that "social knowledge emerges in response to the demands of specific interactive situations" (p. 209), such as trying to enter a play group. In his ethnographies of peer interactions and his examinations of peer communications, Corsaro identified children's developing knowledge about friendship, peer, and adult norms.

In our view, nascent within Corsaro's (1981) microsociolinguistic analyses of preschoolers' behavior was the budding of a series of social rules, governing preschoolers' conceptions of friendship, how to relate to their nonfriend peers, and how to gain access to and defend against involvement with peers. For example, children rejected others by referring to arbitrary rules like the following: "You can't play with bare feet." "I had that first." "That's my house." Or they gave justifications with respect to made-up school policy: for example, "Can I be a little baby?" "No, she can't. We can only have one baby." In addition, children's friendships, which are inherently more situation-specific at this age anyway, were conceptualized by them as being independent of the demands of ongoing activity and can be temporarily dissolved (e.g., "Well, if you keep going 'grr' you can't be my friend anymore") in the service of protecting a particular play scenario from intrusion.

These children were also quick to adjust to the demands of the teaching assistant, who invoked school rules like "The monkey bars have to be shared." Within these play episodes, we see the emergence of social structure in action that foreshadows some of the social rules we identified in Chapters 4, 5, and 6. Although Corsaro's (1981) preschoolers were not yet capable of formally itemizing their social rules, it was fascinating to see their social and linguistic origins.

While few social scientists would minimize the importance of children's developmental changes in coming to terms with their social understandings, we had good grounds for a componential social rule approach that concentrated on itemizing and classifying discrete elements of social experience. We maintained that a valid approach to social relationships during middle childhood is precisely via the social rules that children use. What is more, by not focusing on constructivist stage issues, we were in a better position from which to examine true sociological concerns as they pertain to children, such as how the content of children's social rules changes as a function of social role relationships. However, it is difficult to devise research techniques that clearly capture this interactive nature. Youniss's (1980) Sullivan–Piaget hypothesis converges with Corsaro and Rizzo's (1988) views in that children are seen as consensually validating their social world through mutual co-construction, reflecting the collective and negotiated character of the socialization process. Youniss (1978) claimed that children's social knowledge is simultaneously a product and a component of their social relationships.

Our approach addressed this issue by using an in-depth recursive interview technique (Appendix 1) to examine children's verbalizations of the social rules they use in dealing with others as family members, peers, or nonfamily adults. These verbalizations were then used to develop a comprehensive inventory of social rules, comparable in scope to the adult-based friendship rules identified by Argyle and Henderson (1985). We reasoned that our dependent measure of social rules was sensitive to the cultural content pertinent to children's knowledge of how to manage their relationships with other people.

Because social rules assume such a prominent position in our investigation of social understanding, and since social rules are linguistically represented, it is important to fully appreciate the role that phenomenology plays in relationships. In the next chapter, we connect this microsociology of relationships to several key theoretical accounts of personality, social development, and social relationships, out of which our social rules and relationships approach was derived. We explain why it is so central in an analysis of relationships to appreciate the participants' subjective experiences of them, for only through this subjective window do we gain access to the meaning that relationships have to their participants and to the social rules that are contained within those relationships. The "implicate social order" is then revealed in all its richness.

CHAPTER 3

Phenomenology and Relationships

THE BIRTH OF SOCIAL RULES

In the previous chapter, we argued that personal and social relationships are not only personally experienced but, in addition, are generated and represented as social rules that, by their very nature, are sensitive to the prevailing social order out of which they are constructed. In this sense, people represent the realities of their relationships with persons not only in terms of the unique characteristics of the persons involved (e.g., their temperament, moods, skills, etc.), but also in large part on the basis of the formal and informal roles (e.g., mother, brother, close friend, teacher) that those persons play within the prevailing culture. Social rules are the building blocks of these constructions, and in this chapter we reveal where to find those rules and how to extract them from interviews.

Consistent with our sociological bent, we had proposed, by the commencement of our study, that the nature of children's relationships cannot be properly understood without comparing and contrasting the kinds of social rules they construct to describe their management of those relationships. This is especially interesting during childhood, since the foundation for later social knowledge is formed here. In fact, we found (Tesson et al., 1990) that 85% of the social rules used by adolescents were acquired in childhood. We therefore thought it useful to examine social rules within the context of different relationship types, especially during childhood, where children are very dependent on others to structure their lives.

However, it could be viewed as premature to proceed with an examination of children's social rules and relationships without first tackling the phenomenological nature of social relationships and of the social rules that help to structure them. The importance of relationship phenomenologies is not only that they describe relationships but also that they represent constitutive elements in relationship construction. Aside from its scope, what is being claimed here is nothing new, since it integrates many aspects of others' (e.g., Giddens,1984; Harré & Secord,1973; Kelly,1955; Shotter & Newson,1982; Sullivan,1953; Youniss,1978) views of personality and social relationships. In this sense, it is useful to refresh ourselves with some of the salient features of these works, so that we can see how these various theoretical pieces lead into a phenomenological social rules approach to understanding relationships.

THE IMPORTANCE OF PHENOMENOLOGY
IN RELATIONSHIPS

What is useful about our approach to social rules is that it successfully integrates several bodies of research and theory into a unifying and essential body of elementary constituent parts. For example, Vygotsky (1978) and Butterworth (1982) hold that all cognition is *intrinsically* social, and Fogel (1993) thinks that all cognition is relational. We would like to add that all social cognition is also *intrinsically* phenomenological. Phenomenology is a description of events as viewed from the perspective of the actors. It can even be regarded as a story or script since it often contains a beginning, a middle, and an end (McAdams,1993). As we show at the end of this chapter, these experiences can be carefully content analyzed to reveal the rules and personal themes contained within the subject's expressed experiences. According to Hamlyn (1982), the norm is social in origin: "One who had no form of contact with others could have no concept of a norm, and *a fortiori* no conception of truth or correctness" (p. 19). An important assumption, originally made by Youniss (1978), is that the functions served by these social rules (i.e., to avoid trouble, to assert oneself, to share personal information, to comply, etc.) can best be understood through an examination of their contents.

It then follows that a complete accounting of children's rules is indispensable if we are to properly characterize the normative functions of specific types of social and personal relationships. For example, on what basis can we claim that a relationship with one's mother is any different from a close friendship? What are the unique and shared functions that children have learned through their interactions with people who occupy these nominal positions? It is therefore vitally important to address the role that phenomenology plays in our very understanding and governance of what relationships are and how they work, for through such an examination we may then more readily appreciate the value of social rules in ordering relational lives.

Phenomenological studies of relationships also reduce investigator bias and increase theoretical neutrality. According to Register and Henley (1992):

> The usefulness of any phenomenological study is to describe the phenomenon as it actually is experienced by individuals, a step that is unfortunately usually not adequately done in most psychological research. Questionnaires, no matter how psychometrically sound, typically begin from the experience of the researcher who writes the question, and as such cannot be assured to capture completely the range of the experience of the subjects who respond. (p. 479)

Although we applied scientific discipline to our recordings and classifications, an element of personal bias may inadvertently creep into descriptions. This has been a difficult point for investigators to translate into practice. For instance, as Hinde (1987) argues, the guidelines we observe in everyday life actually help us to be good prognosticators about our own relationships (see Humphrey,1976). We who do the classifying are exemplars of the same or similar cultural expectations held by those whose behaviors are being classified. In fact, this is an important feature of the recent growth of work on the rhetoric of inquiry (Duck,1994), which examines shared meaning in personal relationships. Aside from these assurances, though, we believe that the best safeguard against bias, especially in dealing with children's experiences, rests with a strict fidelity to the content expressed by the child, with a minimum of theoretical filtering. This is particularly so when social rules are at issue, since it is extremely tempting for investigators to "adultomorphize" the meaning of children's social relations.

The value of having children describe their interpersonal relationships has been demonstrated by several investigators of children's friendships. Using a carefully structured interview format designed to measure perspective taking, Selman (1976), Selman and Byrne (1974), and Selman and Jacquette (1978) found that children's interpersonal awareness becomes increasingly more differentiated with age, ranging from the egocentric focus on the self, to the mutual nature of the relationship with the friend, to the group at large. The child eventually becomes a "friendship philosopher" (Selman,1981).

Selman (1980) and Renshaw and Asher (1982, 1983) also asked children to describe how they would handle themselves in various role-taking situations dealing with issues such as peer contact, play entry, jealousy, and peer conflict. While popular children are more likely to verbalize strategies to help them solve these social problems, most children have encoded in their memories peer interactions appropriate to these situations. According to Asher and Renshaw (1981), "70 percent of the three most common strategies given by the popular children to each item were also among the three most common strategies given by unpopular children" (p. 279). It then seemed that there is an encoded or scripted body of social knowledge resembling a set of rules (i.e., "Don't snatch toys away from others," "Don't hit others," "Wait your turn," etc.) that both the child and the researcher can access and that, at least implicitly, contains elements of the prevailing social structure.

Using the more unstructured format of open-ended friendship essays, Bigelow (1977) and Bigelow and La Gaipa (1975) asked children to describe what they wanted or expected in a best friend. This resulted in progressively more differentiated expectations with age (e.g., common activities, global evaluation, proximity, character admiration, acceptance, loyalty and commitment, genuineness, common interests, intimacy potential). The results were broadly comparable to the earlier developmental findings of Scarlett,Press,and Crockett (1971) in children's descriptions of their "liked" peers and comparable to Selman's (1981) work on perspective taking and friendship.

Clearly then, children and early adolescents—and presumably adults as well (see Planalp & Benson,1992; Register & Henley,1992; Stein,1992)— have a fairly rich understanding of their personal relationships. Furthermore, as Duck (1994) has indicated, when people use language to describe their relationships, it not only accesses but also shapes experience: "Relationships are solidly based in the way in which we represent the world to ourselves and to other people, using dialogue, conversations, and talk" (p. xiv). Language transforms as well as describes: it *constructs* (Duck,1973; Fogel,1993; Kelly,1955).

In spite of the apparent utility of having children describe their social relationships, behaviorists stress the inherent unreliability of such projective exercises in predicting children's actual interpersonal behaviors. While, as students of interpersonal relationships, we are certainly interested in social behavior, we do not, at the same time, wish to exclude people's symbolic representations of others and their dispositions toward them. After all, much of what is valid in a relationship is lost to the external observer. In fact, the older that children get, the more abstract and symbolic their relationships become (Hinde,1979). If, as we claim, relationships are experienced subjectively, then, no matter how skillfully trained and disciplined external observers may be, without access to the participants' perceptions of their own social experiences, observers can never *see* what is really there.

Subjective experience forms a large part of our social relationships.

Maccoby and Martin (1983) and Peterson and Rollins (1987) stress that it is very difficult to appreciate a parent–child relationship purely from a vantage point external to the relationship. With respect to relationships, Hinde (1979) asserts the importance of thinking relationally as opposed to simply reporting the independent interactions of the participants. To illustrate, until they interviewed the mothers, Simpson and Stevenson-Hinde (in Hinde, 1987) could not account for the observation that shy boys are more anxious than shy girls. Evidently, mothers feel that it is acceptable for girls (but unacceptable for boys) to be shy. A child's subjective interpretation of experiences in a relationship, such as being anxious about being shy, may have more meaning than the "objective" events themselves. Similarly, La Greca's (1990) review of the clinical assessment of children showed that a reduction of subjective distress is often more indicative of favorable treatment outcome than a change in concrete behavior is. Accordingly, descriptive, qualitative methods are needed to capture the fuller meaning of social relationships, which are otherwise largely inaccessible to the eye of the disinterested observer.

The history of a relationship consists of a collection of memories, general expectations, and more specific verbalized rules—all of which are constructs, not replays of actual events—which may then become defining features of the relationship itself. Consider two children who grew up together as friends and now, as adults, hardly see each other. But when they do, the relationship seems to continue as if there had been no intervening years of separation. During the interim, their relationship existed largely, if not entirely, in their imaginations. There was nothing to "observe."

Phenomenology and Behavior

We were not deterred by concerns that verbal responses are in any way inherently unreliable or unstable. In fact, Ericsson and Simon's (1980) evaluation of verbal reports as data substantiated the reliability and validity of the phenomenological approach: "Verbal reports, elicited with care and interpreted with full understanding of the circumstances under which they are obtained, are a valuable and thoroughly reliable source of information about cognitive processes" (p. 247). Too often in our experience, psychologists tend to dismiss verbal reports as so much cognitive noise: "Pay attention to what they do, not what they say." In the present undertaking, verbal reports are the centerpiece of our endeavors.

Although observable behavior may not represent the essential element of a relationship, people's conceptual representations of their social behaviors are certainly relevant to their conduct. While managing face-to-face behavior is an important component of social competency as manifest in social skills and parenting styles (see Chapters 1 and 7), there is a lot of evidence demonstrating that social competency is acquired through a verbal-conceptual fabric of understanding, representing and framing pertinent concrete behaviors. For instance, Strayhorn (1988) used children's stories in response to vignettes dealing with selected social issues, such as assessing trustworthiness and being kind and helpful. He addressed the problem of the validity of descriptive responses as a "fantasy repertoire" that defines a set of "interactions, thoughts, feelings and behavior patterns that the child is capable of conjuring up in his imagination" (p. 50). The pattern that the child enacts in the fantasy repertoire is then "more available for translation into behavior" (p. 50). More abstractly, Hinde (1987) states: "Thus, the human language-based capacity for culture has consequences . . . affecting virtually all aspects of our behavior and experience" (p. 5).

Accordingly, we cannot understand social behavior simply by looking at it; we must interpret it within the child's linguistic social-relational repertoire. Even in studies of imitation and social learning, Bandura (1977) eventually acknowledged that children who are in the process of observing do not simply replicate others' behaviors; rather, children symbolically represent and transform those behaviors in order to incorporate the behaviors into their own behavior repertoire. Indeed, as the following literature shows, there is a better connection between thought and behavior when there is this fabric of understanding, which helps the child to chunk (Duck,1990, 1994) behaviors into meaningful groupings, which in turn fosters additional social skills through mental rehearsal.

People's relationship phenomenologies are not mental photographs. Although people are capable of uncanny accuracy in their memories for some types of early experiences, such as the circumstances surrounding the birth of a sibling (Sheingold & Tenney,1982), their relationships are constructed, not recorded, as the events giving rise to relationship memories are mutually "co-constructed" (Youniss,1980; Fogel,1993). As Youniss (1978) said, experiences do not flow directly through the child's mind but are transformed in the process. Such transformations also imply that relationships, while having a normative structure, are also in a constant state of flux; relationships are not "stable and arid things" (Duck, 1994, p. xiv). Therefore, we can only conclude that the way people perceive events contains the expectations and rules that compose those events. These constructed experiences, then, leave their footprints on the memories of the participants. As explained by Duck (1990), it is the accounting for regular patterns of social behavior, rather than their descriptions, that is the business of relating.

Even though we have not dealt with overt social behavior in our examination of children's social rules, as we illustrated in Chapter 1, social skills studies themselves often benefit significantly from an inclusion of children's cognitive representations of their social relationships (see also Ladd & Crick,1989). Cognitive representations of social relationships are therefore not "cognitive noise" but have a deep connection to the events that give rise to them. We may not fully understand how this connection comes about, but we know that it is there (see Youniss,1978). The proverbial glue that may help us to bridge a behavioral skill to a conceptual social rule resides in the cognitive representation of means-end relations.

As we indicate near the end of this chapter and in detail in Appendix 1, there is an implicit order encoded within people's personal relationships that is retrievable by means of in-depth interviewing at successive levels of abstraction. For example, in answer to the question, "Tell me some of the ways you use in getting along with your mother?" children typically give an initial volley of description that, when explicated (i.e., "Could you tell me a little more about . . . ?"), reveals a list of "dos" and "don'ts" (e.g., "I do things for her, so I can stay out late," "I stay out of trouble," "I talk to her about my day," etc.) that constitute social rule strategies. Only through this recursive "peeling" does the child articulate the rules that govern the social relationship. By identifying the commonalities and differences in rule use across various social and personal relationships, the investigator is then in a position from which to address the "implicate social order" (Shotter & Newson, 1982):

> Just as the child comes to appreciate the "suckability" of a proffered teat or the "graspability" of a cup handle, so she also apprehends in an equally direct manner, we suggest, the moral force underlying serious maternal prohibition, and begins to distinguish between a deliberately harmful insult to her person and one which is merely a humorous form of play. (p. 38)

However, unlike Shotter and Newson (1982), we do not think that people (even infants) remain oblivious to social actions within relationships (see Fogel,1993), but rather that the rules representing relationships are often not consciously realized until the rules are deliberately extracted. In fact, in our recursive interviews, children often mentioned that the interview itself was an entirely unique experience for them. For children to explicate their management of social relationships and reveal the social strategies involved, the interviewer must probe the children's repertoire of solutions to social situations for the limits of understanding before those solutions are meaningful to social behavior.

As mentioned by Renshaw and Asher (1983), even social-skill-deficient children have social and friendship *goals* similar to their more popular age-mates. However, the in-depth spontaneous verbal representation of social skills was the main discriminating factor between these two groups. Even in social skills training, it has been determined with third- and fourth-grade isolates (Oden & Asher,1977) that explaining the rationales (i.e., to make a game fun to play) of social skills (e.g., paying attention, taking turns, sharing, talking and listening, offering help and encouragement), as well as simply practicing the skills, leads to significantly higher gains in skill attainment. These effects were detected even after one year, showing the significant impact of cognitive-based skills training. It is quite probable that such training helps children to marry their behaviors to their social meanings. For this reason, we analyzed children's social rule rationales (Chapter 9) as well as their social rules.

Oden and Asher (1977) showed that cognitive approaches to reinforcement or modeling techniques result in children's becoming more actively involved in thinking about, talking about, practicing, and imagining the consequences of their actions (Combs & Slaby,1977; Urbain & Kendall,1980). For example, Bandura,Grusec,and Menlove (1966) found that asking children to describe the actions of the model greatly improved imitation. Cognitive coaching has also been successful in training preadolescents to have better conversational skills, such as sharing information about oneself, asking others about themselves, and giving suggestions (Bierman,1986). More recently, Chalmers and Townsend (1990) found that selective rehearsal of social skills in a variety of hypothetical contexts significantly increased the social perspective-taking abilities of socially maladjusted adolescent females.

As Strayhorn (1988) stressed, the use of linguistically mediated symbols transports us beyond the need to deal with behavior as it occurs and allows us to examine social relationships through the use of imagination. We extended this reasoning to claim, as did Duck (1990), that social relationships exist within the cognitive fabric of the child and that if we wish to understand their structure and function we must investigate the content of this fabric through description. In summing up the literature on relationships, Duck (1990) expressed the issue bluntly: "In brief, a problem that faces researchers in the 1990s is to grasp the *phenomenological* nature of relationships as well as those factors that 'objectively' ought to influence them to develop, stabilize or decline" (pp. 12–13).

Critical Incidents

While not dismissing the value of successively reinforced discrete approximations as a major shaping force for behavior, we took the position also expressed by Bandura and Walters (1963) that this theory of approximations is simply too much like erosion to be an elegant paradigm through which to understand how children become socialized, especially when one is trying to determine how children come to represent their relationships with other significant people in their lives. Consider how cumbersome it would be to learn how to function within a parent–child relationship or friendship if one had to memorize each and every occurrence, to shape one's behavior in minute detail each and every part of each and every day. Like Youniss (1978), we also argue that social experience is filtered; that is, children selectively attend to what they and other people say and do. This conceptual chunking (Duck,1990, 1994) is reflected in the child's perception of critical incidents (Harré & Secord,1973) within a relationship that become stored in long-term memory and that provide a basis for a relationship to be understood as meaningful. These conceptual chunks are transformed and updated with experience and development and compose the content of discourse about relationships.

The social rule can be understood as grounded in critical incidents: we propose it as an explanatory construct for charting the themes that children use to understand their relationships with the significant types of people they have to deal with in their lives. According to Harré and Secord (1973), critical incidents reflect the regularities (and, presumably, the irregularities) within the social environment that give order to events and that make the events more predictable. Critical events are the source of normative expectations and rules. Critical incidents range from traumatic events to more mundane occurrences, which form the bulk of day-to-day socialization.

Incidents are critical to the extent that they help the child to define the social order. In perceptual terms (see, e.g., Gibson,1969), critical incidents are the social counterparts of perceptual invariants that afford the child the defining features of objects in the environment. For example, an older infant has learned to identify a triangle simply by locating one of its component angles; perceptual closure fills in the rest. The child learns the implicit rules within each type of social relationship by detecting social invariants: for example, "This is the teacher. I should obey her." It follows then that a phenomenological approach is more than simple open-ended description. As we stress below in our interview protocol (see also Appendix 2), children's representations of social interactions within relationships must occur with respect to specific real persons who occupy legitimate positions within their social space. Such descriptions are anchored behaviorally as well, so that they unearth social rules applying to actual relationship content.

SOCIAL RULES AND RELATIONAL MEANING

For decades, investigators have struggled with the problem of identifying the meaning of a personal relationship (see Duck,1990). While Duck (1990) asserted that meaning is to be found within people's accounts of their relationships, we were also persuaded by Harré and Secord (1973) that social rules are the basis of any attempt to uncover the normative meaning of relationships. According to Harré and Secord critical description is self-directed rule following in which very subtle patterns of human interaction have the force of causal laws. Nonrandom social patterns are taken to be the product of stable, relatively enduring mechanisms. Similarly, with respect to the family system in particular, Minuchin (1985) claimed that friction and change are inevitable as relational boundaries within the family undergo developmental change. Whenever confrontations or disagreements occur, there are bound to be events that are construed to be important and are subsequently stored in long-term memory for present and future use. Family tension is meaningful precisely because it challenges its members to reconstrue or reorder their relationships. Whether this process of personal construction is couched in terms of accounts or social rules, the message is clear: meaning within a relationship is an experience of connectedness and implication that integrates our mental organization of past experience.

We suspect that each one of these kinds of reconstructions of past events forms a fundamental part of our current conceptions and expectations about our social and personal life (Duck,1990, 1994; Duck & Miell,1986; Edwards & Middleton,1988; Kelly,1955; Miell,1987), and some of these memories take the form of social rules that guide our future relationships. McAdams (1993) even claims that our personality, the very sense of who we are, is created through a personal "myth" or story that is a patterned integration of perceived past, present, and future. Although our work does not address individual differences in social rule usage, the conceptual processes that McAdams refers to are every bit as pertinent in governing children's normative social understanding. People selectively assign meanings to items in their environment that include the rules and conventions that people use in monitoring their own social behavior. Much of the meaning of an interpersonal relationship is to be found within its strategies (i.e., rules) and goals (e.g., to initiate, maintain, or dissolve relationships).

While we did not discount the fact that social information may be assessed through other nonverbal channels (see Bigelow,1983) such as picture sequences or nonverbal cartoons, we argued that children's understanding of their encounters with others is encoded and abstracted essentially in the form of verbalized social rules, reflecting the critical features (Harré & Secord,1973) of this understanding. Youniss and Smollar (1985) argued that through content analysis descriptive techniques allow insight into the meaning that the participants give to the interactions between themselves and others. For Vygotsky (1934/1962), it is language and dialogue that shape our thoughts, provide us with meaning, and determine how we construct our relationships with people. According to Vygotsky, "The primary function of speech, in both children and adults, is communication, social thought. The earliest speech of the child is therefore essentially social" (p. 19). Gaskins et al. (1992) made a parallel point by viewing children as active, interpretive agents of their own culture, which they create situationally through language. It is essential for investigators who want to access this meaning system to do interpretive research (such as phenomenology) that records how children themselves represent meaning. Children derive meaning by their participation in cultural practices, in both its individualistic and collective senses. It is children's individual experiences that are meaningful because those experiences are *personally constructed* and connect to the culture at large, which affords and constrains the child's thinking; children "shape" their own developmental experiences. Accessibility to the crucial features giving rise to social rules is obviously not direct and must be investigated by examining the child's naive representations of those rules. After all, the study of history itself is essentially postdictive and constructivistic (Carr, 1961; Collingwood, 1956).

Relationships are meaningful when they are ordered and have a purpose. The idea of a corpus of rules defining a given kind of interpersonal relationship has been germinating for some time in psychology. Similar theoretical ideas include Kurt Lewin's (1943) "life space." Lewin (1935) believed that any good theory is practical, suggesting that our life space is composed of social or "hodological forces" containing meaningful experiences and agenda, dealing chiefly with conflict resolution. Kelly (1955), in his personal construct theory, also obtained evidence supporting the view that we construe our social environment by discerning similarities and contrasts in people's characteristics, which then function as rules of classification. With regard to the family literature, social rules are also implicit in the family "maps" revealed in transactive therapy and family systems theory (see, e.g., Minuchin, 1985; Palazzoli, Cecchin, Prata, & Boscolo, 1978). Indeed, Duck (1994) illustrates this process nicely: "Relationships can be processes that continually (under the right circumstances) reproduce themselves in their own image, and that is what has led us to view them as stable entities" (p. xiv). In short, the purpose of relating is to create and maintain a personal sense of social order.

What is more, like McAdams (1993), we feel very strongly that social rules are efforts to isolate the core ingredients of social encounters by rendering them to a miniplot, which orders the interaction and gives rise to regulation of future events. In a real sense, then, people construct their social reality by telling stories about it (Duck, 1994). Edwards and Middleton (1988) describe verbal accounts of family relationships as a "deixis," which is the process by which acts of speech are "rooted" in "particular contexts of time, place, speaker and hearer" (p. 9). For instance, knowing how to deal with siblings and getting around one's parents' authority are major childhood tasks, tied mainly to occasions where the child is confronted with a problematic situation: for example, "I can't come out and play, I'm grounded. But call me back later."

We extended this argument further by claiming that people press on to seek explanations for virtually any novel social encounter, especially when it occurs within an otherwise predictable relationship: for example, "What got into him?" Because relationships can seldom be concretely validated, people seek to reduce uncertainty by locating or even imposing a social order on their relationships without which they are inherently ambiguous (Duck,1990, 1994). The need for this conceptual order is glaringly obvious after the termination of a "good" relationship, since the participants often go through a long period of "working through" what went wrong. The relationship dissolution violates the very order that previously existed, and a new one must be constructed to manage the breakup (McCall,1982; Harvey,Weber,& Orbuch,1990). In the following section, we illustrate how social rules are identified within an interview and what the information-processing demands are that give rise to those rules.

EXTRACTING SOCIAL RULES: THE RECURSIVE INTERVIEW

As we argue in this chapter, we needed a theory-neutral method of interviewing children about their social rules. We adapted Kiss's (1972) recursive concept analysis (RCA) for this purpose. This is a powerful interview technique that employs a reductive information-processing strategy resembling a tree shape, with successive branches providing progressively more exhaustive information. (The reader interested in replicating this procedure should consult Appendices 1 and 2 for complete details.) Recursive interviewing requires the interviewee to explicate to exhaustion a concept, in this case how to get along with the person in the specific relationship in question (e.g., "your mother"). Our interviews consisted of three stages: the initial listing phase, the explication phase, and the rationale phase.

Interviewees were first asked to provide an initial list (i.e., phase 1) of the ways (i.e., the strategies) they use to get along with (i.e., "dealing with," "keeping things smooth with") each person in their social lives (phase 1). After providing this initial list of strategies for the first target relationship (e.g., mother), each strategy (e.g., "playing games," "talking," "going for walks," "keeping things to yourself") was then in turn used as a target concept for the next recursive level of interviewing (phase 2): for example, "You said that you talk to your close friends as one of the ways you deal with them. Tell me a bit more about this. Give me some examples." This procedure permitted the interviewer to probe relational concepts until the respondent could no longer offer additional information or until information became redundant with items overflowing from other target concepts. Kiss found that information could typically be probed to three levels of explication: but because we were working with children, we typically stopped interviewing after two levels had been completed or when distress was noticed. (For ethical reasons, a training period and pilot study are advisable, so that the interviewers can become attuned to the sensitivities of the respondents.) The interview format dealt separately and in turn with each of three social domains (i.e., family, peers, other adults).

The interviewers copied all responses onto a rule-by-relationship grid sheet (Appendix 2) so that interview contents could be periodically verified with the respondent: for example, "You said that it is important for you to 'be loyal' to your close friend and that this involves 'doing things you promised you would do.' Is this what you meant?" In this way, we were able to document the social rules that children use in dealing with the various people in their lives, and we were able to help the interviewees clarify in their own minds which strategies were most relevant for persons in each relationship.

We made every effort to keep responses relational (e.g., "I don't hurt her feelings") and behavioral ("Give me some examples of how you avoid hurting her feelings") rather than superficial (e.g., "I try to be nice") or vague (e.g., "He likes me and I like him"). Relational validity was also reinforced in the third phase of the interview by asking the respondent to provide a rationale for the use of each strategy: for example, "You said that it is important to protect her feelings. How does protecting her feelings help you to deal with your close friend?" To enhance validity, we also used the help of our "peer investigators" children in the same age range as our sample (Appendix 1), whom we treated as colleagues, to help design the interview protocol (Appendix 2), construct the content analysis categories, and develop the social rules checklist, which is described below.

THE SOCIAL RULES

Our interviews resulted in 6,125 statements that were then content analyzed into 63 social rule categories (Table 3.1). Before classification, each interview statement was split into its social strategy (e.g., "I help her") and, if present, its rationale (e.g., "So you can have fun with them later").

TABLE 3.1. Social Rule Themes

NOT UPSETTING OTHERS

Don't bug or bother.
Don't argue.
Don't be rude.
Don't fight with or physically hurt another.
Don't fool around.

FOLLOWING RULES

Do what you are told and obey.
Do obligatory work.
Respect property.
Act correctly.

SHOWING DEFERENCE

Be polite, have manners, show respect.
Accept others as they are.
Go along with others' initiatives.
Listen and pay attention to what others are saying.

PLEASING OTHERS

Work hard, do well, do your best.
Give to or buy things for others.
Please others and make them happy.

HELPING OTHERS

Offer to help others.
Help by doing things for others.
Teach and show others how to do things.

BEING ASSERTIVE

Be yourself and don't be phony.
Say what you really think.
Be and act independent.
Stand up for your rights and opinions.
Be manipulative to get what you want.
Let others know when they've upset you or made you mad.
Retaliate.

BEING SOCIABLE

Be nice and pleasant and say "Hi."
Joke and fool around, or be humorous and funny.
Invite others over or out.
Visit each other.
Do things together, such as playing.
Include others in your group or in things you do.

(cont.)

TABLE 3.1 *(cont.)*

RECIPROCATING

Share things.
Help each other.
Cooperate and be fair.

TALKING

Talk, tell things, and discuss (general).
Reveal your personal experiences and feelings to others.
Talk over problems.

FIGURING OTHERS OUT

Get to know and learn about other persons and find out what they are like.
Know about those who are close to other persons.
Monitor other persons' moods.
Figure out your effect on other persons and vice versa.

AVOIDING AND IGNORING

Keep some things to yourself.
Compromise to prevent conflict.
Don't take notice of bothersome people.
Leave bothersome situations and find something else to do.
Avoid people or situations that are troublesome.
Don't take what people say or think too seriously.
Invoke third-party authority and advice.

BEING LOYAL AND TRUSTING

Be honest and don't lie.
Don't use or take advantage of others.
Trust others.
Seek help.
Be loyal and dependable.

EXPRESSING FEELINGS

Demonstrate affection.
Let your anger out and be aggressive.
Cheer others up and be nice to them.

CONTROLLING FEELINGS

Control your feelings.
Be sensitive to others' feelings.
Don't be hurtful by calling names or criticizing.

REPAIRING DAMAGE

Talk and make up after fighting.
Help with problems or give support.
Try to stop others from fighting with each other.

The rationales were coded and analyzed separately (Chapter 9, Table 9.1) from the rules themselves. The coding system for both rules and rationales was very reliable (see Appendix 2), and discrepant statements were coded to consensus or discarded.

THE SOCIAL RULES CHECKLIST

A 56-item Likert-type questionnaire was constructed that incorporated items from ideal examples of the 63 social rules identified from the interview transcripts. As can be seen in Table 3.2, these items were divided into Form A (Study 1) and Form B (Study 2), so that children could complete a representative sample of items within a single classroom period. Respondents were asked to rate how often they used the given rule in dealing with people in the following eight relationships: "mother," "father," "brother(s)," "sister(s)," "close friend(s)," "other friend(s)," "other kids," and "teacher."

ANALYSES

The 63 interview-derived social rules were conceptually grouped into 15 themes (Table 3.1), which were then reported on the basis of simple occurrence (Table 3.3) as percentage of usage by domain (family, peers, other adults), age, and sex (Figures 4.1–4.2, 4.4–4.5, 4.8–4.9, 4.11–4.12, 5.1–5.3, 5.5, 5.8–5.9, 6.1–6.3, 6.5–6.8, 6.10–6.11, 6.13, and 6.15). The ratings on the social rules checklist were also analyzed for each of the 15 rule themes. Each theme was subjected to a multivariate $8 \times 5 \times 2$ ("relation × age [9 to 13] × sex") analysis of variance, with repeated measures on relation. Results of the MANOVAs are reported in Table 3.4 and specific themes are also reported (Tables 4.1–6.5 and Figures 4.3, 4.6–4.7, 4.10, 4.13, 5.4, 5.6–5.7, 5.10–5.11, 6.4, 6.9, 6.12, 6.14, and 6.16).

Since several investigators (e.g., Furman & Buhrmester, 1992) have found that many of the key features of children's personal relationships are heavily intercorrelated, we chose to report our findings exclusively as relational differences. There is no mathematical connection between correlations and mean differences, and parsimony and reductionism were singularly inappropriate goals in an exercise such as ours that sought description and differentiation. Turiel (1978) is very clear on this point:

> The correlational method, however, is an inadequate way of dealing with the proposed structural relations between different domains of

TABLE 3.2. Social Rules Checklist Items

Theme	Form A (Study 1)	Form B (Study 2)
Not upsetting others	Don't bug or bother them. Don't be pushy or argue with them. Don't fool around when they are there.	Don't be rude to them. Don't get into fights with them or hurt them.
Being sociable	Joke around, try to be funny. Invite them over.	Be nice and pleasant to them, like saying "Hi." Visit each other. Do things with them, like playing. Get them to join in things with you.
Repairing damage	Make up with them after a fight or argument.	Help them out when they are having a tough time. Try to stop them from fighting with each other.
Being assertive	Don't keep things inside, tell them what you really think. Don't always depend on them—try to do things on your own. If you feel you are right, then tell them so.	Be yourself and don't put on an act with them. Let them know when they've upset you. Get back at them for things they do to you.
Talking	Talk with them about everyday things.	Tell them about your feelings and other personal things. Talk over problems with them.
Avoiding and ignoring	If they really bother you, then leave or go and do something on your own. Don't get involved with them. If you can't deal with them, get someone else to help out.	You shouldn't tell them some things. Work things out with them rather than disagree. Ignore them when they do things you don't like.
Following rules		Do what they tell you. Do the work that they ask you to do. Be careful with their things.
Showing deference	Be polite. Go along with what they want to do.	Listen and pay attention to what they are saying.
Helping others	Offer to help them. Show them how to do things.	Help them out, like by doing things for them.
Figuring others out	Find out what they are like. Watch out for their moods.	
Reciprocating	Share things with them. Help each other out.	Be fair with them, like by taking turns.

(cont.)

TABLE 3.2 *(cont.)*

Theme	Form A (Study 1)	Form B (Study 2)
Being loyal and trusting	Be honest with them, don't lie or cheat.	Trust them. Ask them to help you out. Be loyal to them and be sure that they can count on you.
Expressing feelings	Show them that you really like them. Get mad at them if they do things you don't like. Cheer them up when they're down.	
Controlling feelings	Don't say things that hurt their feelings.	Try not to show it if they've upset you—keep it inside. Try to understand their feelings.
Pleasing others	Do your best for them, like in work and sports. Do things that please and make them happy.	Give them things, like gifts.

> conceptual development. Correlations only show that there is (or is not) a systematic relationship in the rates of development of the two measures being used. They do not indicate the nature of the relation between two measures, nor do they provide evidence for their interdependence. (p. 32)

Accordingly, there was no valid point at this stage in our research in reducing social rules to a few larger sets. The importance of social rules to our respondents was reflected validly by the collective expression of those rules in interviews and in the rated importance of those rules on questionnaires. In like manner, the reliability of particular rule and rule themes was not in correlational coefficients but in the pattern of fit, which was usually identical or close, between a given pattern of mean differences across social relationships from one rule to another rule within the same group. In this way, the relative magnitudes of importance are shown.

In the following three chapters, the social rules are presented in three respective "macro" groupings (see Tables 3.3 and 3.4), which contain broad conceptual categories of social rule themes. These "macrorules" are: "compliance" ("following rules," "showing deference," and "pleasing others") and "autonomy" ("avoiding and ignoring," and "being assertive"); "self-control and conflict management" ("not upsetting others," "controlling feelings," "expressing feelings," "repairing damage," and "figuring others out"); and "mutual activities" and "obligation" ("being

TABLE 3.3. Social Rule Theme Occurrences by Social Domain, Age, and Sex ($N = 320$)

		Domain																							
		Family (age)								Peers (age)								Other adults (age)							
Rule themes	Gender	6	7	8	9	10	11	12	13	6	7	8	9	10	11	12	13	6	7	8	9	10	11	12	13
All domains																									
Not upsetting others	Males		+	+	+	+	+					+a	+	+	+	+	+	+a	+	+	+	+a	+	+	+
	Females	+	+	+	+	+	+				+								+	+	+	+	+a	+	+
Being sociable	Males	+	+	+	+	+	+	+	+		+	+	+	+	+a	+	+	+	+	+	+	+	+	+	+
	Females	+	+	+	+	+	+	+	+		+	+	+	+	+	+	+	+a	+	+	+	+	+a	+	+
Family and peers																									
Repairing damage	Males				+							+	+	+	+										
	Females			+	+				+		+	+	+	+											
Being assertive	Males		+		+	+	+	+						+	+	+	+					+a		+	+
	Females			+	+	+	+	+	+		+		+a	+	+	+	+						+		+
Talking	Males					+	+	+	+					+	+	+									
	Females				+a	+	+	+	+a		+	+	+	+	+a	+a	+a								+
Avoiding and ignoring	Males		+	+	+	+	+	+	+	+a	+	+	+	+	+	+	+				+				+
	Females	+a	+	+	+	+	+	+	+		+	+	+	+	+a	+	+a				+	+	+	+	+
Parenting and other adults																									
Following rules	Males	+a	+	+	+	+a	+	+	+									+a	+	+	+a	+a	+a	+	+
	Females	+	+	+	+	+	+	+										+	+	+	+	+	+	+	+
Showing deference	Males		+	+	+		+	+	+a			+a				+	+a	+	+	+	+	+	+a	+	+
	Females			+	+	+	+	+a											+	+	+	+	+	+	+

(continued)

57

TABLE 3.3 *(cont.)*

Domain

Rule themes	Gender	Family (age)								Peers (age)								Other adults (age)							
		6	7	8	9	10	11	12	13	6	7	8	9	10	11	12	13	6	7	8	9	10	11	12	13
Parenting and other adults (cont.)																									
Helping others	Males	+a	+	+	+	+	+a	+	+										+	+	+	+	+	+	+
	Females	+	+	+	+	+												+		+	+	+	+	+	+
Peers and other adults																									
Figuring others out	Males																+								+	
	Females																									
Peers only																									
Reciprocating	Males						+a				+	+	+		+		+									
	Females	+	+							+	+	+	+	+											
Being loyal and trusting	Males												+		+	+									+	
	Females												+			+			+							
Controlling feelings	Males							+	+				+			+										
	Females												+		+	+										
Adults only																									
Pleasing others	Males																	+	+	+	+	+	+	+	
	Females																	+	+						

Note. Occurrences (+) represent frequencies ≥ 7%, *t*-test for proportions. *a* = significant sex differences, $p < .01$, *t*-test for proportions. Macrorules = compliance (following rules, showing deference, pleasing others); autonomy (avoiding/ignoring, being assertive); self-control and conflict management (not upsetting others, controlling feelings); mutual activities and obligation (being sociable, helping others, repairing damage, figuring others out, talking, being loyal and trusting).

TABLE 3.4. Means and Standard Deviations of Ratings of Social Rule Themes by Relationship, Age, and Sex (*F*-values [$N = 181$])

Macrorules, rule themes	Form	Relationship								*F*-values			
		Mother	Father	Brother	Sister	Close friends	Other friends	Other kids	Teacher	Relationship	Relationship × age	Relationship × sex	Relationship × age × sex
Compliance													
Following rules	B(n=81)	3.38** (.55)	3.45** (.62)	2.69 (.72)	2.57 (.76)	2.97* (.58)	2.66 (.62)	2.21 (.69)	3.50** (.69)	24.20 $p < .00$			
Showing deference	A(n=99)	3.31** (.60)	3.34** (.58)	2.52 (.77)	2.55 (.72)	2.99 (.63)	2.64 (.67)	2.39 (.69)	3.20** (.76)	24.96 $p < .00$			
	B(n=89)	3.28 (.81)	3.92** (.83)	2.67 (.91)	2.66 (1.01)	3.23** (.78)	2.65 (.79)	2.24 (.81)	3.30* (.86)	25.03 $p < .00$			
Pleasing others	A(n=96)	3.43** (.57)	3.45** (.58)	2.76 (.80)	2.78 (.74)	3.13** (.64)	2.72 (.69)	2.44 (.71)	3.17* (.80)	23.93 $p < .00$			
	B(n=89)	3.26** (.81)	3.28** (.85)	2.92** (.94)	2.93** (.93)	2.61** (.95)	2.00 (.80)	1.54 (.80)	2.46** (.99)	25.03 $p < .00$			
Autonomy													
Avoiding and ignoring	A(n=91)	2.34 (.66)	2.32 (.68)	2.43 (.57)	2.34 (.56)	2.23 (.48)	2.29 (.59)	2.22 (.59)	2.06 (.66)	4.34 $p < .00$			
	B(n=85)	2.57 (.60)	2.58 (.62)	2.43 (.54)	2.44 (.58)	2.60 (.56)	2.36 (.53)	2.23 (.59)	2.49 (.63)	5.22 $p < .00$			
Being assertive	A(n=95)	2.83 (.59)	2.75 (.57)	2.70 (.68)	2.69 (.61)	2.76 (.60)	2.58 (.58)	2.35 (.66)	2.40 (.67)	8.63 $p < .00$			
	B(n=87)	2.39 (.65)	2.40 (.68)	2.61 (.67)	2.64 (.66)	2.42 (.62)	2.46 (.53)	2.40 (.60)	2.23 (.76)	4.75 $p < .00$	1.52 $p < .05$		

(continued)

59

TABLE 3.4 (cont.)

Macrorules, rule themes	Form	Relationship								F-values			
		Mother	Father	Brother	Sister	Close friends	Other friends	Other kids	Teacher	Relationship	Relationship × age	Relationship × sex	Relationship × age × sex
Self-control and conflict management													
Not upsetting others	A(n=94)	2.61 (.72)	2.59 (.78)	2.29 (.62)	2.35 (.58)	2.37 (.64)	2.25 (.51)	2.10 (.60)	2.60 (.93)	4.34 $p<.00$	2.44 $p<.00$		
	B(n=87)	2.26 (.88)	2.36 (1.00)	2.27 (.75)	2.37 (.70)	2.26 (.71)	2.26 (.61)	2.36 (.67)	2.29 (1.05)				
Controlling feelings	A(n=98)	2.86 (1.31)	2.83 (1.33)	2.63 (1.03)	2.55 (1.06)	2.67 (1.11)	2.46 (.89)	2.41 (.93)	2.74 (1.31)	2.02 $p<.06$	1.57 $p<.04$		1.90 $p<.01$
	B(n=87)	3.02 (.73)	2.94 (.78)	2.82 (.82)	2.85 (.79)	3.00 (.68)	2.62 (.73)	2.43 (.81)	2.71 (.88)	8.71 $p<.00$		2.22 $p<.04$	
Expressing feelings	A(n=100)	3.10* (.52)	3.11* (.49)	2.90 (.60)	2.97 (.57)	2.98 (.55)	2.72 (.55)	2.41 (.64)	2.41 (.65)	25.06 $p<.00$			
Repairing damage	A(n=94)	3.53** (.80)	3.53** (.79)	2.88 (1.09)	2.99 (1.01)	3.39** (.82)	2.94 (.96)	2.44 (1.11)	2.81 (1.19)	13.06 $p<.00$			
	B(n=86)	3.10** (.85)	3.08** (.90)	2.92 (.87)	2.92 (.89)	3.16** (.75)	2.71 (.78)	2.29 (.88)	2.43 (1.09)	18.06 $p<.00$			
Figuring others out	A(n=95)	3.06 (.84)	3.98 (.81)	2.92 (.80)	2.87 (.82)	3.00 (.81)	2.76 (.80)	2.44 (.88)	2.76 (.84)	6.47 $p<.00$			

Mutual activities

									F	p
Being sociable	A(n=96)	2.47 (.83)	2.38 (.89)	2.38 (.87)	3.21** (.66)	2.81 (.75)	2.21 (.76)	1.74 (.71)	43.47	p < .00
	B(n=83)	2.81 (.72)	2.80 (.71)	2.70 (.72)	3.34** (.48)	2.74 (.62)	2.18 (.72)	2.17 (.70)	39.08	p < .00
Helping others	A(n=94)	2.93* (.66)	2.76 (.73)	2.75 (.74)	2.86 (.63)	2.50 (.64)	2.25 (.72)	2.30 (.80)	16.96	p < .00
	B(n=87)	3.22** (.88)	2.81 (.94)	2.84 (.95)	3.03* (.84)	2.45 (.79)	2.06 (.85)	2.81 (1.10)		

Obligation

									F	p
Talking	A(n=99)	3.26** (.93)	2.55 (1.06)	2.69* (1.05)	3.06** (.91)	2.47 (.92)	1.91 (.93)	2.02 (.95)	28.88	p < .00
	B(n=88)	2.94** (1.09)	2.09 (1.04)	2.22 (1.06)	2.64** (.99)	1.98 (.78)	1.50 (.64)	1.96 (.89)	31.03	p < .00
Being loyal and trusting	A(n=181)	3.01* (.95)	2.55 (.96)	2.68 (.94)	2.95 (.99)	2.66 (.93)	2.45 (.98)	2.91 (1.13)	Sing. 1.91	p < .00
	B(n=82)	3.50** (.58)	2.81* (.81)	2.76 (.81)	3.08** (.65)	2.57 (.59)	2.10 (.65)	3.01 (.80)	39.03	p < .00

Reciprocity

									F	p
Reciprocating	A(n=93)	3.46** (.65)	2.93 (.87)	2.96 (.80)	3.26** (.66)	2.75 (.69)	2.30 (.75)	2.45 (.96)	31.88 3.05	p < .00 p < .01
	B(n=87)	3.60** (.67)	3.10 (.88)	3.08 (.94)	3.33 (.84)	2.98 (.85)	2.61 (.93)	3.22 (1.12)	11.64	p < .00

Note. Scheffé ex post facto analyses were used for testing mean differences. Significances are illustrated only for comparisons with the "Other Kids" means.
** p < .01; * p < .05; p < .10 (italics only).

61

sociable," "helping others," "talking," "being loyal and trusting," and "reciprocating"). These macrogroupings were a good match between the natural content of our data and the organizational principles governing companion works (e.g., Youniss,1980). Using data from interviews as well as the social rules checklist, each of the chapters first addressed the overall domain (i.e., family, peers and other adults) similarities and differences of its macrorule groupings (e.g., "compliance"), followed by relational, age, and sex patterns of the specific social rule themes contained within this macrogroup. These comparisons were followed by a more detailed "micro" examination of the relational distributions of particular rules, along with illustrative examples taken from the interviews themselves. These sample social strategies are identified in the child's gender (M, F), age (9 to 13), and social domain ("family" = 1; "peers" = 2; "other adults" = 3). We turn now to "compliance" and "autonomy."

CHAPTER 4

The Rules and with Whom They Are Used

COMPLIANCE AND AUTONOMY

In this and the next two chapters, we acknowledge that the broad structural organization of the child's social environment is revealed, in part, by examining the macrolevel distributions of social rule themes (e.g., "compliance" and "autonomy") across social domains (i.e., parents, peers, other adults) and their component relationships (e.g., mother, close friend, etc.). In Chapter 2, we argued that there should be a significant degree of distinctiveness between family, peer and other-adult domains, as well as differences within the family and peer groups. These differences would reflect not only varying patterns of authority and compliance, which are addressed specifically in this chapter, but differing degrees of closeness (e.g., *close* friend) as well, mirroring the formal and informal social functions within each type of relationship.

We also reasoned that there should be a notable degree of overlap or *fuzziness* (mathematically) in the functions served by different social domains, as between the family and the peer group. We maintain that it is the contiguity between social domains that fosters the efficient transmission of salient social competencies from adults to children and then in turn between children and other children. While acknowledging their broadly distinctive features at a macrolevel, we show below and in the following chapters that there is also a striking degree of overlap between the family and peer domains when examined not only "macroscopically" as social domains and rule themes but also "microscopically" as individual rules (i.e., the component rules within rule themes) and specific relationships. We show that parent–child relationships are remarkably similar to *close* peer relationships on a number of compliance and cooperative rule themes that have elsewhere been taken as the exclusive preserves of either parent–child relations or child–child friendships (e.g., Youniss, 1980). Herein, we see the origins of friendship and how it is governed in part by examining the parent–child bond as a source of the rules of friendship (see Chapter 7).

Perhaps more important from the point of view of our arguments on relationships and their meanings (Chapter 3), we also show that there is indeed a lot to be learned by examining particular relationships in terms of their specific social rules and sample strategies, since the overlaps and distinctions between relationships are especially revealing at this interpretive microlevel of analysis (see Gaskins et al., 1992). It is very useful therefore to compare macrorule distributions, on the one hand, and specific rules and relationships, on the other, since there is a different and valid implicate order at each of these two levels of analysis.

This is particularly true with regard to "compliance" issues ("following rules," "showing deference," "pleasing others"), which are especially relevant to a child's getting along with adults, including both parents and teachers, and also with close friends. As we shall see below, in the examination of particular rules and sample social strategies, the kinds of cooperative "compliance" rules that are specific to a close friendship are revealed only by the particular content of the rules in this relationship in comparison with the rules of "compliance" used in adult–child relations.

As we shall also see in Chapters 5 and 6, this same kind of fine-grained analysis of rules and relationships was useful in examining several other types of issues and indicated our case for a complete descriptive analysis of social and personal relationships. It is especially true at this level of analysis that the interconnections between social relationships become evident and then provide a basis from which to consider how socialization actually transpires.

RELIABILITY AND VALIDITY

Our approach to reliability rested squarely on the determination of whether a particular profile of significant relational mean differences was consistent from one rule (or rule theme) to another. Regarding rule themes, Table 3.4 shows that for all 12 of the 15 rule themes that were measured across two samples (Form A/Study 1; Form B/Study 2), patterns of significant relational differences were very consistent (78% agreement). There was also a 94% agreement when the overall relational profiles of these mean ratings were compared between the two samples.

Therefore, our rule themes were very reliable, especially considering that the rule items within each theme were heterogeneous.

Examination of significant ratings for particular rules within a given theme (i.e., the microanalyses) were also reported. We guarded against type 1 post hoc errors in these instances by calculating the probability of finding a significant mean as a proportion of the total rule-by-relationship matrix within a theoretically meaningful "family" of comparisons (see Myers & Well, 1991). Thus, a rule-by-relationship pattern was significant if it exceeded a chance binomial error rate ($p < .05$) within this family of means. In our study, a family was defined as two or more relationships within the same rule or two or more rules within the same relationship. For example, if a given rule was rated more highly for dealing with brothers and sisters, then it was a robust finding. Alternatively, a rating on only one relationship (e.g., father) was significant if it was highly rated on two or more rules.

Validity, particularly for phenomenologically derived rule statements used for illustrating microanalyses, must be understood within the framework of what Gaskins et al. (1992) refer to as "interpretive inquiry" (p. 5) in which the meaning is expressed in cultural context. In our study, the content of the rule statement is therefore sensitive to the rule-by-relationship issues dealt with in the rule theme. We could not determine at this microlevel whether the same child would express the same kind of social rule strategy if interviewed again. Such considerations of reliability were not appropriate for this kind of analysis. The validity of social rules rests squarely with their content; they are a valuable datum in their own right.

COMPLIANCE

As the interview content reported in Table 3.3 shows, the 15 social rule themes were distributed cleanly into the three domains. In particular, the "compliance" themes of "following rules," "showing deference," and "pleasing others," were distributed almost exclusively within the family and other-adult (i.e., grown-up) domains. While "following rules" applied exclusively to family and other-adult domains in the frequency of interview replies (Figures 4.1 and 4.2), as seen in Figure 4.3 and Table 3.4, it had significantly higher ratings for parents, teachers, *and* close friends.

"Compliance" generally applied more to males than females. This was mostly true for "following rules," with a reversal in preadolescence (Figures 4.1 and 4.2). There was also a consistent sex difference for "showing deference" only for the grown-ups (i.e., other adults) domain. "Pleasing others" was not mentioned frequently enough to be reported.

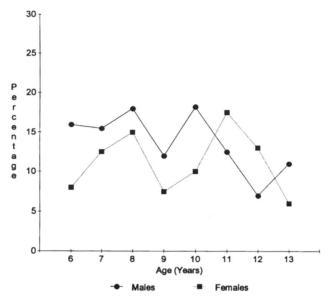

FIGURE 4.1. Percentage interview distribution of "following rules" in the family domain by age and sex.

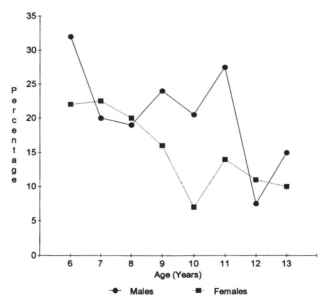

FIGURE 4.2. Percentage interview distribution of "following rules" in the grown-ups domain by age and sex.

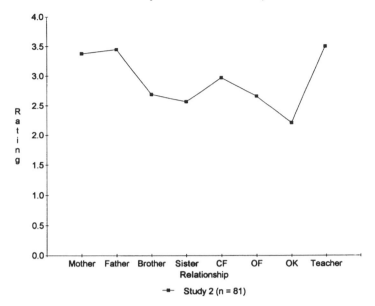

FIGURE 4.3. Ratings of "following rules" by relationship.

While Table 3.3 does not identify usage of rules with siblings separate from those used with parents, our interviewing experience and our subsequent checklist data indicate that, except for "being loyal and trusting" and "reciprocating" (Table 3.4), most rule themes prominently identified within the family domain were generally reflective of the parent–child relation. This pattern was confirmed by the virtual replication of "following rules" and "showing deference" in the other-adult domain, signifying the emphasis on adult authority. While these other-adult rules encompassed all nonparental adult–child relationships, the most common one cited during the interviewing was the teacher–child relationship. This relationship was thus incorporated into the rule checklist.

There was only one "compliance" theme applicable to the other adults only (i.e., teacher) domain: "pleasing others." Interestingly, as well, there were no "compliance" themes that uniquely applied to getting along with peers and other adults together, suggesting that these two worlds are quite distinct for children. The world of other adults seems to be quite alienating for children. In fact, compared to being with family, friends, and being alone, Larson, Ham, and Raffaelli (1989) found that children recorded a resounding sentiment that when in school "they wished they were doing something else" (p. 54). These authors argue that there is not much intrinsic motivation within a task-oriented, socially restrained environment, such as school. However, our data (Tables 3.3 and 3.4) also show that the clear advantage of parent–child interactions is that the task-oriented authority, especially associated with "following rules," and "showing deference," which is shared with the teacher–child relationship, is tempered with cooperative rules (i.e., "self-control and conflict management," "mutual activities," "obligation") that are almost indistinguishable, at this macrolevel of analysis, from those found in the close friend relationship. If we left the analyses at this macrolevel, it would then appear, contrary to Piaget (1932/1965) and Youniss (1980), that the rules of friendship are forged primarily within the family, an issue that we address directly in Chapter 7. We deal with the cooperative rules in Chapters 5 and 6. The following text addresses each "compliance" social rule theme, paying particular attention to domain and relationship similarities and differences, with specific rule examples used to highlight the social functions served within them.

Interestingly enough, from our interviews, "helping others," on the face of it not a "compliance" social rule, was empirically distributed across domains much the same as the "compliance" rules were. This was a robust finding ($p < .001$) since it represents a coherent family of three rules (Table 3.1). On the other hand, the relatively contextless peer literature (see, e.g., Mannarino, 1980; Sullivan, 1953; Youniss, 1980) includes mutual helping as one distinguishing feature of a close friendship, not parent and other-adult authority. Clearly, our contextual interviews portrayed helping in a much different light.

Because the distribution of our interview data included "helping others" as a form of "compliance" to adult authority, this suggested that children use a prosocial *language* to describe the obligatory household and school chores that they must do. This was confirmed in our microanalyses. But the checklist data (Table 3.4) clearly included "helping others" within both the parent–child *and* close friend relationships, supporting our argument that the meaning of social relationships is often only evident in light of specific rule-by-relationship contexts (in this case differentiating close friends from peers in general) and the language in which it is expressed. This finding illustrated the value of a phenomenologically informed and contextual approach to ratings of social relationships (Chapter 3), since without it inaccuracies surely prevail.

As with "helping others" the "compliance" themes of "following rules," "showing deference," and "pleasing others"—themes of adult authority in the interviews (Table 3.3)—were also rated in the checklist (Table 3.4) as frequently used in the close friend relationship. Normally, "compliance" issues have been reported exclusively as parent–child concerns (e.g., Youniss, 1980), but here we find that "compliance" rules on a wide basis are also close friend issues. As we shall see below though, by inspecting the finer content of specific "compliance" rules and examining the way in which children express them in the interview, it will become evident that the relational difference between parents and close friends is still apparent. As we show below, the overarching parental governance evident at the macrolevel trickles down in the form of the language used by children to express "compliance" with other kinds of people.

Compared with the aggregate domain (i.e., family, peers, other adults) comparisons derived from interviews, the checklist ratings, which compare individual rules with particular social relationships, show that there are instances in which selected kinds of "compliance" rules are germane to dealing with a peer, particularly when the peer is a close friend. It is precisely for this reason that the "compliance" rules, and the rules contained within all the other rule categories dealt with in this book, are also examined at this secondary (i.e., "micro") level of analysis. As we argued above, the overlap, or fuzziness, between types of relationships permits socialization to work more efficiently. In retrospect, this only makes sense, for it is difficult to imagine that a child has to learn a set of rules for relating to friends that is completely different from the rules for relating to parents, since one essential goal of parenting is presumably to help socialize the child to be competent in a wide range of relationships—formal, informal, and personal. It is within the finer contexts of this highly descriptive level of analysis that the fuller meaning of social relationships can be differentiated from the larger overarching social structures of authority and cooperation. Both levels of social rules analysis are indispensable and complementary.

Following Rules

The checklist distributions of "compliance" rules raised an interesting theoretical point, since Youniss (1980) found that unilateral authority, which is addressed directly by this theme, is chiefly an adult–child preserve. Maccoby and Martin (1983) also found that "compliance" is the very cornerstone of parent–child relationships. While our interview data, which compared parents and peers, certainly showed this, when confronted with "compliance" strategies in the checklist, such as those dealing with "following rules" (e.g., "Do what they tell you" and "Do the work that they ask you to do") (Table 3.2) within parental and close friend relationships, children seemed to recognize the fact that friendship has obligations of its own. The power of a peer group to control its members finds its expression in extensive use of "compliance" rules (Table 3.4). In retrospect, this finding is not surprising since children within this age band are very concerned with acceptance by their peers. By age 12 or so, the time that children spend with same-sex friends exceeds the time spent with parents (Buhrmester & Furman, 1987).

That this obligatory character of close peer relationships was not detected as a marked feature of peer relationships during the interviews is in itself an interesting phenomenon, perhaps reflecting the influence of normative role expectations and indicating that, when given the opportunity, children acknowledge that parents and teachers take precedence over peers. However, since the ratings (Table 3.4) for father and mother on "following rules" were higher—but not significantly higher— than the ratings for close friends, the issue of "compliance" in adult versus peer relationships contrasted with the assumptions contained within the Sullivan–Piaget hypothesis (see Youniss, 1980), which imply that unilateral adult authority and child "compliance" are necessarily structurally separated from peer reciprocity and negotiation, when close friend relationships replace peers in general. A similar pattern of relationship differences was found for "showing deference," which appears in the next section. It should be noted that the consistency in the overall pattern of mean ratings across rules and relationships underscored the very high reliability of these data.

When specific rules and personal relationships are examined, the validity of the Sullivan–Piaget hypothesis depends on the interaction of a particular kind of compliance rule with a specific kind of peer relationship. Evidently, close relationships, whether or not they are adult–child or child–child in nature, contain certain control functions intrinsic to the relationship. Certainly, a macrolevel analysis of the interview data shows very clear support for the Sullivan–Piaget hypothesis, but the scope and limitations of the hypothesis are revealed within a fully contextualized analysis, such as ours. The following account of specific rules draws on both the fine-grained detail of the interview material and the comparative analysis of the checklist data.

Specific Ways of Following Rules

"Do what you are told and obey."

The message here is clear and unambiguous: authority has to be obeyed. The only thing that does vary is the reason given for obeying others, such as doing things to please (here and in subsequent sections and chapters interviewee responses are identified by letter and number codes that immediately follow each quotation): "Do what they say. It makes them feel good" M6 (1); concern with sanctions: "When Mommy tells me to go to bed, I don't like it, but I do it. Then she won't yell at me" F7 (1); or a recognition that the obligation is in the nature of the situation, rather than an arbitrary imposition: "Obey and do not insist on your own way with adults. Try to understand their position" F10 (3). However, as Table 4.1 shows, obeying fathers was more frequently ($p < .05$) endorsed with respect to "Do what they tell you" than obeying a close friend was, suggesting that this type of unilateral "compliance" rule applies to parental authority in particular and in this specific sense confirms the overarching structural parent–child distinction reported by Youniss (1980). Given that there are three rules at play here, it is unlikely ($p > .17$) that this specific mother–father difference is due to chance.

"Do obligatory work."

At one end of the continuum, this is clearly a response to an imposed obligation backed by sanctions: for example, "Do your homework. She gets mad at you if you don't" M10 (3). At the other end, the obligation is cloaked in more voluntaristic terms: for example, "Help with jobs you have to do, so that others don't have to do it" F13 (1). While this rule can express an obligation in response to unilateral authority, either at home or in the classroom, it nevertheless can also be expressed in more altruistic terms, such that it almost blends into the "helping others" theme, illustrating its applicability for parental, sibling (brother and sister), and close friend relationships alike. Perhaps, also, some of the "helping" is less voluntary than its label would otherwise suggest.

"Respect property."

There are two elements to this strategy, the first being that one should take care with things, especially if they belong to other people: for example, "Try and take care of valuable toys" F7 (1). The second element has to do with respecting the property rights of others: for example, "Don't touch something that doesn't belong to you" M6 (1) or, perhaps more directly, "Stay out of Mom's purse, or she'll get mad and ground me" F7 (1). In absolute terms, this strategy ("Be careful with their things") seems readily applicable to all relationships (Table 4.1) although one suspects that parental preaching lies at its source, since ratings are highest for parental and close friend relationships. These findings are not due to chance because they reflect a family (parents and close friends) of identical differences.

"Act correctly."

This category subsumes various conventions that children feel they have to follow but that are too specific to merit a separate category.

TABLE 4.1. Means and Standard Deviations of Social Rule Ratings in the Theme "Following Rules"

	Relationships							
Rule	Mother	Father	Brother	Sister	Close friend	Other friend	Other kids	Teacher
Do what they tell you.	3.33** (.77)	3.67** (.80)	2.33 (.87)	2.29 (.92)	2.66** (.82)	2.24 (.78)	1.81 (.80)	3.41 (.84)
Do the work that they ask you to do.	3.17** (.76)	3.26** (.83)	2.49 (.93)	2.33 (.90)	2.72** (.86)	2.33 (.79)	1.92 (.84)	3.42* (.87)
Be careful with their things.	3.78 (.58)	3.75 (.66)	3.28 (.94)	3.25 (.99)	3.65 (.63)	3.42 (.77)	3.17 (.96)	3.70 (.78)

Note. Nominal Ns were 315 (Form A) and 344 (Form B), but actual sample sizes varied depending on the particular rule and relationship. Means were compared by means of Scheffé ex post facto tests. Calculations employed the multivariate within-cells error.
** $p < .01$; * $p < .05$; $p < .10$ (italics only).

Some examples are the following: "Don't get up from supper until the whole family is finished; it disturbs them"; "Don't say bad words, or you get punished"; "If you don't know them, it's not polite to just go up and say 'Hi' "; and "Follow rules of games, or you'll lose friends." Because it lacked a concrete reference to which it could be anchored, this category was among the few not included in the checklist. In the interviews, these conventions were justified by a mixture of references either to unilateral power (e.g., "You get punished") or to a recognition of the practicality of these conventions within the social order (e.g., "It disturbs them" or "You'll lose friends"). The value of these kinds of rules rests squarely in their inherent interpretive validity (Gaskins et al., 1992).

Showing Deference

As Table 3.3 indicates, "showing deference" is verbally constructed primarily as a family (i.e., parent) (Figure 4.4) and other-adult (i.e., teacher) (Figure 4.5) rule theme. There were also relationship differences for the checklist ratings (Table 3.4, Figure 4.6). However, as with "following rules," these "deference" items were generally rated more highly in the parent, teacher, and close friend relationships, but the close friend relationship was included only for "Listen and pay attention to what they are saying" (Study 2/Form B, Table 3.2). "Be polite" and "Go along with

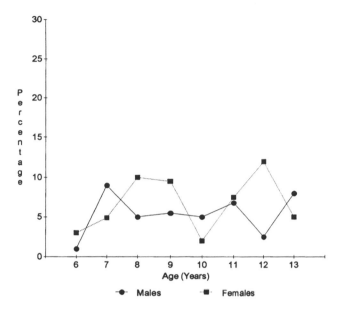

FIGURE 4.4. Percentage interview distribution of "showing deference" in the family domain by age and sex.

what they want to do" were more relevant in the parents and teacher relationships for Study 1/Form A (Table 3.2). Obviously, the rule "be polite" was, on the surface, more appropriate for dealing with adult authority than with one's friends (Table 4.2) and this pattern was replicated with the larger sample ($N = 315$), indicating that these are valid and reliable findings.

This theme of "showing deference" revealed more about the adult and child worlds than the "following rules" theme did, the subtle differences residing in the way in which authority and "compliance" are exercised in parent–child and close friend peer relationships. For smooth functioning with authority figures it is necessary to "be polite" and "go along with what they want to do," but to "listen and pay attention to what others are saying" applies to virtually any relationship in which there is an expectation of either obedience or cooperation. Being polite serves as much to acknowledge the other person's more powerful position. One can even make a reasonable case for manners that reflect "deference" as hindering the free flow of peer relationships, which serves to allow children to challenge one another's authority (Piaget, 1932/1965) and to co-construct (Sullivan, 1953; ,Youniss 1980) the terms of an egalitarian relationship. In fact, informal observation of peer culture reveals that

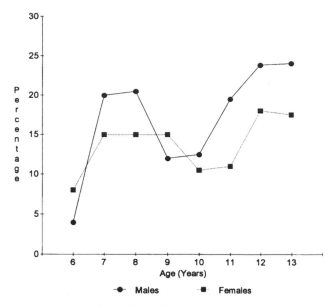

FIGURE 4.5. Percentage interview distribution of "showing deference" in the grown-ups domain by age and sex.

swearing and other forms of rudeness are often seen by children as a natural part of casual discourse. On the other hand, manners affirm authority distinctions inherent in adult–child relationships. Here, we are making the important distinction between manners as a vehicle for showing respect (e.g., not swearing in front of your teacher; saying "please" and "thank you") and social skills or conventions, such as not interrupting a conversation without waiting your turn, which are presumably relevant in getting along well with anyone.

Specific Deference Rules

"Be polite, have manners, show respect."

For many of our subjects, being polite and showing respect are one and the same thing; that is, politeness is essentially a "deference" behavior to adult authority: for example, "Be polite with them; it helps them know you have respect for them" M7(3). In this sense, this category is understandably very close to "Don't be rude" (Table 3.1) in the universal theme of "not upsetting others" and emphasizes the fine but essential discriminations that children need to learn in order to function competently. It

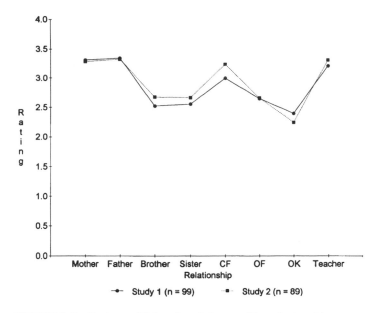

FIGURE 4.6. Ratings of "showing deference" by relationship.

is one thing to ignore manners with one's close peers and another thing to hurt their feelings. Or, to put it differently, there is a difference between acting rudely and being rude to someone. Evidently though, there is less risk in children's being too informal or rude in their actions with close friends than there is in children's behaving like this in front of a parent or teacher. Being polite can also signal a recognition that manners facilitate social interaction: "Act civilized, so they'll think more of me" M10 (3).

"Go along with others' initiatives."

We might call this the "reluctant 'compliance' " strategy. Unlike the obedience category (i.e., "Do what you are told and obey")—which seems more appropriate to relationships with those in positions of formal authority, such as parents and teachers who have to be obeyed—this rule implies recognition of more general and diffuse kinds of social superiority that call for "compliance." As a consequence, it is equally appropriate to close relationships with peers (Table 4.2) as it is to relationships with adults. The logic of this kind of "compliance" may presumably vary according to different relationships. Thus, it may involve straightforward

TABLE 4.2. Means and Standard Deviations of Social Rule Ratings in the Theme "Showing Deference"

Rule	Relationships							
	Mother	Father	Brother	Sister	Close friend	Other friend	Other kids	Teacher
Be polite.	3.48^{**}	3.51^{**}	2.69	2.77	*3.14*	2.82	2.56	*3.43**
	(.70)	(.70)	(1.04)	(.94)	(.79)	(.92)	(1.01)	(.81)
Go along with what they want to do.	3.02^{**}	3.12^{**}	*2.30*	*2.33*	2.80^{*}	2.39	2.02	*3.06*
	(.86)	(.85)	(.88)	(.87)	(.80)	(.76)	(.81)	(1.01)
Listen and pay attention to what they are saying.	3.37^{**}	3.40^{**}	2.70	2.68	3.21^{*}	2.75	2.29	3.36^{*}
	(.75)	(.81)	(.91)	(.97)	(.73)	(.77)	(.86)	(.84)

Note. Nominal Ns were 315 (Form A) and 344 (Form B), but actual sample sizes varied depending on the particular rule and relationship. Means were compared by means of Scheffé ex post facto tests. Calculations employed the multivariate within-cells error.
$^{**}p < .01$; $^{*}p < .05$; $p < .10$ (italics only).

peer ingratiation: for example, "Play with what the other wants to play, so that they'll keep playing with you" F7 (2); it could be a question of recognition of necessity: for example, "Go along with whatever they like, because they'll win in the end" F9 (3); or it could be largely a matter of avoiding conflict: for example, "By going along with what the other wants to play, you avoid hassles" F8 (1).

"Listen and pay attention to what others are saying."

There is often an important unilateral element to this strategy, suggesting that it is primarily appropriate to all salient authority relationships: for example, "You listen to them, because what they tell you is important" M8 (1), with sanctions often lurking in the background: for example, "Listen to them so I won't get yelled at" M7 (3). For some children, the rationale is quite logical: others should be listened to because they know better, for example, "Pay attention to them so that you will know what to do and understand things better" M11 (3). Clearly, too, the relevance of this rule for close friends (Table 4.2) derives from the necessity of attending to one another in order to sustain the interaction: deference in this sense is, therefore, a very practical matter intrinsic to a close relationship. For others, it seems more a matter of etiquette: "Try to be patient and understand what someone is saying when they talk to you" M13 (3). Attending is a logical and natural prerequisite to information processing.

Pleasing Others

As can be seen in Table 3.3, this social rule theme occurred only with respect to other adults during the interview stage of the investigation. Figure 4.7 and Table 3.4 show that "pleasing others," a moderately mentioned theme at best during the interview, was rated very highly on the checklist in getting along with both parents, with teachers, and with close friends, particularly for rules in Study 1 (Table 3.2): "Do your best for them, like in work and sports" and "Do things that please and make them happy." This relational pattern was consistent for specific social rules as well (Table 4.3). Surprisingly, this theme was also rated moderately high for siblings too (Study 2/Form B). However, the item that contributed to the high rating for siblings was "Give them things, like gifts" (Table 3.2), which is a ritualistic feature in family life, as on birthdays. Close friends are frequently treated as an extension of the family during middle childhood, as evidenced symbolically by this gift giving. Teachers have direct evaluative control over the child's work and behavior within a task-defined environment, so gift giving may also betoken this status difference. In fact, some children often give little gifts to teachers whom they particularly like.

Specific Rules for Pleasing Others

"Work hard, do well, do your best."

The key element here is not so much the actual work or the effort that is expended, which is nonetheless high, but rather that the effort is made to please others or to make them proud: for example, "Do the best that you are able to do, to please them" M11 (1) or "Study and get better grades, so they will be proud of me" M13 (1). This kind of rule attests to the power that parents have to motivate their children and reminds us of the responsibility of parenthood.

"Give to or buy things for others."

This is a rather superficial strategy aimed at social acceptance: "Give them presents, so they'll like you and talk to you" M8 (3). Sometimes, it is the expression of affection: "Give them gifts to show you love them" F6 (3); but at other times there is the expectation of reciprocation: "Give little presents to them and maybe they'll do the same for you" F8 (2). Clearly,

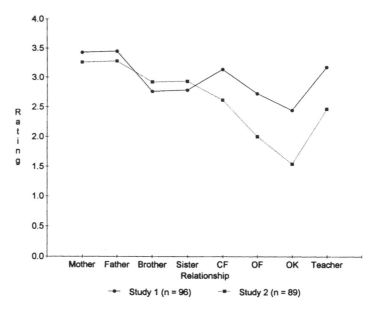

FIGURE 4.7. Ratings of "pleasing others" by relationship.

in our society, gift giving is essentially symbolic and serves as a potential entry point for establishing or maintaining a closer personal relationship rather than being the actual basis of it, and children seem to understand this. Clearly also, gift giving serves as a convenient mechanism for cultivating reciprocity.

"Please others and make them happy."

Another social facilitator—and again not at a very complex level—this category groups together those strategies designed to please others and to generally create a good impression or atmosphere. Sometimes these strategies are expressed at a quite simple level: for example, "Do favors for them" M6 (1). At other times these strategies display quite high levels of social perception: for example, "Give them compliments so that they know that I've noticed, and then they appreciate me making them feel good" F8 (3).

This rule is deceptively simple in its appearance. The complexity does not become evident in the rule itself because, after all, even infants show that they understand the social value of pleasing others. Rather, complexity is shown through the appropriateness of the occasions when such rules might be judiciously used. One cannot please everyone all

TABLE 4.3. Means and Standard Deviations of Social Rule Ratings in the Theme "Pleasing Others"

Rule	Relationships							
	Mother	Father	Brother	Sister	Close friend	Other friend	Other kids	Teacher
Do your best for them, like in work and sports.	3.40^{**} (.78)	3.45^{**} (.80)	2.83 (1.02)	2.83 (.94)	3.11^{*} (.87)	2.67 (.89)	2.34 (.95)	3.23^{**} (.95)
Give them things, like gifts.	3.45^{**} (.77)	3.36^{**} (.84)	2.97^{**} (.96)	2.92^{**} (.92)	2.67^{**} (.94)	2.06 (.85)	1.53 (.80)	2.45^{*} (.96)
Do things that please and make them happy.	3.34^{**} (.75)	3.35^{**} (.75)	2.71 (.90)	2.75 (.85)	3.13^{+} (.81)	2.66 (.80)	2.30 (.86)	3.16^{*} (.91)

Note. Nominal *N*s were 315 (Form A) and 344 (Form B), but actual sample sizes varied depending on the particular rule and relationship. Means were compared by means of Scheffé ex post facto tests. Calculations employed the multivariate within-cells error.

$^{**}p < .01$; $^{*}p < .05$; $p < .10$ (italics only).

of the time, and, furthermore, there are times when one just does not feel like pleasing other people. Children are in fact very careful not to appear to be "sucking up" to their parents or "brownnosing" their teachers, which can result from lack of judgment as to the timing and extent of pleasing those in authority. For instance, children who fail to exercise such caution in dealing with their teachers can be accused of being "teacher's pet," which is a traditional control tactic of classmates to police one another in the face of school authority so that no one gains an unfair advantage. On the other side of the coin, teachers must find it difficult to strike a balance between being supportive and encouraging to students while preserving the authority boundary that is inherent in the role.

AUTONOMY

"Autonomy" and "compliance" have a dialectical relationship to each other. "Autonomy" themes include "avoiding and ignoring," and "being assertive," which stand in direct contrast to those rules that reflect acquiescence to external pressures. "Autonomy" reflects the need to assert one's independence from the social order, as well as to oppose conformity. This can be achieved either by distancing oneself physically from the group or people within it: for example, "Avoid those I don't like, so they don't get on my nerves" F10 (2), or by detaching oneself psychologically from the influence of others: for example, "Go along with what others say the first time, but think it over the next time" F12 (2). As can be seen in Table 3.3, these two themes are salient in all three domains in the interview but more so for family and peers and for older children in dealing with other adults.

The checklist data (Table 3.4) also revealed no post hoc relationship differences in either of these two themes. We therefore considered "autonomy" as a "universal" rule theme governing children's relationships with most types of people and with all types of people at older childhood ages. However, there were relational differences nested within specific rules in "avoiding and ignoring" ("Work things out with them rather than disagree") for parents and close friends and in "being assertive" ("Get back at them for things they do to you") for siblings and other kids. Both of these post hoc differences exceeded chance ($p > .38$) occurrence. There was also a singularly higher rating for "Don't get involved with them" for the "avoiding and ignoring" theme in the teacher relationship, which by itself was not a significant post hoc finding but was retained because of its conceptual similarity in its distancing function compared with the age-by-relationship interactions found for three of the assertiveness rules.

Avoiding and Ignoring

As the interview data in Table 3.3 show, "avoiding and ignoring" rules are essentially family (Figure 4.8) and peer (Figure 4.9) concerns, with generally greater usage by females; and as the ratings in Table 3.4 and Figure 4.10 indicate, these kinds of rules are applicable in dealing with virtually every kind of social relationship at a moderate level of usage. As can be seen in Table 4.4, the only two rules that clearly delineated autonomy within a close relationship (i.e., with mother, father, or close friend) as opposed to a task-oriented one (e.g., teacher) were "Work things out with them rather than disagree" (for parents and close friends) and "Don't get involved with them" (for teachers). The emphasis here is on compromising one's assertiveness in order to avoid conflict within a valued relationship and avoiding conflict outright within a distanced task-oriented relationship, as with a teacher.

Clearly then, there are times when ignoring or avoiding a parent or close friend is not possible, and so it becomes necessary to give some ground on an issue (i.e., to work things out) to extricate oneself at least partially from a given situation. Because the child is a captive within the

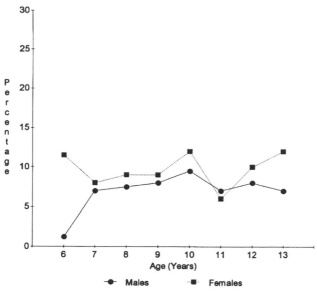

FIGURE 4.8. Percentage interview distribution of "avoiding and ignoring" in the family domain by age and sex.

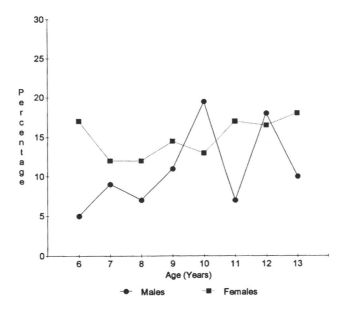

FIGURE 4.9. Percentage interview distribution of "avoiding and ignoring" in the peer domain by age and sex.

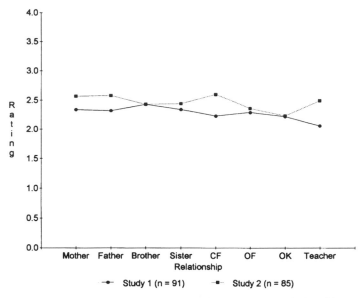

FIGURE 4.10. Ratings of "avoiding and ignoring" by relationship.

task-defined classroom environment, the teacher's role as instructor and disciplinarian may clash with a child's efforts to ignore, leave, or negotiate. Not getting involved personally with teachers is wise strategy since it keeps the boundaries clearly defined. We now turn to some specific examples to more fully illustrate the meaning behind each rule.

Specific Avoiding and Ignoring Rules

"Keep some things to yourself."

This rule involves being guarded about giving out information: for example, "Don't give private things away to other people" F10 (2), and is the converse of "Reveal your personal experiences and feelings to others" in the theme "Talking," which is dealt with at some length later in Chapter 6. One would expect this strategy to discriminate on the basis of intimacy, that is, one can be free and open with those whom one feels close to (e.g., close friends) but guarded with more superficial acquaintances (e.g., other kids). However, such was not the case.

Even though it has been well documented (Berndt, 1981; Bigelow & La Gaipa, 1975; Buhrmester & Furman, 1987; Jones & Dembo, 1989) that, beginning during early adolescence, an intimate exchange of informa-

TABLE 4.4. Means and Standard Deviations of Social Rule Ratings in the Theme "Avoiding and Ignoring"

	Relationships							
Rule	Mother	Father	Brother	Sister	Close friend	Other friend	Other kids	Teacher
You shouldn't tell them some things.	2.44 (.95)	2.45 (.98)	2.41 (.96)	2.34 (.96)	2.45 (.96)	2.26 (.84)	2.20 (1.04)	2.27 (1.05)
Work things out with them rather than disagree.	3.21* (.85)	3.24* (.90)	2.59 (.91)	2.56 (.95)	3.09* (.79)	2.68 (.81)	2.29 (.87)	3.18 (.97)
Ignore them when they do things you don't like.	2.21 (1.04)	2.25 (1.09)	2.30 (1.30)	2.40 (1.07)	2.30 (.96)	2.30 (.91)	2.34 (1.01)	2.16 (1.12)
If they really bother you, then leave or go and do something on your own.	2.48 (1.06)	2.43 (1.09)	2.66 (1.08)	2.49 (1.00)	2.37 (1.03)	2.50 (.97)	2.56 (1.11)	2.06 (1.17)
Don't get involved with them.	2.19 (1.14)	2.21 (1.13)	2.19 (1.09)	2.20 (1.00)	2.27 (1.09)	2.20 (.89)	2.07) (.93)	2.97* (1.06)
If you can't deal with them, get someone else to help out.	2.19 (1.12)	2.12 (1.09)	2.29 (1.09)	2.24 (.98)	2.24 (1.02)	2.15 (.90)	2.03 (.94)	1.95 (1.04)

Note. Nominal Ns were 315 (Form A) and 344 (Form B), but actual sample sizes varied depending on the particular rule and relationship. Means were compared by means of Scheffé ex post facto tests. Calculations employed the multivariate within-cells error.

** $p < .01$; * $p < .05$; $p < .10$ (italics only).

tion, such as sharing secrets and confidences, becomes increasingly more prevalent—if not the defining feature of a best friend (Berndt, 1981)—it was evident among our participants that keeping some things to yourself (i.e., "You shouldn't tell them some things") is a strategy to hold in reserve in dealing with virtually any relationship, even with a close friend (Table 4.4), and underscores the value of our approach, which is to start with a comprehensive account of personal relationships from the child's point of view. To our knowledge, this is the first time in the child literature that the control of intimacy has been raised as an issue of social maturity, although parallel findings have been unearthed for college students by Duck, Rutt, Hurst, and Strejc (1991). Researchers including ourselves (e.g., Bigelow, 1977) have been couching unfettered disclosure as a mark of competency, when children themselves inform us, on the contrary, that one must be prudent in sharing information.

This rule also suggests that no matter how disclosive a personal relationship may become, there are still aspects of one's self and one's activities that one chooses to keep private. For example, we suspect that one of the cardinal lessons of romantic involvements in adolescence and young adulthood is that the perceived dissolution of personal boundaries that so often accompanies the absorption of romantic love (Rubin, 1973) diminishes as the relationship progresses over time. Participants eventually must come to grips with the inherent separateness of personhood, which is showing its earlier forms of expression here. Such boundary issues offer provocative material for subsequent investigations made possible by a growing corpus of social rules in children (Bigelow et al., 1992), adolescents (Tesson et al., 1990), and adults (Argyle & Henderson, 1985).

"Compromise to prevent conflict."

This strategy is similar to "Cooperate and be fair" (Table 3.1, "reciprocating"). The difference here is less the pursuit of fairness than the avoidance of conflict, so that one can distance oneself from further entanglements. The rule applies more to dealing with parents and close friends (Table 4.4), reflecting the vested interest that the child has in these relationships. In general, there is some personal sacrifice involved: for example, "If there is a fight in a game, volunteer to be 'it' so the fighting stops and the play can continue" F9 (2). In the analysis of the interview data, this category also included some statements about intervening as a peacemaker to prevent others from engaging in conflict: for example, "Try to stop fights between two people, because it can spread to involve you and more people" F13 (2); but this was conceptually closer to "repairing damage," which is dealt with in the next chapter. In the first case, by compromising, the child backs down on something in order to meet others halfway; in the other case, the child intercedes in a situation in order to influence its outcome. Even during middle childhood, there are the building blocks of diplomacy. Notice that compromising seems more motivated by expediency than by principles of justice or fair play; it is in reality a miniretreat in response to the needs of the other person, so that harmony can continue. One chooses to ignore the encroachments of the other for the time being.

"Don't take notice of bothersome people."

There are a number of different "avoiding and ignoring" strategies (Tables 3.1 and 4.4), each of which differs in at least one important respect. This rule involves not paying attention to (i.e., ignoring) some aspect of another individual's behavior in an otherwise ongoing relationship: for example, "When [another] calls me names, I ignore him, and he gets tired. It helps him realize he's done wrong" M12 (1). This statement illustrates nicely the discriminations required between not being polite, such as swearing, which may be tolerated, and being offensive, such as calling someone names, which is not acceptable, as discussed above in relation to "deference" rules. A significant number of children's relationships are of an involuntary nature, either because of family ties, as in the above example, or because there are unavoidable encounters with others in the school context or in the street and children have to find some way of dealing with conflicts that might ensue: for example, "Try to be nice and ignore it when [others] bug you" M9 (2) or "Just let [others] do what they want if they're doing things like swearing that you don't like" F7 (2). Here, the child has to try to make the best of a bad situation.

"Leave bothersome situations and find something else to do."

This is a rather different response from not taking notice of bothersome people, but to a similar irritant. In this case, the response involves physically leaving, rather than ignoring, which may be considered a stronger response that is sometimes aimed at teaching the other person a social lesson: for example, "Go home if [others] fight, and then they'll get mad and want you back again" F6 (2). A more pointed message can be made by finding something else to do when offended: "If [others are] mad, go outside and play with somebody else" M6 (2). Leaving also has the advantage of allowing one to collect one's thoughts: for example, "If having a disagreement, take a break so as to think it over and review your opinion" F13 (1), or to cool off: for example, "If [others are] mad at you, go to your room and read to get your mind off it" F10 (1). This rule has even been incorporated in a common expression of children that is used as a warning that others are becoming offensive: "Take off!"

"Avoid people or situations that are troublesome."

This is a distance-keeping strategy. Clearly, it is best to avoid certain situations or categories of people. The avoidance may be either temporary: for example, when someone is in a bad mood: "Stay away from [others] when they are grouchy or disagreeing" F13 (1). Or the avoidance may involve not entering into a relationship with others who have certain undesirable characteristics: "Avoid those I don't like, so they don't get on my nerves" F10 (2). Indeed, several children would not tolerate some forms of behavior: "If [others] are using you, then forget them as a friend" F11 (2). This is a good example of a relationally specific phenomenon, such as being used, which distinguishes the parameter of a friendship from the characteristics involved in being popular or "liked." Being "used" addresses disloyalty, which can be very damaging to close friendships (Bigelow & La Gaipa, 1980). Children also seem aware that association with some individuals can get them into trouble: "Sit away from friends that will tempt you to talk and get into trouble" F11 (3).

"Don't take what people say or think too seriously."

Unlike the above rule, this one proposes overlooking negative behaviors of others rather than treating those behaviors as grounds for keeping others at a distance: for example, "If [others] call me names, let it go in one ear and out the other" M12 (2). While the rule "Don't take notice of bothersome people," proposes merely ignoring such behaviors, the focus of the current rule is on reducing the psychological effect of such behaviors: "Don't take it seriously when [others] bug you. Get away and don't worry about it" F10 (2). The impression here is that behaviors normally not tolerated in a stranger are tolerated to some degree within a friendship. Either the relationship takes priority over irritating behavior or, as argued in Chapter 1, relationships and social skills simply occupy different social spaces and are therefore often unrelated.

It must be remembered that children are not always in a position to avoid those who trouble them (see "Don't take notice of bothersome people" above). Adolescents do often recognize that the effects of the "imaginary audience" (Elkind, 1981) can be neutralized: for example, "Don't be overconcerned with what [others] are thinking about you" F13 (2). In speculating about what other people think of them, children can also eventually learn to transform input through an appreciation of the interplay between their own and others' thoughts, intentions, feelings, emotions, and values (Damon & Hart, 1988). The adult phrase "Rise above it" may have its roots here. This rule was not in the checklist.

"Invoke third-party authority and advice."

This strategy involves children's getting some third party to intervene in a relationship, usually in the face of some difficulty. It may involve calling on an adult to exercise a superior level of power or authority: for example, "When [others] make me mad, I go to another adult who knows the person, so that they can talk to them, and it makes me feel better" F9 (3); or it can be a case of children's drawing on peer support to sustain them in the face of adult authority: for example, "Get support from friends when teacher is being unfair" F13 (2). The thrust here is to ignore or avoid further attempts to deal with the problem yourself and to call in the social "troops." With this rule, we are reminded again of the danger of viewing social relationships as isolated dyads. For any given relationship, the other relationships in which one is involved are interlaced to some extent and can all, in varying degrees, exert an influence right up to the point of direct intervention, as in the present case.

Being Assertive

As with "avoiding and ignoring," this theme was essentially con-structed as a family (Figure 4.11) and peer (Figure 4.12) one and was rated with moderate frequency in virtually every relationship (Tables 3.4 & 4.5, Figure 4.13) at this macrolevel. There were no consistent sex differences here. However, there was a significant age-by-relationship rating interaction effect in Form B/Study 2 (Table 3.4). As we can see in Table 3.2, the Study 2 rules were "Be yourself and don't put on an act with them," "Let them know when they've upset you," and "Get back at them for things they do to you." Univariate F-tests located this effect in the other-friends and teacher relationships. At age 11, other friends were rated more highly on these assertiveness rules than were all other relationships on these rules. On the other hand, this interac-tion also showed that assertiveness is more difficult to manage with one's teacher (see also Table 4.4), especially at age 10, when it is easier to self-assert with virtually anyone else. Children are less likely to tolerate offenses from those with whom they do not have a close relationship, except when there is a formal authority boundary, as with a teacher. Interestingly enough, these results also show that it is not easier to be assertive with one's close friends, only with one's other friends. Perhaps, the closer the relationship, the less likely that of-fenses will occur.

It is not entirely clear why this group of rules achieved such a unique profile during early adolescence in relation to other friends. The tempo-rary appearance of retaliation at ages 10 and 11 with respect to other friends may simply signal a transition point from adult to more intense peer relationships. Other friends may serve to bridge these two worlds at a time when peers begin to assume a relatively more intimate and powerful role in the child's social life (Buhrmester & Furman, 1987). As

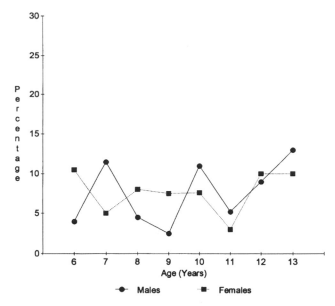

FIGURE 4.11. Percentage interview distribution of "being assertive" in the family domain by age and sex.

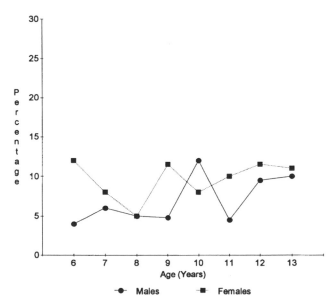

FIGURE 4.12. Percentage interview distribution of "being assertive" in the peer domain by age and sex.

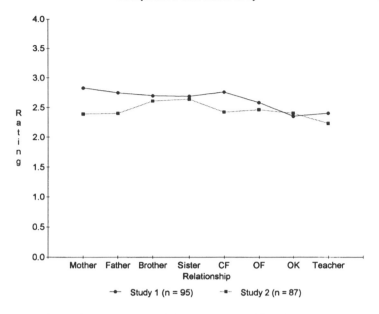

FIGURE 4.13. Ratings of "being assertive" by relationship.

we surmised in Chapter 2, children's peer relationship distinctions are important because the relationships involve quite different categories of interactions (Oden, Herzberger, Mangione, & Wheeler, 1984), ranging from friends who share and help on a personal level to social friends, activity participants, and mere circumstantial acquaintances. Bigelow and La Gaipa (1980) also found that during early adolescence, children's conceptual distinctions between different levels of friendship begin in earnest. We suspect then that at this juncture the world of peers requires a social "stepping stone" of other friends to bridge the gap between parents (and teachers) and close friends, on the one hand, and close friends and unacquainted or strange children, on the other, who up until this age are seen as less socially relevant.

It is also intriguing to inspect Table 4.5, which indicates that among the six rules, only retaliation (i.e., "Get back at them for things they do to you") had a significant overall relationship main effect, with siblings and other kids rated more highly on this rule compared to the parental relationships, where it was decidedly of low frequency suggesting that opportunities for getting back at one's mother or father are strictly limited. Because of the coherency of these findings within the sibling relationships, it was deemed unlikely that the results were simply due to chance, although replication in this case might be advisable. The sibling

TABLE 4.5. Means and Standard Deviations of Social Rule Ratings in the Theme "Being Assertive"

	Relationships							
Rule	Mother	Father	Brother	Sister	Close friend	Other friend	Other kids	Teacher
Be yourself and don't put on an act with them.	2.87 (1.23)	2.90 (1.23)	2.67 (1.11)	2.70 (1.10)	2.79 (1.09)	2.63 (1.00)	2.48 (1.06)	2.71 (1.27)
Don't keep things inside; tell them what you really think.	2.56 (1.01)	2.42 (1.08)	2.41 (1.10)	2.40 (1.04)	*2.62* (1.01)	2.24 (.99)	1.89 (1.11)	1.96 (1.16)
Don't always depend on them; try to do things on your own.	2.72 (.93)	2.72 (.92)	2.55 (1.05)	2.56 (.96)	2.55 (.96)	2.48 (.94)	2.39 (1.14)	2.60 (1.09)
If you feel you are right, then tell them so.	3.15 (1.01)	3.03 (1.08)	3.07 (1.10)	3.14 (1.04)	3.12 (1.01)	2.92 (.99)	2.69 (1.11)	2.61 (1.16)
Let them know when they've upset you.	2.75 (1.11)	2.76 (1.12)	2.63 (1.18)	2.60 (1.16)	2.49 (1.03)	2.30 (.95)	2.15 (1.05)	1.99 (1.13)
Get back at them for things they do to you.	1.66 (.96)	1.68 (1.04)	2.45[*] (1.09)	2.49[*] (1.06)	2.07 (.97)	2.33 (.90)	2.51[*] (.96)	1.76 (1.09)

Note. Nominal *N*s were 315 (Form A) and 344 (Form B), but actual sample sizes varied depending on the particular rule and relationship. Means were compared by means of Scheffé ex post facto tests. Calculations employed the multivariate within-cells error.

[**]$p < .01$; [*]$p < .05$; $p < .10$ (italics only).

issue notwithstanding (Stoneman et al., 1984), it is easy to see why retaliation is more likely to occur with relative strangers (i.e., other kids), since there is nothing to lose when there is no investment in the relationship. The high usage of retaliation for siblings at first seems anomalous in that siblings are enduring and meaningful relationships; but as we argued in Chapter 8, the rules for their governance are relatively "cooler" compared to those of close friendships.

Specific Assertiveness Rules

"Be yourself and don't be phony."

We suspect that this is a separate category that does not fit very well with any other. It seems to imply a recognition of the fact that, in contrast with the "being sociable" strategies presented in detail in Chapter 6, there is a certain danger in trying to be all things to all people. Throughout one's relationships, one must try to maintain a sense of who one really is, and people will accept you just as you are. This rule is similar to the therapeutic purpose behind Carl Roger's concept of "unconditional positive regard" and has been used in the content analysis of children's friendships in several studies (e.g., Canfield & La Gaipa, 1970; Bigelow & La Gaipa, 1975). The danger is that others will catch on and find you not believable: for example, "Be yourself and don't try to act cool. [Others will] know you're not really like that" M13 (2), or, perhaps more perceptively, that others will simply be confused by the signals being put out: for example, "Don't put on an act, because you'll get into a confusing situation if people don't know what to expect" F13 (2). One might hypothesize that widespread utilization of this rule could be taken as evidence of the child's attempt to construct a coherent self out of the different social relationships in which the child must engage. In this sense, "Be yourself" recalls Goffman's (1959) portrayal of social life as a stage, where one enacts different roles within a grand play but is required to sustain a single identity throughout them.

"Say what you really think."

Again, this is a fairly advanced strategy. If we compare this with other self-assertiveness rules outlined above, in principle this category seems much more appropriate to stable relationships (Table 4.5, close friends) in that it places a value on providing accurate feedback and is less concerned with whether this feedback will temporarily offend or irritate the other person. However, such was not the case. Because there was no significant ex post facto difference (Table 3.4) within this rule theme and because this was the only rule within this theme to reach overall significance (Table 4.5), it was likely due to chance.

Children seem aware that this is an appropriate strategy within any social interaction, from those interactions that are close: for example, "Don't think ahead; speak freely if you know each other" M13 (1), or "Be open and say what you think, so you let others know you trust them" F13 (2), to those interactions that are not: for example, "If somebody asks me to play with them, I will tell them whether I want to or not" F6 (2).

Clearly, a sound and stable relationship, as well as a weaker one, must allow members to express themselves freely; and conversely, the tendency to only say what the other wants to hear to please the other seems likely to achieve its objective only in the short term. Indeed, one can make the case that one of the key provisions of any relationship is that it provide the necessary conditions within which frank exchanges can be obtained.

If we had not examined this rule by itself, along with its subtle meanings, it would have escaped our attention, and our misunderstanding of close relationships would have persisted. Naturally, given its importance, this finding bears replication. Our emphasis on comprehensive description of relationships is reinforced here and cautions those who rush headlong into reductionistic analyses without first establishing a fuller appreciation of the phenomena under examination.

"Be and act independent."

One important dimension along which our social rules varied was the extent to which the children either are passively responding to others because of their superior authority, power, or status or are actively asserting themselves in order to impose their own stamp on the enveloping social relationships. This rule may involve not depending on others to extricate oneself from difficulty: for example, "I fight my own battles" M6 (2); trying to work things out for oneself: for example, "Go along with what others say the first time, but think it over the next time" F12 (1); and avoiding blind conformity: for example, "Don't try to do everything that others are doing just to fit into a group" F13 (2). Note that these examples are as much a reflection of mental as they are of behavioral autonomy; they do not express assertiveness in the ordinary sense of pushing oneself forward, but rather in the sense of desiring to work things out for oneself: for example, "Try to do things by yourself, even if it's hard, so as not to be just a child" F8 (3). Surely, this must be a latent sign of the struggle to be mature.

"Stand up for your rights and opinions."

Another manifestation of "autonomy," but which goes beyond internal acts as well, involves children's actually defending their own point of view in the face of opposition: "When [others] say I'm wrong, I try to find out what's right and prove them wrong" M12 (1). It may involve intellectual autonomy, as in the example just cited, or it may involve an issue of social justice: "When someone blames you for something you didn't do, then you tell them so" M13 (1).

"Let others know when they've upset you or made you mad."

This rule appears as quite an advanced strategy in that it involves giving others feedback about one's reaction to them, especially about negative things. It presupposes the social perception that others simply may not realize that they are causing annoyance: for example, "If [others] keep bugging me and they don't know that I am bothered, then I tell them" M9 (2). Compared to the various avoidance techniques cited above, one might expect this strategy to be more successful in modifying offending behavior and less drastic than retaliation, which may really damage the longer-term prospects of a relationship. For example, the statement "Always discuss things that are bothering you about others, so that they either change or else you get an explanation" F12 (1) seems to be an excellent piece of advice about social relationships. It could be hypothesized that this strategy would be used more frequently in close relationships, as with family and close friends, but Table 4.5 suggests otherwise.

"Retaliate."

Taking self-assertiveness a step further, here we have the time-honored "eye-for-an-eye" strategy: "If others pick on me, I pick on them back, so as to teach them not to do it to me again" F12 (1). In some cases, retaliation (e.g., "Get back at them for things they do to you") may have the aim of modifying the offending behavior, as in the example just cited; in other instances, the motive may simply be one of bald revenge: "If I'm insulted, then I just insult them back. It gives me satisfaction." One would expect retaliation to be more important in dealing with negative behavior on the part of more "distant" social encounters, and Table 4.5 confirms this with respect to other kids and siblings, compared with parents. The coherency of these findings militates against chance occurrence ($p > .38$).

We found this rule particularly intriguing for sibling relationships (Table 4.5) since it betrayed an element of hostility and lack of attention to the quality of the relationship not found in close friend relationships. Understandably though, the lack of this rule in dealing with adults in general reflects the relative power of adults to neutralize social strategies of this sort. Relationships between siblings then are relatively cool, and we will have more to say about sibling relationships in Chapter 8.

Retaliation is a fitting transition to our next chapter which deals with "self-control and conflict management." These kinds of rules form the bedrock of successful relating, but, as we illustrate below, their universal applicability at a macrolevel of analysis belies children's intricate sensitivity to the appropriateness of specific types of rules that apply to specific types of relationships. As we also illustrate, while "conflict management" is the very stuff of interpersonal relationships, there is a rich conceptual corpus of strategies that children use in its execution when dealing with many kinds of social and personal relationships.

SUMMARY

The current chapter examined children's social rules with respect to "compliance," which is an overarching issue of social relationships. Our contextualized analysis, addressing groups of relationships, or "domains" (e.g., parents, peers, other adults) and types of "compliance" rules, reveal a level of specificity and meaning that would have been otherwise impossible. Firstly, the distribution of "compliance" varies as a function of how relationships are grouped. When grouped as parents, peers and other adults, "compliance" is clearly reserved for dealing with parental and other-adult (i.e., teacher) relationships.

However, when specific relationships (e.g., close friends) are examined at a microlevel, there is clearly a similarity in the usage of compliance across relationships of adult authority and close friends alike. Our examination of the contents of specific rules and strategies in our microanalyses yields a pattern of similarity and difference in compliance rules for dealing with adults versus peers. For example, one is polite with one's parents and teachers but one listens and pays attention to, and goes along with, both adults and close friends.

In like fashion, the "autonomy" rules, which had very few significant relational differences at either level of analysis, nevertheless show that the way in which one asserts oneself with parents and close friends is decidedly more cooperative than with others with whom there is less vested interest. Similarly, one may retaliate more freely with relatively more distant relationships, which ironically include one's siblings. But, as we explain in Chapter 8, this finding is quite consistent with the literature.

Perhaps the most significant appeal of these findings is the way in which they address the meaningfulness of children's personal and social relationships. In order for meaning to be clear, it has to be specific, and it is at this level of the particular rule and relationship and how it is expressed that this meaning is detected in all its fullness of form. On the other hand, the overarching governance of adult authority, especially parental authority, is reflected both at macro- and microlevels. Compliance may occur with close friends, but its nature is clearly more cooperative.

CHAPTER 5

The Rules and with Whom They Are Used

SELF-CONTROL AND CONFLICT MANAGEMENT

The conceptual distinction between "autonomy," on the one hand, and "self-control and conflict management," on the other, is a subtle but necessary one. The assertiveness rule of retaliation (i.e., "Get back at them for things they do to you") illustrated in the previous chapter (Table 4.5) is a case in point, since it helps children to assert themselves and to establish their sense of self-worth, but this is seldom done bluntly within a close relationship, where restraint operates in the service of cooperative relationship preservation (e.g., "Work things out with them," Table 4.4). In a close relationship, in particular, especially a voluntary one such as friendship, there is often the need to manage harmony, which is the thrust of this chapter. "Self-control and conflict management" rules serve precisely this function by illustrating how one's own views and emotional reactions can be tempered by the need to avoid alienation from the relationship. As we shall see below, this is particularly true with respect to rule themes like "repairing damage," which are especially useful, if not indispensable, in preserving close relationships.

The macrocategory examined in this chapter embraces rule themes such as "not upsetting others," "controlling feelings," and "repairing damage." These themes have in common the need to restrain oneself in order to prevent problems from occurring or to facilitate the resolution of these problems once they have occurred. As can be seen from the interview data reported in Table 3.3, "not upsetting others" is a fairly universal rule theme, with the single exception that it is more pertinent for males ($p < .01$) than for females in the peer domain. "Controlling feelings," and "repairing damage" are chiefly peer domain rules, suggesting that voluntary peer relationships require significantly more self-restraint and diplomacy than do family and other-adult relationships, which are more compulsory in nature. If a child wants a friend back, the child has to make up with the friend and hold anger in check. Parents and teachers will, like the rising sun, be there the next day, although our analyses of specific rules and relationships at the microlevel of analysis suggests that even these relationships require some attention to maintenance. The other side of control is knowing when to express rather than inhibit feelings and how to understand people or "analyze" their behavior. However, "expressing feelings" and "figuring others out" were mentioned too infrequently in the interviews to be reported in Table 3.3.

The above rule distribution alters considerably when specific rule themes are rated within the context of specific relationships. These checklist data (Table 3.4) paint a comparable picture of relationship differences with the interviews, with respect to "not upsetting others" which was moderately high on children's social agenda for all types of relationships. However, contrary to the interviews, "controlling feelings" was rated moderately highly in all types of relationships and "repairing damage" was rated highly in relationships with parents and close friends. These were confident findings ($p > .38$). Evidently, children associate controlling feelings with peer relationships when interviewed, but recognize the importance of self-control in getting along in virtually any relationship when specific relationship comparisons are put to them. That participants rated "expressing feelings" more highly for their parents ($p > .25$) signified the relative relational support and safety inherent in this most robust of relationships.

The importance of parents and close friends is revealed by efforts to repair relationships with those parties. We argued that while children indicated in their ratings that they control their feelings equally as often in dealing with their family, peers and teachers, the *costs* of not keeping feelings in check for peers is higher; peers can simply walk away from a relationship, but family members and teachers cannot. Hence, the motivation to mention this type of social rule for peer relationships is higher in the interview situation, since it is uppermost in children's minds, even though it may in fact be used as often in managing peer relationships as any other. Thus, the rated frequency of rule use may underestimate its greater peer salience. The same logic applies to "not upsetting others."

"Expressing feelings" was rated as more appropriate in relating to parents (Table 3.4), suggesting that parents are more tolerant and supportive of their children's emotional displays. In itself, this is an intriguing aspect of parent–child relationships not fully appreciated in the literature on children. Unlike the peer group, where the control of feelings rather than their expression is the rule, parent–child relationships afford the opportunity to demonstrate and ventilate feelings. This is a significant feature of parent–child relationships that reflects the relative safety and acceptance embraced in parental support and not seen in the other relationships we examined. To our recollection, this supportive aspect of parenting has been given scant attention in the family literature and further underscores the value of a phenomenological approach to investigating relationships. Since our checklist ratings were only administered to children with both parents, an avenue of enquiry is then open to compare this supportive feature of parent–child relationships within other patterns of parenting, as within single-parent and dysfunctional families.

Not Upsetting Others

Figures 5.1, 5.2, and 5.3 also show that there was a significantly higher mention of this rule theme by younger children, and by males generally, at age 8 in all three social domains, but it continued at a high rate at all age levels in the other-adult domain. We found this a fascinating result from a socialization perspective because one would predict that, for socialization to be at all effective, it must produce a gradual reduction over time in unacceptable behavior, making "not upsetting others" rules less necessary over the course of middle childhood. That is, as behavior becomes more socially acceptable over time, there is less of a need to consciously inhibit any abrasiveness, which is presumably decreasing. There is also less of a need for others to police it.

The decreases in age in this group of rules in the family domain corresponded with the decreases in age in the authority-based structure of parent–child relationships (Youniss, 1980; Youniss & Smollar, 1985; Fischer & Bullock, 1984a, 1984b) as children develop toward adolescence. As Maccoby (1984b) noted, perhaps by the time children begin to enter preadolescence, their behavior within the family is more self-regulated; perhaps too, this self-regulation generalizes to relationships with peers as well, as our interview data suggests. Note that although this theme does not address "compliance" directly, the appeal to inhibition is intrinsic to it and attests to the inherent *fuzziness* of social rules and reflects a necessary amount of overlap between various contexts of socialization, as between parent–child and peer relationships. We will have more to say about this in Chapter 7.

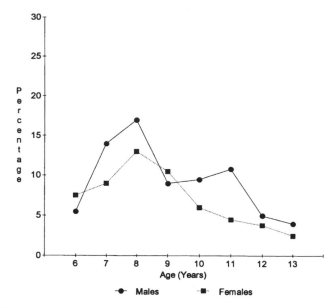

FIGURE 5.1. Percentage interview distribution of "not upsetting others" in the family domain by age and sex.

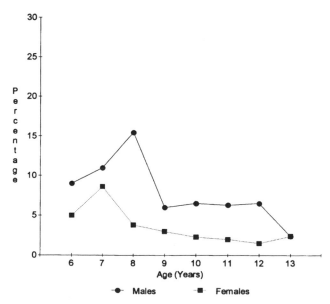

FIGURE 5.2. Percentage interview distribution of "not upsetting others" in the peer domain by age and sex.

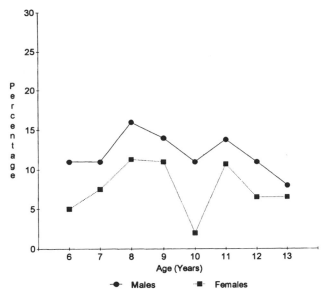

FIGURE 5.3. Percentage interview distribution of "not upsetting others" in the grown-ups domain by age and sex.

The relative constancy with age for the ratings of these rules in dealing with other-adult authority (Figure 5.3) may signal the unilateral nature of the classroom teacher–student relationship. Upsetting the teacher is unwise at any time, considering that one cannot change one's teacher or retreat to one's room if things don't go accordingly. As unilateral authority with respect to the parents reduces over time (Youniss & Smollar, 1985), teachers continue to be authority figures and older children are obliged to continue to show teachers respect. Nevertheless, our interview data (Table 3.3), as well as our checklist data (Table 3.4), show that this kind of "conflict management" rule (i.e., "not upsetting others") may be normative, not only in peer relationships (Shantz, 1987), but to some extent in all specific relations. In retrospect, this should not surprise us, since it is difficult to conceive of a world where giving offense is totally unavoidable; therefore, children must learn to deal effectively with offending others.

As noted in Table 3.3 and Figures 5.1, 5.2, and 5.3, through interviews, this group of rules was mentioned much more by males at almost all age levels in all three domains. Perhaps, this is due to the fact that during middle childhood, males are more aggressive than females are (Hartup, 1974, 1979) and must therefore exercise more inhibition than girls in getting along with others. Moreover, since females hardly ever mentioned these rules with respect to the peer culture after age 7 (Figure 5.2), we suspect that they do not irritate one another to the same extent that males do. These findings were particularly intriguing since they were derived from children's self-reports. Evidently, males consciously acknowledge their relative abrasiveness compared with their female counterparts and have acquired rules with which to deal with this.

With respect to "conflict management" rules, the above findings suggest a unique twist to Renshaw and Asher's (1983) claim that socially skilled children are more likely than unskilled ones to spontaneously verbalize social skills. In our study, children who were more socially skilled—particularly the females (Hartup, 1979; Tesson et al., 1990)—from their ratings clearly recognized the rules that are needed in order to function effectively with others but because these children are less conflictual, they do not need to consciously invoke such rules in practice; therefore, these children expressed conflict management rules less readily during an open-ended interview. In any event, this issue of expressivity and the transition to actual behavior is more complex than had first been assumed. Obviously, further examination of the variables mediating the thought-to-behavior connection needs to be done, since this connection is at the very heart of scientific investigations of social phenomena. Nevertheless, "not upsetting others" is a rule theme that males mention ($p < .01$) more often, and therefore that theme is more salient in their personal relationships.

Since children in middle childhood select friends primarily from within their own gender (see, e.g., Gronlund, 1955), it also makes sense that males invoke this class of rules more than females in getting along with their peers; that is, males are likely to be bothered more by other males than by females. This gender difference in rule use may well explain why there is so much gender segregation during middle childhood (Maccoby & Jacklin, 1987) since males as a group are less socially adept and are more likely to give rise to offense. Females may then seek refuge within their own less abrasive gender relationships. This is a fertile field for future investigations.

There was a relationship-by-age interaction (Table 3.4), illustrating that sibling relationships are especially unique in the functions they serve, as we explain in more detail in Chapter 8. The first part of the interaction showed that there was an overall pattern of a transition from not upsetting siblings at ages 9 and 10 to not upsetting parents and teachers at older age levels. It was noteworthy that while children usually make a transition from parents to peers over time (Youniss, 1980), here we found evidence of the opposite age trend when siblings are involved, suggesting that siblings serve a different social function than peers do. As we discuss in

Chapter 8, siblings offer children an advanced training ground within which to prepare themselves for the wider world, which includes non-family adults and peers. After all, sibling relationships are largely involuntary, whereas peer relationships and relationships with some adults stand or fall squarely on their own merits.

The second part of the interaction shows that there is an equivalent age-related transition reminiscent of the watershed age-by-relationship effect observed for self assertiveness at ages 10 to 11 in the previous chapter, reflecting a status change in the relative importance of close friends versus siblings at this time. Specifically, close friends were rated more highly on "not upsetting others" than siblings were at ages 12 and 13. Adolescence signals the onset of finer distinctions between levels of friendship (see also Bigelow & La Gaipa, 1980), thus making checklist ratings for close friends more germane at this age level. In addition, consistent with the gender difference noted above, sisters were rated more highly than other kids were at ages 10, 11, and 13; that is, in recognition of sisters' improving social skills, it is progressively more important not to upset them. This training is particularly important for boys who tend to offend more and who need this extra training.

Age differences aside, sibling relationships, along with the rest (Table 3.4 and Figure 5.4), are not rated any differently in relation to other kids

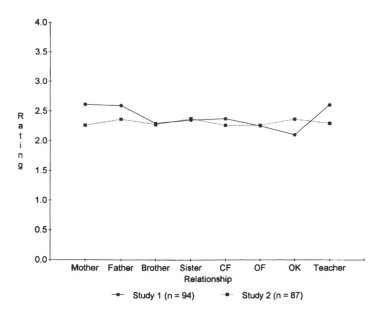

FIGURE 5.4. Ratings of "not upsetting others" by relationship.

on this rule theme. This does not by any means allow us to conclude that siblings are any less hostile to one another than peers are, which would be somewhat anomalous in light of the sibling literature. Conflict (Furman & Buhrmester, 1985b), ambivalence (Furman & Buhrmester, 1985a), and harshness (Stoneman et al., 1984) have been shown to be more common among siblings than among other relationship types. One must bear in mind though that our data addresses social rules for getting along with other people; hence, siblings are as aware as anyone else that it is important not to upset people if one wishes to get along with them. As the following microaccount of specific "not upsetting others" rules indicates, whilst some rules are specifically tailored for managing one's parents, other rules apply to getting along with virtually anyone within the family.

Perhaps one of the most important features of these rules is their inherent moral appeal, as embodied in the injunction "Do no harm." Weston and Turiel's (1980) data are particularly relevant here, because these authors found that children regard many social rules as social-conventional (e.g., nakedness, leaving toys on the floor, or refusing to share a snack) but make clear distinctions about rules that pertain to persons who cause harm to others, which are uniformly disapproved of. The five rules within our theme (Tables 3.1 and 5.1) can be viewed as variations of moral rules, ranging from the obvious "Don't fight with or physically hurt another" and "Don't get into fights with them or hurt them" to being considerate: for example, "Don't bug or bother them," "Don't be pushy or argue with them," "Don't be rude to them," "Don't fool around when they are there." Obviously, our subjects considered it a relatively short distance between irritating others and actually fighting with them, although the family and other-adult domains (Table 3.3) provide children with a more formal support structure that enhances and reinforces the need to inhibit offensive behavior.

The domain differences (Table 3.3), permitted us to address the implications that these analyses have for training children to be more socially effective. Foremost, as checklist ratings in Table 5.1 show, there was a universal and moderately high recognition of the appropriateness of these rules in all eight social and personal relationships, a finding that was also reflected in the interview frequencies (Table 3.3, Figures 5.1, 5.2, and 5.3), but more particularly for the other-adults domain after age 8. In light of the specific examples reported in the following section, we infer that getting children to actually behave more appropriately is accentuated by their school attendance that requires teacher supervision. While we recognize that children need to work things out for themselves (Shantz, 1987; Youniss, 1980), the contexts that enhance such rule awareness of adult (i.e., teacher) authority are essentially one-sided.

Given that the family is the initial and most important social context

TABLE 5.1. Means and Standard Deviations of Social Rule Ratings in the Theme "Not Upsetting Others"

Rule	Relationships							
	Mother	Father	Brother	Sister	Close friend	Other friend	Other kids	Teacher
Don't bug or bother them.	2.51 (.74)	2.62 (.89)	2.40 (.96)	2.40 (.87)	2.46 (.94)	2.36 (.83)	2.30 (.95)	2.70 (1.12)
Don't be pushy or argue with them.	2.71 (1.03)	2.75 (1.10)	2.24 (.93)	2.37 (.86)	2.52 (.90)	2.37 (.80)	2.20 (.84)	2.73 (1.23)
Don't be rude to them.	2.49 (.96)	2.54 (1.06)	2.37 (.79)	2.49 (.78)	2.49 (1.04)	2.37 (.82)	2.34 (.80)	2.56 (1.22)
Don't get into fights with them or hurt them.	2.30 (1.20)	2.28 (1.25)	2.28 (1.01)	2.34 (.97)	2.38 (.99)	2.35 (.84)	2.36 (.85)	2.29 (1.32)
Don't fool around when they are there.	2.63 (1.05)	2.63 (1.07)	2.32 (1.04)	2.37 (.95)	2.30 (1.02)	2.24 (.90)	2.12 (.98)	2.67 (1.22)

Note. Nominal Ns were 315 (Form A) and 344 (Form B), but actual sample sizes varied depending on the particular rule and relationship. Means were compared by means of Scheffé ex post facto tests. Calculations employed the multivariate within-cells error.

$^{**}p < .01$; $^{*}p < .05$; $p < .10$ (italics only).

in which children find themselves, and given that relationships with teachers and other supervisory adults also continue to be governed in later years by the same kinds of inhibitory rules as those found in the family, it makes sense to us that deficiencies in children's conduct stem largely from inadequacies of adult supervision (see Chapter 7). Perhaps social rules training needs to be a more prominent feature of school curricula, either as a preventative measure or, more pointedly, as a means of dealing with children who are showing early signs of conduct problems. This rule theme also raises important questions about the role of the modern family: for example, Why do older children feel that it is more acceptable to upset their parents? Is this a simple aspect of more openly expressing one's feelings, or does it signal a reduction in parental supervision and guidance? Perhaps, as we explain in Chapter 7, older children and adolescents begin to treat their parents more like peers, a point also made by Youniss and Smollar (1985). What is more, since meaningful social relationships can only be properly understood within a relationship matrix, assessment of social rule knowledge deficits, in addition to children's overt social behaviors may help us to detect early social deficiencies.

Specific Rules for Not Upsetting Others

"Don't bug or bother."

Strategies in this category of rules generally address the simple fact that others will get irritated, angry, or uncomfortable as a result of certain behaviors that should be inhibited: for example, "Don't bug [others] a lot and then they will not get grouchy" F8 (3). Children also realize that pestering is generally not an effective way to get what they want from their parents: for example, "Don't keep on asking them to do things or they'll just get mad" M8 (1). Furthermore, these strategies appear to help the child learn to understand perspective-taking skills so that treating others with consideration encourages them to be treated nicely in return: for example, "Be quiet when others are asleep, so you won't be disturbed when you are asleep" M9 (1). As with other rules in this theme (Table 5.1), children recognize its universal appeal. They recognize the greater power of parents and teachers expressed in the common refrain " . . . or they'll get mad," although they can infer an element of reciprocity, as in the third example. However, regardless of motive, displaying aversive behaviors is likely to incur effective reprisals (see "Retaliation" in Chapter 4).

"Don't argue."

Although arguing is an essential component of social relations (e.g., Shantz, 1987), there are limits as to its use. Consequently, there are shades of meaning here that vary within and between different social contexts, such as avoiding challenges to authority (e.g., "Don't argue with them because they know best" M13 (1), not provoking needless conflict (e.g., "Don't start arguments; I'd rather go along with others than fight about it" M11 (1) or assuming too aggressive a posture (e.g., "Don't be too bossy" F13 (2); "Don't tell them to get out of your yard, or they'll do the same to you" M6 (2).

"Don't be rude."

These strategies are especially sensitive to dealing with people in higher status and authority (e.g., "Don't talk back or they'll get mad" M8 (1) but also reflect a form of social etiquette (e.g., "Don't interfere in adult conversation; wait until they stop to make your point" F12 (3)). The subtle difference between not being rude with adults versus peers is exemplified in this strategy: "Don't say rude things to them because you know how it feels" F13 (2). Evidently then, one must follow some protocol, even with one's peers. It seems clear that children acquire a better sense of empathy from peers because the reason for the strategy is not principally to respect authority but to sustain harmony (see Chapter 9).

"Don't fight with or physically hurt another."

Although not hurting others implies a straightforward moral overture, the reasons for these strategies often appeal both to altruistic and ulterior motives: for example, "Don't fight, so then things are better" F12 (1), "Don't push when playing because you might hurt [others] and they'll stop being friends" M7 (2), "Try not to fight with people in my family because I have to live with them" M12 (1).

"Don't fool around."

Here, as well, the logic of these kinds of strategies changes with the social context. It might reflect a sense of compliance with teacher: for example, "Don't fool around in class with friends; it let's her know I'm doing my work" M11 (3), or "Don't act silly" M6 (3) or an attempt to preserve friendly peer relationships through cooperation: for example, "Don't act stupid, then she'll want to be with me and won't get embarrassed" F9 (2). There is an interesting contrast here between avoiding misbehavior in adult-dominated situations, on the one hand, either to favorably impress or to avoid sanctions, and, on the other hand, avoiding a breach in a peer relationship by stepping out of line and causing embarrassment as a result. It is theoretically interesting at a macrolevel of analysis that these two kinds of motives seldom seem to coexist (cf. Youniss, 1980), that is, the same action is reinforced by different consequences, according to the relational context. However, there are occasions when these two motives *do* coexist within the parent–child relationship, as illustrated in Chapter 7.

"Don't be hurtful by calling names or criticizing."

Strategies such as not calling names or criticizing were not very prevalent in the interview transcripts and were therefore not included in the checklist. Needless to say, this does not diminish their value in preserving relationships (see, e.g., Bigelow & La Gaipa, 1980), since low frequency does not necessarily indicate low importance. Such strategies reflect simple self-admonition: for example, "Don't tease or call names" M7 (2), or a more complex sensitivity to another's welfare in a specific situation:

for example, "Don't criticize when [others] are doing well" M13 (2). A sense of empathy is central to this theme: for example, "Don't hurt others' feelings because you know how it feels" F13 (2). Obviously, the closest of relationships can be severely damaged by hurtful behavior, and, as we have indicated before (Bigelow & La Gaipa, 1980), children are keenly aware of this.

Controlling Feelings

Several investigators (e.g., Harris & Olthof, 1982; Hoffman, 1983; McCoy & Masters, 1985) have noted the considerable array of emotions among children, but the social strategies children use to control their feelings have not been examined very extensively. This is particularly germane since empathy is an essential foundation of sociability. Accordingly, how children govern their feelings should have implications for a wide variety of social relationships.

Shantz, in her 1987 review, noted that by age 6, there are significant increases in children's understanding of others' emotions and the situations that elicit those emotions. McCoy and Masters (1985) found that, with age, children become more skilled at changing another's emotional state and, consistent with Gnepp and Gould's (1985) data, react more to negative than to positive states. In addition, Weiner and Handel (1985) found that children at most age levels are reluctant to hurt a classmate's feelings. In fact, ego-degrading remarks are one of the most important causes of the break up of early adolescents' friendships (Bigelow & La Gaipa, 1980). These findings agree with those of Saarni (1977), who noted that children in the middle years may hide their real emotions to simply express norms, avoid trouble, maintain self-esteem, avoid embarrassment and derision, but also to support relationships. Certainly, our own accounting of children's rules within the theme "controlling feelings" (Tables 3.1 and 3.2) mirrors these findings with respect to preventing others from hurting one's own feelings (i.e., "Control your feelings," "Try not to show it if they've upset you") and not hurting others' feelings (e.g., "Be sensitive to others' feelings," "Try to understand their feelings"; "Don't be hurtful by calling names or criticizing," "Don't say things that hurt their feelings").

As we can see in Table 3.3 and Figure 5.5, "controlling feelings" is essentially the preserve of the peer domain for the interviews, again suggesting that the price paid for hurting a peer's feelings is particularly high. However, in the ratings, there are no significant thematic mean differences as a function purely of relationship (Table 3.4, Figure 5.6), indicating that these rules are nevertheless valuable in dealing with

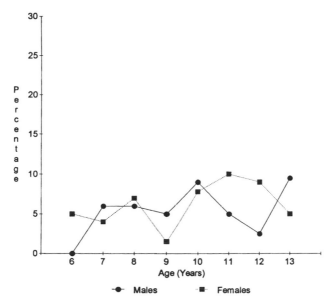

FIGURE 5.5. Percentage interview distribution of "controlling feelings" in the peer domain by age and sex.

anyone. There was only an elevation of one rule ("Try to understand their feelings") for the parental relationships (Table 5.2). Since these two elevated ratings occurred within a family of relationships for the same rule, binomial theory suggested that it was likely a reliable finding ($p > .25$).

As we have been arguing throughout, the relevance of these rules depends on their relational contexts, which in this case also includes considerations of age and gender. Interactions (Table 3.4) show that females rated these rules more highly for their peers, which is consistent with the interview distribution of domain differences (Table 3.3). Again, we interpreted the enhanced use of this theme in peer relationships as reflecting the overall voluntary, cooperative nature of peer relationships (Youniss, 1980), which makes controlling feelings around one's peers a more serious concern if one wants to keep one's friends.

Interactions also show that as age increases, children extend their purview of feelings control beyond family to include other friends and teachers. In Study 1 (Form A), there was a significant relationship-by-age effect, indicating that "controlling feelings" ("Don't say things that hurt their feelings," Table 3.2) was rated as more frequently used with other friends, parents, siblings and teachers after age 11. Teachers were also

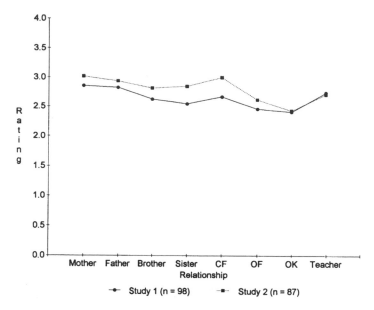

FIGURE 5.6. Ratings of "controlling feelings" by relationship.

rated higher on this rule than were relationships with siblings, close friends and other kids at ages 11, 12, and 13. These age interactions show that distinctions among levels of friendship begin in earnest during early adolescence (Bigelow & La Gaipa, 1980; Bigelow et al., 1992). Although not hurting feelings is still a moderately appropriate rule for getting along with close friends during early adolescence, this rule is subtly more pertinent for other less-intimate levels of friendship because the relative impermanence of the relationship places a premium on watching what you say. Perhaps close friends are more indulgent with each others' expressiveness or are simply less likely to hurt one anothers' feelings in the first place, making "controlling feelings" somewhat less of an issue. As we saw in the previous chapter with respect to "Say what you really think," the issue of free expression in a closer relationship has yet to be fully resolved.

In Table 3.4 (Study 1) there is also a sex-by-age-by-relationship interaction showing that males used "Don't say things that hurt their feelings" more often with their parents, brothers and teachers than with their sisters at age 13. These findings suggest that the onset of adolescence poses significant challenges for males in dealing with same-sex siblings and adults, perhaps reflecting the adultlike reserve that adolescent males

TABLE 5.2. Means and Standard Deviations of Social Rule Ratings in the Theme "Controlling Feelings"

	Relationships							
Rule	Mother	Father	Brother	Sister	Close friend	Other friend	Other kids	Teacher
Try not to show it if they've upset you—keep it inside.	2.57 (1.08)	2.56 (1.10)	2.45 (1.13)	2.48 (1.14)	2.71 (1.06)	2.60 (1.05)	2.49 (1.19)	2.77 (1.19)
Try to understand their feelings.	3.45* (.74)	3.35 (.84)	3.14 (.94)	3.17 (.90)	3.31 (.80)	2.82 (.86)	2.41 (.99)	2.72 (1.11)
Don't say things that hurt their feelings.	2.93 (1.26)	2.95 (1.29)	2.64 (1.00)	2.55 (.99)	2.76 (1.12)	2.60 (.94)	2.47 (.98)	2.91 (1.31)

Note. Nominal Ns were 315 (Form A) and 344 (Form B), but actual sample sizes varied depending on the particular rule and relationship. Means were compared by means of Scheffé ex post facto tests. Calculations employed the multivariate within-cells error.

**$p < .01$; *$p < .05$; $p < .10$ (italics only).

are encouraged to adopt in our culture. The old saw "Act like a man" takes on an earnest meaning at this age.

It is left to the females to be more considerate and understanding of their friends. For the other two rules, "Try not to show it if they've upset you—keep it inside" and "Try to understand their feelings," Table 5.2, females rated "controlling feelings" more with their close friends than their male counterparts did and, compared to teachers, used these two rules more with peers at all levels. These findings support the view that females' peer relationships involve more feelings and control than male peer relationships do and also encourage us to revise the preconception that females are somehow more emotionally expressive than males, when clearly this is far from the case (Table 3.4). However, parallel to males' greater use of the "not upsetting others" theme for curtailing their aggression, females may have learned through the internalization of control rules to keep any latent emotionality in check in the service of harmony with others. With males, the focus of socialization is clearly on inhibiting overtly atavistic behaviors, but with females the focus is clearly on moderating emotional displays. The pronounced gender difference at ages 11 and 12 seen in the interviews (Table 3.3), suggests to us that female pubescence makes emotional control a more salient issue for females at this time.

Specific Rules for Controlling Feelings

"Control your feelings."

This may be considered the converse of venting your feelings (e.g., "Let your anger out," Table 3.1) or asserting them ("Let them know when they've upset you," Table 3.2). Instead of letting other people know when you are mad, it counsels containing anger: "When [others] do things to upset me, then I'm a little angry or sad, but I try not to show it so as not to upset them" M9 (3). It is clear that for some children, thinking things through appears a wiser course of action than externalizing anger: "If [another] says you're not as exciting as other kids, just keep it to yourself and remedy it yourself; keep it inside" M12 (2).

"Be sensitive to others' feelings."

This should be considered in comparison with "Don't be hurtful," which warns against behaviors that might offend, such as teasing and bugging, and carries with it an implication of empathy. The current rule specifically enjoins a concern about other people's feelings: "Be understanding: know what another person is going through" M12 (1). However, this does not just appear as generalized empathy; rather, it emphasizes the value of reading what another's feelings might be and adjusting one's own behavior accordingly: for example, "Know when others need time to themselves and leave them alone" M13 (1). Note that these sensitivities seem uniquely relevant to a close relationship, and, as argued in Chapter 1, are not brought to light simply by observing children's behaviors or recording their social skills. Examined in this light, this rule is an essential component of social competency

"Don't be hurtful by calling names or criticizing."

This appears as a self-admonition to avoid a very specific behavior: for example, "Don't tease and call names" M7 (2). It can, however, be more complex, as, for example, when it involves the recognition that criticizing may not always be appropriate: "Don't criticize when [others are] doing well" M13 (2). This and other statements clearly imply a sense of empathy: for example, "Don't hurt others' feelings because you know how it feels" F13 (2). Either implicitly or explicitly then, this theme shows an awareness of others' feelings and a recognition that to hurt others through ridicule damages relationships.

Expressing Feelings

Bretherton, Fritz, Zahn-Waxler, and Ridgeway (1986) recognized the importance of children's talking about their emotions and being aware of and regulating each other's feelings. As indicated in the self-control theme, several investigators (Harris & Olthof, 1982; Hoffman, 1983; McCoy & Masters, 1985) have noted that children are indeed aware of the role that emotion plays in their social relationships; and, as mentioned before, empathy is an essential foundation of sociability (Hoffman, 1983). Nevertheless, control always assures a particular expression, and we should therefore not be surprised to find children using strategies that, at their face value, are diametrically opposed. Indeed, we might argue that it is precisely the ability to experiment with different, even seemingly opposing, strategies and to adapt to different contexts that defines the essence of social competency. Our findings have led us to be quite appreciative of the arduous task facing children in their acquisition of socially competent behavior, since their social world is full of seeming contradictions such as: "expressing your feelings," "controlling your feelings," "speaking your mind," "holding yourself in check."

The ways in which feelings can be expressed depend on the different kinds of feelings there are to express. For example, when one demonstrates affection, one does not usually express affection in the manner of letting out pent-up anger. In contrast to the kind of rules found in this theme (e.g., "Demonstrate affection," "Let your anger out and be aggressive"), rules reflecting less intense forms of emotional expression are included in the "being assertive" theme presented in the previous chapter: "Say what you really think" "Let others know when they've upset you or made you mad" (Table 3.1). As well, the subtler expressions of positive feelings, such as "being nice," do not lend themselves to bald declarations (like "I really feel nice towards you!") but rather are usually expressed indirectly through kind deeds.

Rule statements reflecting the expression of feelings did not occur very frequently during our interviews. Clearly, most children are not consciously aware of the rules they use to convey positive and negative emotions to others. However, based on the checklist statements, we were able to detect significant relationship differences (Study 1 and Table 3.4) in the frequency of their usage (Table 3.4). In particular, Figure 5.7 shows that "expressing feelings" is more likely to occur in interactions with

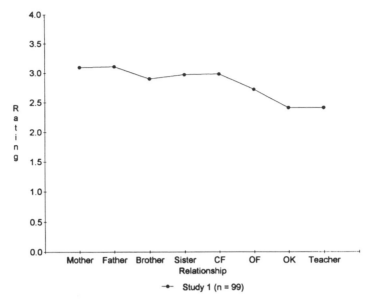

FIGURE 5.7. Ratings of "expressing feelings" by relationship.

TABLE 5.3. Means and Standard Deviations of Social Rule Ratings in the Theme "Expressing Feelings"

	Relationships							
Rule	Mother	Father	Brother	Sister	Close friend	Other friend	Other kids	Teacher
Show them that you really like them.	3.54** (.74)	3.52** (.78)	2.93** (1.02)	2.98** (.97)	3.18** (.88)	2.65 (.92)	2.09 (.93)	2.50 (1.08)
Get mad at them if they do things you don't like.	2.26 (1.02)	2.19 (1.03)	2.61 (1.06)	2.68 (1.00)	2.25 (.95)	2.38 (.93)	2.46 (1.00)	2.80 (1.10)
Cheer them up when they're down.	3.44** (.82)	3.42** (.84)	3.17 (1.04)	3.27* (.94)	3.43** (.78)	3.01 (.87)	2.58 (.98)	2.40 (1.12)

Note. Nominal Ns were 315 (Form A) and 344 (Form B), but actual sample sizes varied depending on the particular rule and relationship. Means were compared by means of Scheffé ex post facto tests. Calculations employed the multivariate within-cells error.

mother and father. Table 5.3, which itemizes individual rule ratings, shows that two of these rules ("Show them that you really like them" and "Cheer them up when they're down") are actually rated significantly higher in the mother, father, brother (only for "Show them that you really like them"), sister and close friend relationships, a very confident finding indeed ($p > .63$). That parents receive the highest rating for positive feelings from the child is consistent with Reid, Landesman, Treder, and Jaccard's (1989) finding that parents constitute the most important support structure the child has.

The rule strategy "Get mad at them if they do things you don't like" was used at a moderate level (2.00–2.99 range) for each of the eight types of relationships, perhaps indicating that demonstration of anger is relatively more explosive in nature and therefore less given to social discrimination. It could also indicate that the sorts of things that make older children angry, such as insulting remarks and talking deceitfully behind one's back (Bigelow & La Gaipa, 1980; Gottman & Mettetal, 1986), are universally aversive, independent of the person from whom the offense is received.

Specific Rules for Expressing Feelings

"Demonstrate affection."

This is a fairly simple and straightforward category that amounts to showing some outward sign of affection: for example, "Kiss [others] and show you love them" F6 (1). The form of the demonstration may vary, but the point is letting others know you care about them: for example, "Let [others] know you care: say nice things" M12 (1).

"Let your anger out and be aggressive."

On the surface, this rule looks like a case of emotional self-indulgence, but the nature of the statements subsumed under this rule suggest that it is more sophisticated than that. The key message seems to be that if other people make you angry, it is healthier to express that emotion than it is to contain it: for example, "Have a fight once in a while: it gets out the anger, and you can talk about the problem later and become better friends" F12 (2).

"Cheer others up and be nice to them."

This might appear similar to "Please others and make them happy" in the theme "pleasing others" (Table 3.1). However, the meaning is quite distinct, since "pleasing" is aimed at creating a good impression on others. On the other hand, cheering someone up signifies a genuine concern for others' feelings and a willingness to do something about it: for example, "If a person looks for a compliment once in a while or is down on [her]self, go along with it and tell [her], 'Yeah, it looks nice' " F13 (3). In this sense, then, it is more of an empathy strategy akin to "Be sensitive to others' feelings" in the theme "controlling feelings" (Table 3.1).

Repairing Damage

This social rules theme addresses the diplomacy side of social relationships. Patching things up is a very real and necessary part of dealing with other people, and is an important social skill in its own right. Children learn to restore equilibrium within a relationship by apologizing or by making amends in some other way and by preventing or stopping others from fighting so that there is less of a chance that the behavior of others will in some indirect way diminish relationships. Problems in a relationship may also stem from problems the partner is having, such as needing help or support, without which the personal relationship may suffer. By assisting the other person, the relationship itself is repaired. As illustrated

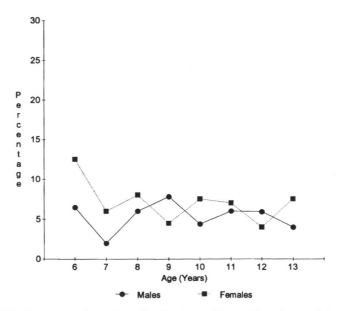

FIGURE 5.8. Percentage interview distribution of "repairing damage" in the family domain by age and sex.

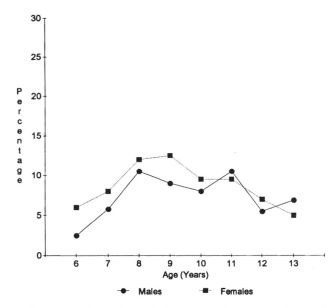

FIGURE 5.9. Percentage interview distribution of "repairing damage" in the peer domain by age and sex.

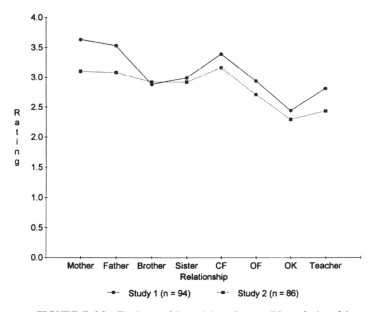

FIGURE 5.10. Ratings of "repairing damage" by relationship.

TABLE 5.4. Means and Standard Deviations of Social Rule Ratings in the Theme "Repairing Damage"

Rule	Relationships							
	Mother	Father	Brother	Sister	Close friend	Other friend	Other kids	Teacher
Make up with them after a fight or argument.	*3.51*[**] (.84)	*3.51*[*] (.84)	2.86 (1.11)	3.03 (1.03)	*3.48* (.82)	2.93 (.96)	2.46 (1.06)	2.80 (1.20)
Help them out when they are having a tough time.	*3.50*[*] (.72)	*3.40*[*] (.85)	3.21 (.94)	3.17 (.95)	*3.35* (.80)	2.88 (.84)	2.35 (.95)	3.15 (1.14)
Try to stop them from fighting with each other.	2.84 (1.19)	2.83 (1.20)	2.66 (1.14)	2.66 (1.13)	3.02 (1.02)	2.63 (.97)	2.15 (1.04)	2.05 (1.25)

Note. Nominal Ns were 315 (Form A) and 344 (Form B), but actual sample sizes varied depending on the particular rule and relationship. Means were compared by means of Scheffé ex post facto tests. Calculations employed the multivariate within-cells error.

[**] $p < .01$; [*] $p < .05$; $p < .10$ (italics only).

in Table 3.3 and Figures 5.8 and 5.9, this theme appears for both family and peer domains, with more of a stress on peer relationships. We hesitated to classify this theme as peers only since family use was as high as some other themes in the peer domain. There were no significant gender differences.

The rule ratings (Tables 3.4 and 5.4, Figure 5.10) also indicate that these kinds of rules are important in dealing with problems with parents and peers alike, especially close friend relationships. Post hoc analyses showed that parents and close friends were rated most highly ($p > .38$) for "Make up with them after a fight or an argument" and "Help them out when they are having a tough time." Accordingly, reparation is most pertinent for parents (i.e., the family domain) and close friends (i.e., the peer domain), emphasizing the point made in Chapters 4 and 7 that children share with their parents as well as with their friends aspects of mutual involvement.

Interestingly, while the other adult relationships were very low on these rules in the interview data, certain kinds of rules (Table 5.4: "Make up with them after a fight or an argument" and "Help them out when they are having a tough time") were moderately to highly rated for teachers as well on the checklist, perhaps indicating that reparations are potentially useful in getting along with virtually anyone with whom one interacts frequently, but particularly more with parents and close friends. The profile of usage between interviews and ratings was similar, with a higher stress on peers in the interview.

Specific Rules for Repairing Damage

"Talk and make up after fighting."

The emphasis here is on making up after a conflict rather than on talking as such: for example, "If you fight with a friend, then make it up later" F6 (2); "Say I'm sorry and then she will get along with you" F8 (1). This rule may be contrasted with avoidance strategies, which consist of diminishing the importance of a relationship in order to minimize the effects of conflict. Here, we have an expression of concern about maintaining a relationship by repairing the damage caused by conflict, and our data confirm that this rule is more apparent in the context of stronger and more permanent relationships, since it heralds a certain commitment to the relationship itself: for example, "Make up after arguments because we're really good friends and we wouldn't have anything to do if we didn't play together" M8 (2). We might also compare this rule with those that aim at preventing conflict in the first place, as was addressed in the "avoiding and ignoring" theme (Table 3.1), the difference being that the current rule proposes an after-the-fact repair strategy.

Talking and making up strategies also hint at a cultural norm of sorts within relationships that allows a partner a face-saving way back into the good graces of the other person. A child may speak in plain terms about restarting a relationship: for example, "Well, when we're in her pool, sometimes we'll get into a little fight, but then she will say, 'Jamie, do you want to make up and be friends again?' and then I will make up with her" F8 (2). Other ways of making up involve a "cooling off period": for example, "We just argue, and we just don't talk to each other for about an hour or so, and then we make up again, make friends again" M9 (2). However, there are limits to forgiveness. If an offense is perceived to be intentional, then the road back to harmony is very difficult: for example, "If you did it on purpose, then you say 'sorry,' and they know that you did it on purpose and that, and then they don't like you" F10 (2).

Interestingly, this latest child's subsequent comment in discussing her mother could have been lifted from the pages of Piaget's (1932/1965) *The Moral Judgment of the Child* by suggesting that apologies are in order only when the damage is relatively large, in which case the intentionality or fault is perceived to be greater: for example, "Sometimes I'll do something bad and, then she, my mom, will give me a spanking, and I'll tell her that I'm sorry if I broke a vase or then, but I don't really break a vase, I just, if it drops on the floor, so, then it probably won't break" F10 (1). Yet another way to make up is to change the routine: for example, "If it's a dumb reason to argue about it, you just let it pass, you know, try and forget about it" F10 (1).

Restoring balance in a relationship can sometimes take a rather blunt twist, which not surprisingly may occur more in harsher siblings relationships. For example, an 8-year-old girl said of her siblings: "Sometimes I hurt them, and then I tell them that they can do stuff to me if they don't tell my mom. I don't want to get into trouble, and then we'll be even" F8 (1). Notice here that the intent is not to preserve a mutual relationship per se but to duck parental reprisals. Perhaps this is the reason why siblings are not rated very highly on this theme compared with close friends and parents.

"Help with problems or give support."

This rule appeals to the old bromide "A friend in need is a friend indeed." The two key elements of this rule are, first, the recognition that someone is in difficulty or has a problem and, second, a willingness to intervene and do something about it: for example, "If you realize [others] have a problem on their mind, ask if you can help" F12 (2). It is thus partly a problem-solving strategy like "Talk over problems" and partly a helping strategy like "Offer to help others" or "Help by doing things for others" (Table 3.1) but appeals to the friend who is having more than usual difficulties that need to be rectified in order to repair the relationship. Failure to come to the person's aid during these times may diminish the other person's capacity to live up to the relationship. This rule entails a higher degree of empathic understanding than is usual for the other helping rules.

"Try to stop others from fighting with each other."

This rule involves preventing others from fighting or arguing or actually stopping them while in the midst of conflict, because such unpleasantness can quickly spread to include more people and may ultimately undermine the relationship that the child has with one of the antagonists. One example sums this rule up nicely: "Try to stop fights between two people, because it can spread to involve you and more people" F13 (2). It may be considered a more active, interventionist strategy.

Figuring Others Out

This theme encompasses rules such as "Get to know and learn about other persons and find out what they are like" as well as "Monitor other persons' moods" (Table 3.1). As Table 3.3 indicates, this theme was hardly mentioned at all during the interviews, but was rated on the checklist as frequently used in getting along with mother, father and close friends; these relationships were not rated significantly higher (Figure 5.11) on this theme than other kids were (Table 3.4). As Table 5.5 also reveals, there were no significant relationship differences on these particular rules either. Nonetheless, this theme was relatively important to children when they filled out the social rules checklist, suggesting that "figuring others out" is not a particularly conscious social process but nevertheless one that is quite relevant in successful social and personal relationships.

Perhaps more than any other social rule theme, "figuring others out" captures the naive psychological approach to dealing with people, that is, it assumes that the vital element in keeping matters smooth and conflict free is to first examine how others *are* as individuals. Perhaps also, the low frequency of this rule in children's interviews conveys to us the relative weakness of its approach in achieving social competency.

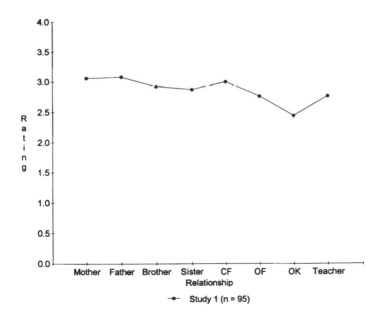

FIGURE 5.11. Ratings of "figuring others out" by relationship.

Of course, this is not to say that people's idiosyncrasies and dispositions (e.g., moodiness and irritability) are socially irrelevant; in fact, the contrary seems to be the case, as the ratings (Table 3.4) indicate. Rather, as we argued in Chapter 2, it seems that competent social understanding stems in the first instance from appropriate social rule application. Knowledge of the uniqueness of the person with whom one is interacting occurs as a *result* of unexpected reactions to normally appropriate social behaviors. To illustrate, a boy is more likely to first ask his mother for help with his homework, but discovers that she is grouchy, then leaves her alone and tries to figure things out by himself. He is less likely, according to our data, to first assume, without feedback, that his mother is grouchy, not bother to ask her to help out with his homework, and then leave her alone.

Since children do not have "figuring others out" rules encoded as readily accessible social rules, but have them stored in recognition (i.e., "implicit") memory, we have concluded that a psychological approach, which assumes that social behaviors originate within persons rather than between them, is not very useful in achieving socially competent behavior. Interestingly though, if a person with whom the child interacts has consistently unique personal characteristics (e.g., excessive strictness), then these traits may become incorporated into the child's construction of the role that person occupies (e.g., "Aren't all fathers like that?"). We also infer from the lack of significant relationship differences on this theme that children make adjustments to their behavior in interacting with other people, regardless of their formal or informal social relationship with them.

TABLE 5.5. Means and Standard Deviations of Social Rule Ratings in the Theme "Figuring Others Out"

	Relationships							
Rule	Mother	Father	Brother	Sister	Close friend	Other friend	Other kids	Teacher
Find out what they are like.	2.96 (1.09)	2.79 (1.08)	2.76 (1.10)	2.77 (.95)	3.12 (.95)	2.79 (.93)	2.44 (1.04)	2.55 (1.16)
Watch out for their moods.	3.23 (.95)	3.26 (.92)	3.07 (1.11)	2.99 (1.11)	3.01 (1.01)	2.66 (1.03)	2.35 (1.12)	2.99 (1.08)

Note. Nominal Ns were 315 (Form A) and 344 (Form B), but actual sample sizes varied depending on the particular rule and relationship. Means were compared by means of Scheffé ex post facto tests. Calculations employed the multivariate within-cells error.

[**] $p < .01$; [*] $p < .05$; $p < .10$ (italics only).

Specific Rules for Figuring Others Out

"Get to know and learn about other persons and find out what they are like."

"Getting to know" is a somewhat ambiguous term in the English language, since it means becoming acquainted in the sense of entering into a relationship with, as well as deepening the relationship by finding out more about the other person. While we find some children using the phrase in the first sense, for example, "Get to know and like them" F9 (3), others reflect the second sense of strengthening a relationship, for example, "Ask things about [others] to get to know them better" M11 (2). The predominant use of these rules, however, seems designed to gather intelligence about other persons in order to act accordingly toward them: for example, "Watch out for what kind of person they are so you know how to act around them" F10 (1). But, as we saw in the interviews, this type of rule is apt to be realized after the fact rather than as a preplanned strategy. This is perhaps the most metacognitive of our rules since it involves the fine-tuning of behavior in the light of social feedback. It is also a rule that contains within it a major goal of relating: to learn about others and yourself (Chapter 9).

"Monitor other persons' moods."

There is nothing very complicated about this strategy, which offers a sound piece of social wisdom: "Don't ask for favors when [others are] in a bad mood" M10 (1). We might have expected that children are much more vulnerable to the bad moods of parents, siblings, close friends and teachers, as is suggested by the mean ratings in Table 5.5; however, these differences were not statistically significant. Hence, the implication is clear that virtually anyone, even a relative stranger, can have a bad mood that might affect how he or she reacts.

In our next chapter, we introduce "mutual activities" and "obligation," which emphasize the content rather than the process of relating. While "compliance" and "autonomy," on the one hand, and "self-control and conflict management," on the other, serve to protect the boundaries of a relationship, rules appealing to social activities, such as helping, talking, loyalty and trust, and reciprocity, reveal what transpires within a relationship.

SUMMARY

The issues involved in this chapter, such as universality, on the one hand, and relational specificity on the other, were amply illustrated in the rules for "self-control and conflict management." When rule themes are examined constructively at a "macro" level of family (parents), peers and other adults (teachers), a different picture emerges than when specific rule-relationship distributions are considered at a "micro" level. For example, the theme "not upsetting others" presents a universal moral dictum (see, e.g., Weston & Turiel, 1980) as the basis of both interviews and questionnaires. However, the interview findings for "controlling feelings" and "repairing damage" were primarily apparent as peer concerns. Also, specific rule-relationship checklist ratings painted "controlling feelings" as a universal rule theme, and "repairing damage" applied to parents and close friends alike.

Moreover, the meaning of a particular rule depended on the content of its particular expression in conjunction with the specific relationship to which it was applied. For example, "Try to understand their feelings" (in "control feelings") applied more to dealing with parents, an exception to its otherwise universal appeal. Similarly, ratings of "express feelings," which also applied more to dealing with one's parents, acquired a meaningful application in parental, sister, and close friend relationships when expressed as "Cheer them up when they're down."

These rule-relationship analyses have also permitted us to address selected issues about how children govern their relationships as a function of relational saliency. Take, for example, emotional expression, reparation, and control: evidently, parental and close friend relationships are as germane to "express feelings" and "reparation" as parental relationships are to "control feelings." In particular, positive feelings (e.g., "Show them that you really like them") were more appropriate for expressing feelings with parents and close friends.

With regard to self-regulation, younger children are more likely to express rules within the theme "not upsetting others" in the family, which of course means the parents for the most part. This finding appears to offer additional support for the Sullivan–Piaget hypothesis (Youniss, 1980), which portrays unilateral parental control as giving way serially over time to peer cooperation, but extended control to the peer domain. Such rules do not directly tap into compliance, which was addressed in the previous chapter, but they are implicit in elementary social governance. On the other hand, the declining usage of these rules in both parental and peer domains with age suggests that socialization of proper conduct is accomplished in parallel within both of these domains.

The importance of peers as socializers is redoubled here. Adult authority extends to the world of peers, which up to now has been portrayed as a world unto itself (see, e.g., Shantz, 1987; Youniss, 1980). This issue of authority in our findings is neatly hived off from parental governance since teachers were rated more highly on "controlling feelings" at ages 11 to 13, precisely when rules of "not upsetting others" are declining in perceived salience for parents and peers. As we observed in the last chapter, issues of "compliance" as well as milder forms of authority dealt with here are socially governed and are not necessarily limited to parenting as such.

Perhaps equally as interesting is the fact that sibling relationships would not have been appreciated for the unique functions they serve unless such rules and relationships were examined at an intricate microlevel. For example, at age 13, males control feelings less with their sisters; and since sisters are more likely to control their own feelings with close friends, their brothers may learn a great deal about self-control by interacting with them. This is especially useful for boys when it is important for them not to offend their close friends who assume a new significance at this time. Boys are more likely to give rise to offense (e.g., Hartup, 1974, 1979) than girls are. As we discuss in Chapter 8, the specific role provided by siblings is a hotly contested issue.

CHAPTER 6

The Rules and with Whom They Are Used

MUTUAL ACTIVITIES
AND OBLIGATION

The social rules reported in this chapter are relatively unique in that they address the content that transpires within relationships as opposed to the mechanisms children use to preserve them. In the previous chapters, we dealt with "compliance" and "autonomy" as well as "self-control and conflict management," which serve to define the boundaries within which a relationship is contained: one complies with authority in its various forms, as with one's parents and teachers, or even in some senses with close friends, and one also invokes strategies that appeal to the conflict processes that help to govern the relationship itself. In a close relationship, there are also rules that govern "mutual activities," such as "being sociable" and "helping others," which often occur within a fabric of "obligation," which also requires "talking" in all its forms and "being loyal and trusting." Hence, the focus in this chapter is less on what children do when relationships go awry, and what to do to prevent that from happening, and more on how to interact with a person with whom one has established or is establishing a close relationship.

The rules contained in "mutual activities" contain a variety of functions (Zarabatany et al., 1990) that form a continuum of interactions that may culminate in "obligation," the foundation of a stable relationship. "Obligation" binds one individual to the needs of another. These obligations are expressed in several different forms, ranging from helping one another; sharing personal information; honesty and trust (see Mannarino, 1980). Of course, while mutual activities are often the precursors of intimacy and trust, they are not necessarily so; and certainly not all people with whom the child has trusting interactions began as playmates. However, because mutual activities (e.g., play) constitute the best predictor of children's friendship formation (see, e.g., Gottman, 1986; Youniss & Volpe, 1978), we view "mutual activities" and "obligation" as a natural continuum. This chapter also reports on rules of "reciprocating" because this theme appeals explicitly to the mutual nature of a close peer relationship (see Youniss, 1980).

MUTUAL ACTIVITIES

These social rule themes span "being sociable," reflecting the rather socially demanding exchanges characteristic of peer interactions during middle childhood, to "helping others," which serves to cement coordinated play and connects to feelings of obligation. The theme "talking" has aspects of mutual activities even though it is also dealt with in a more obligatory context with respect to sincerity and trust issues, which are expressed directly in the theme "being loyal and trusting" in the second section of this chapter.

Being Sociable

These rules refer to efforts on the part of children to become involved with others or to get others involved with them. As can be seen in Table 3.1, this is a large category that our interview data (Table 3.3) indicates applies to both genders and to all three domains of persons (Figures 6.1, 6.2, and 6.3). Males were much more frequent in their mention of this group of rules than females were in the peer domain (ages 6, 9, and 11) and females cited these rules slightly more in the other-adult domain (ages 6, 10, and 11). This gender difference in the peer domain may reflect the fact (see, e.g., Eder & Hallinan, 1978; Erwin, 1985; DiPietro, 1981; Hallinan, 1981; Lever, 1976; Maccoby, 1990) that females during middle childhood, and perhaps beyond, have a smaller, more intimate friendship network than boys do and that boys tend to play in larger, more organized groups, where active social commerce plays a larger part. Girls often have only one best friend to depend on and are consequently more vulnerable to and distressed at the breakup of friendship than boys are (Maccoby & Jacklin, 1987; Waldrop & Halverson, 1975). These gender differences, though, detract from the main idea that "being sociable" is a widely used component of children's social relationships, particularly with their peers (Figure 6.4).

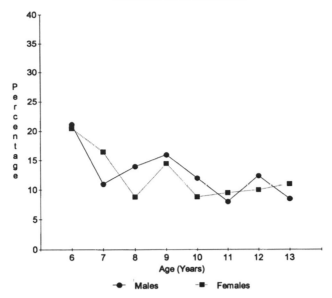

FIGURE 6.1. Percentage interview distribution of "being sociable" in the family domain by age and sex.

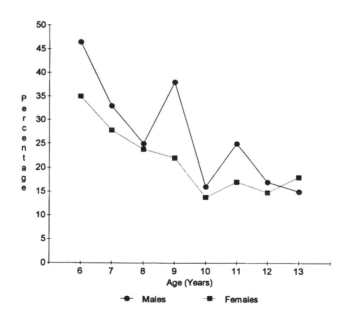

FIGURE 6.2. Percentage interview distribution of "being sociable" in the peer domain by age and sex.

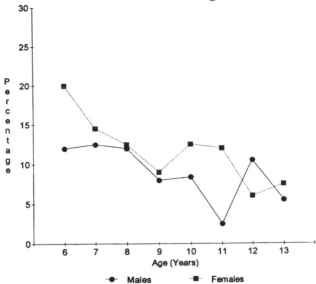

FIGURE 6.3. Percentage interview distribution of "being sociable" in the grownups domain by age and sex.

In addition, although children are relatively more influenced by and more involved with peers as they get older (see, e.g., Berndt, 1979; Youniss & Smollar, 1985), there is a discernible decrease with age in the frequency of mention of these rules in the interviews, regardless of domain (see Figures 6.1, 6.2, and 6.3). However, there is no such age decrease in the checklist data, which shows the highest usage of these rules for the close friend relationship (Table 3.4). The age decrease in spontaneous mention apparent in the interviews may reflect unmeasured but operative environmental restrictions on children's free behavior, restrictions that are apt to motivate children to reduce the perceived relevancy of sociability rules (Youniss, 1980). With age, the demands of school and structured extracurricular activities, such as sports (e.g., Bigelow & La Gaipa, 1975; Bigelow, Lewko, & Salhani, 1989), chores and work, take up progressively more of children's free social time. Such activities are less apt to be perceived as meaningful to adolescents (Csikszentmihalyi & Larson, 1984; Larson et al., 1989). These structural influences may be occurring precisely as the peer group gains in its relevancy and attractiveness, resulting in constancy over time in the rated frequency of use of sociability rules. The age decrease seen in the interviews may well reflect a corresponding decrease in the voluntariness of peer contacts. Thus, while sociability is important at all age levels, it may be less of a conscious focus

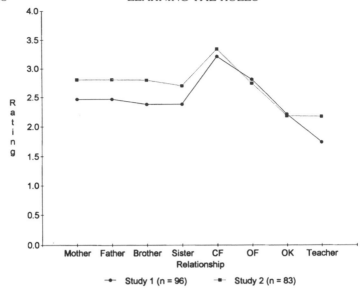

FIGURE 6.4. Ratings of "being sociable" by relationship.

during later childhood and adolescence, and interviews would be more sensitive to this.

The above gender difference was not replicated for the checklist data (Table 3.4). We surmise that while both genders judged these rules as equally applicable to close friend relationships at all age levels, the gender difference noted in the interviews also reflects the perceived saliency of "extensive" (Erwin, 1985) social activities for boys. Since females have smaller, more "intensive" (Erwin, 1985) intimate friendship groups, they change friends less often, which makes active social commerce less crucial to them as a means of making themselves available in the social "market-place" (Goffman, 1983). However, as we shall see when we introduce "talking" rules, it is the females who use "talking" rules more, so it is likely that it is the form of sociability that is at play here; males place more emphasis on overt activities than girls do, and females stress verbal discourse more than boys do. Even in the overall interviewing, we found that, on average, girls provided one-third more rule statements. This sex difference in "talking" has also been found in young adults (Duck et al., 1991). These findings also strike a wider chord, since it is often heard that males express their affection by doing things, and females by saying things. Gender differences aside, we also feel that more than simple method effects are at play here. Interviews and questionnaires may be tapping into different aspects of social perception that complement each other in ways that are not yet fully understood.

As children develop through the middle years, the foundation of their peer social activity undergoes profound change from the activity-based world of the preschooler and early school age span to the complex world of sharing private thoughts and feelings out of a sense of mutual respect and affection (e.g., Berndt, 1981; Bigelow, 1977; Mannarino, 1980; Youniss & Volpe, 1978). A separate project not reported in this volume used social rule categories to content analyze preschoolers' peer behavior in a university day care. Consistent with Gottman (1986) and Youniss and Volpe (1978), it was found (Bigelow & Deck, 1996) that the most common form of peer interaction for these preschoolers was "social facilitation," accounting for 63% of all interactions. Other categories such as "prosocial behavior" (3.9%) and "conflict" (6.4%) were comparatively rare. "Mutual activities" are nevertheless preconditions for the later exercise of these other more abstract functions that only work well within a framework of "obligation."

To elaborate, Gottman (1986) noted that the goal of peer interaction for young children (ages 3 to 7 years) is coordinated play, but Gottman and Mettetal (1986) noted that during middle childhood (ages 8 to 12) the goal changes from playful interaction to social acceptance within the peer group and that verbal activities such as gossip enter heavily into peer exchanges at this time. By age 13 (and age 11 in our study; Figure 6.5), the quality of peer interaction changes again to a combination of gossip and self-disclosure, with its attendant emphasis on problem solving and intense honesty. This shift from cooperative play to intense verbal discourse can be clearly seen in Figures 6.5 and 6.6, where the theme "talking" increases significantly ($p < .01$) at age 11 for females in the family domain and for both genders in the peer domain. "Talking" categories include "Talk, tell things, and discuss," "Reveal your personal experiences and feelings to others," and "Talk over problems."

As Table 6.1 and Figure 6.4 show, with the exception of "Invite others over or out," ratings of "being sociable" rules are operative to a moderate degree in most personal and social relationships, but this group of rules appears to capture the essential distinctiveness of close friend relationships ($p > .63$). While these rules may seem to be somewhat superficial, this belies their functional significance. What sets friendship apart from other social relationships is that its integrity is totally dependent on how it is managed on a day-to-day basis. For example, one cannot change who one's siblings are, but one can and often does change one's friends.

Thus, friendship is in reality formed out of the general "social marketplace." Without the social interaction skills that permit children to involve themselves effectively with one another, friendships cannot take place, and those that manage to get off the ground are likely to dissolve back into the wider social world from which they originally emerged. As

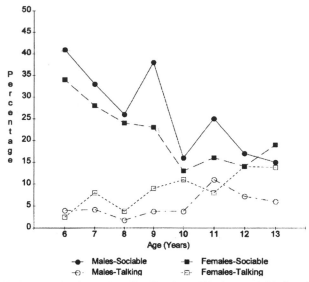

FIGURE 6.5. Percentage interview distribution of "being sociable" and "talking" in the peer domain by age and sex.

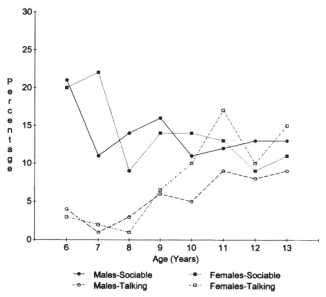

FIGURE 6.6. Percentage interview distribution of "being sociable" and "talking" in the family domain by age and sex.

TABLE 6.1. Means and Standard Deviations of Social Rule Ratings in the Theme "Being Sociable"

	Relationships							
Rule	Mother	Father	Brother	Sister	Close friend	Other friend	Other kids	Teacher
Be nice and pleasant to them, like saying "Hi."	3.54** (.72)	3.52** (.76)	3.09 (.97)	3.00 (1.00)	3.46** (.76)	3.05 (.81)	2.51 (.95)	*3.13* (1.00)
Joke around, try to be funny.	2.80 (1.01)	2.80 (1.00)	2.70 (1.01)	2.72 (.96)	3.10 (.87)	2.81 (.92)	2.45 (.98)	2.14 (1.09)
Invite them over.	1.86 (1.28)	1.87 (1.27)	1.96 (1.22)	1.94 (1.25)	3.21** (.83)	2.58 (.88)	1.82 (.90)	1.33 (.80)
Visit each other.	2.69* (1.44)	2.66 (1.44)	2.65* (1.38)	2.62* (1.39)	3.22** (.86)	2.58 (.87)	1.83 (.92)	1.67 (1.06)
Do things with them, like playing.	2.80 (1.02)	2.78 (1.05)	2.95* (.93)	2.73 (.97)	3.37** (.80)	2.84 (.87)	2.15 (.87)	1.85 (1.03)
Get them to join in things with you.	2.71 (1.00)	2.63 (1.01)	2.58 (1.01)	2.49 (.98)	3.23** (.80)	2.70 (.84)	2.07 (.84)	1.90 (1.09)

Note. Nominal Ns were 315 (Form A) and 344 (Form B), but actual sample sizes varied depending on the particular rule and relationship. Means were compared by means of Scheffé ex post facto tests. Calculations employed the multivariate within-cells error.

**$p < .01$; *$p < .05$; $p < .10$ (italics only).

Erving Goffman (1983) has indicated, the day-to-day mechanics of social interactions are legitimate social data. In addition, following Mannarino (1980), our findings also suggest that children's close friendships provide, in turn, an important context within which such interactional competencies are learned.

Specific Rules for Being Sociable

"Be nice and pleasant and say 'Hi!'"

These kinds of strategies are often used as superficial elements of the initiation stage of a relationship: for example, "Say 'Hi' when [others] go by to make friends" F7 (3). The relevance ($p > .38$) of such strategies in getting along with parents and close friends (Table 6.1) also attests to the fact that such apparently simple actions are nevertheless also meaningful, if not indispensable, in everyday interactions with significant people in children's lives. Obviously, too, these strategies are not used here simply for acquaintanceship purposes, but are meaningful in close ongoing relationships as well. Thus, their superficial appearance is deceptive. For instance, try ignoring someone close to you and see what happens.

"Joke and fool around, or be humorous and funny."

Such strategies dispel tension and help others to like you: "Make [others] laugh so that they will like you and you will have more friends" F6 (2); "Joking around is one way to deal with shyness: it lets me know [others], and they know me better" M13 (3). Thus, this rule is not reserved for any relationship in particular. Joking around can also avert conflict: "Try and make [others] laugh so you won't be fighting later" F6 (1), which makes it useful in a closer relationship as well.

"Invite others over or out."

This category seems by its very nature to be a peer-oriented one (Table 6.1). While one could, in principle, invite one's teacher over, and there could be occasions to invite siblings or even parents out to join in some activity, children seldom say they do. It is peers who are singled out for this kind of strategy, with the aim of establishing a firm relationship: "Having kids over means you get more used to them" M7 (2). In addition, inviting others over signals that a certain stage of the relationship has been reached: "Invite kids to birthday parties and let them play with toys and eat cake: makes them think I'm a good friend" M9 (2).

"Visit each other."

This is very much like the previous strategies, being largely peer oriented and aimed at cementing a relationship: for example, "Visit each other's houses to get to know each other" M11 (2). These kinds of strategies seem like a cultural norm of friendship, that once you know someone as a friend, then you visit that person's house and that person can visit yours. But as Table 6.1 shows ($p > .75$), visiting is normative for virtually any relationship, except for persons whom one does not routinely socialize with.

"Do things together, such as playing."

This is clearly a bedrock rule. What better way is there of getting along with other people than by doing things with them? Certainly, this comes out in the friendship literature (e.g., Berndt, 1983; Bigelow, 1977; Youniss & Volpe, 1978), where playing together is a key component in forming friendships and in dealing with one's brother as well ($p > .25$), a fact that children seem very conscious of, as in the observation "Play with [others] so that they like you" M6 (2). It would thus be a mistake to view the current rule as simply an early childhood strategy for becoming friends; it can also serve to make people closer throughout the whole range of relationships at any age: for example, "Do family activities together as a way to get to know others better" F11 (1), and can also in some instances avert tension and conflict: for example, "Play together: it gets things out of your mind that made you mad at the person" M8 (2). It would be difficult to find a better illustration of the way in which cooperation reduces conflict and promotes harmony than that reported by Sherif, Harvey, White, Hood, and Sherif (1961) in their classic Robbers Cave experiment. This third example also foreshadows Chapter 9, which illustrates that children often explain the use of one rule by invoking another. As we can see through many such examples, there is support for Gottman and Mettetal's (1986) claim that emotional control is "critical for the management of conflict, for without it, coordinated play would be impossible" (pp. 200–201).

"Include others in your group or in things you do."

The main thrust here is to initiate activities in order to get to know new people: for example, "Try to include other kids in what I'm playing: helps me to be friends with lots of people" F8 (2); but this approach also shows a solicitousness toward those who have been left out: "Introduce them to others, so they'll have someone to play with when you're not around" M8 (2). This rule betokens a certain independence, a willingness to actively make things happen rather than passively respond to what others do, especially with one's close friends (Table 6.1: "Get others to join in things with you"). The special significance of close friends here is especially informative in that a child's close relationship with a peer must be coordinated with the activities of the wider peer group.

Helping Others

This theme of helping others captures the obvious altruism and prosocial behavior rules but does not explicitly include notions of empathy and guilt, which are covered in other social rule themes, such as "pleasing others," "controlling feelings," and "repairing damage" (Table 3.1). While altruism and concern for others are two sides of a common coin, empathy and guilt are germane to several other types of social rules in addition to altruism, which is more narrowly defined here.

As we can see from Table 3.3 interview data, "helping others" is essentially a family (Figure 6.7) and other adults (Figure 6.8) rule theme. The checklist ratings (Table 3.4, Figure 6.9), on the other hand, include both parents and close friends among those with whom "helping others" is a moderately to frequently used rule. As we shall see below in the description of individual rule items, altruism for children often carries with it an element of "obligation" or even "compliance" to authority, which explains why children mention "helping others" primarily within a parental and teacher context (Table 3.3) (see also Chapter 4, "compliance"). However, this is not to say that helping is irrelevant to peer relationships—far from it. "Helping others" was rated highly in getting along with close friends. In fact, when the means of individual rules (Table 6.2) are inspected, "Offer to help others," and "Help by doing things for others,") are significantly ($p > .38$) elevated for both parents and close friends alike.

Specific Rules for Helping Others

"Offer to help others."

This is an unambiguous prosocial category. Not only does this rule show concern and consideration for others, but it also addresses behavior that is initiated purely by the subject and is therefore an indication of altruistic intent and of individual autonomy, particularly for parents and close friends (Table 6.2). At one level, this may be viewed as a "social facilitation" behavior designed to create a good impression—"Offer to help, to get on their good side, and then they might understand you" F9 (3)—and we might suspect that all children are aware of this effect whether they say so or not. On another level, the language used indicates a noncalculative, empathic attitude: "Ask [others] if they need help, so that they don't have to do it all by themselves" M6 (3). The feeling one has, reading the statements under this category, is that offering to help is primarily an adult-oriented category designed to give the child some leverage in an otherwise powerless situation: "I feel sorry for adults who need help, so I offer to help" F9 (3). In this sense, it signifies the role that parents play in teaching children how to deal with close friends. We deal with this issue at length in the next chapter.

"Help by doing things for others."

This category could be considered as allied to "Do obligatory work" (Table 3.1), since it often involves doing work, but with the difference that it is

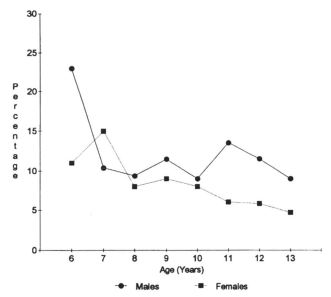

FIGURE 6.7. Percentage interview distribution of "helping others" in the family domain by age and sex.

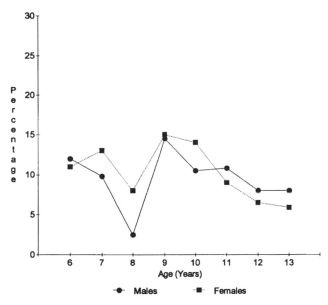

FIGURE 6.8. Percentage interview distribution of "helping others" in the grown-ups domain by age and sex.

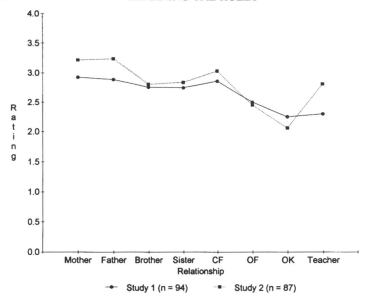

FIGURE 6.9. Ratings of "helping others" by relationship.

expressed as a voluntary act, which applies to both parents and close friends (Table 6.2). While one suspects that a lot of helping, especially with household chores, is a response to parental urging, it is nevertheless important to note that many children describe helping as a prosocial act, showing consideration for others: "Help out and do things, so others will have time to do things" M7 (1). Some children seem to recognize that the obligatory character of household chores derives less from parental pressures than from the nature of the situation: "Help around the house, because if I didn't, the jobs wouldn't get done" M6 (1). For others, it is an occasion for social interaction: "Help Mom with the chores: it's a way for me to spend time with her" M9 (1).

In this, as in other contexts, such as helping other kids with their schoolwork, helping can be a means of strengthening a relationship: "Help others to do things, so you can be more close and come to understand each other more" F13 (1) or "If they ask me to do something for [others] I will, as this makes us better friends" F11 (2). The point here is that although helping may start out as adult-initiated behavior when children are "asked" to help with chores around the house, helping nevertheless assumes a more voluntary and prosocial form as reflected in the language used to describe it. Very few children cite fear of sanctions as a reason for helping. This "scaffolding" (Bruner, 1975) function of competent social relationships by parents is discussed in detail in Chapter 7.

TABLE 6.2. Means and Standard Deviations of Social Rule Ratings in the Theme "Helping Others"

| | Relationships | | | | | | | |
Rule	Mother	Father	Brother	Sister	Close friend	Other friend	Other kids	Teacher
Offer to help them.	3.27^{*} (.84)	3.29^{**} (.87)	2.67 (1.01)	2.58 (.95)	3.08^{*} (.85)	2.65 (.85)	2.28 (.91)	2.79 (1.01)
Help them out, like by doing things for them.	3.38^{**} (.80)	3.32^{**} (.86)	2.79 (.94)	2.82 (.95)	3.10^{*} (.82)	2.53 (.77)	2.06 (.83)	2.86 (1.07)
Show them how to do things.	2.48 (.98)	2.36 (1.02)	2.67 (1.01)	2.58 (.98)	2.74 (.87)	2.38 (.78)	2.09 (.87)	1.94 (.97)

Note. Nominal *N*s were 315 (Form A) and 344 (Form B), but actual sample sizes varied depending on the particular rule and relationship. Means were compared by means of Scheffé ex post facto tests. Calculations employed the multivariate within-cells error.

$^{**}p < .01$; $^{*}p < .05$; $p < .10$ (italics only).

"Teach and show others how to do things."

This rule shows even more assertiveness than the previous one, and we would expect it to be primarily oriented to peers and perhaps siblings: for example, "Teach other kids to do things that they can't do, so that they can do the same things as me" M7 (2). In a curious role reversal, however, both parents and teachers are also possible candidates for children's teaching (Table 3.4), although this result is not a stable one (Table 6.2). Sometimes, one finds these kinds of strategies explicitly framed in a reciprocal mode: for example, "Teach each other our skills," reminiscent of Piaget's (1932/1965) and Youniss's (1980) contention that peer relationships are built on a foundation of mutuality and reciprocity. However, the value of our contextualized analysis is shown here, in that "Show them how to do things"—superficially quite cooperative—is not chiefly a friendship rule.

OBLIGATION

The rule themes included in the above category embrace the truth and vulnerability aspects of personal relationships. Wherever openness of communication occurs, there is the simultaneous need to be loyal and trusting, lest potential harm to the participants occurs as a result of lack of care in receiving and caring for this shared information. In referring to adolescents, Gottman and Mettetal (1986) commented:

> The most salient social process of adolescence involves the application of intense scrutiny and logic to the turbulent world of emotions and unstable personal relationships. Because of this fact, intense honesty can almost be "derived," in a mathematical sense, as a necessary corollary concern of adolescence. In a climate of deceit, none of this analysis is possible. Hence, the adolescent's great concern with loyalty and betrayal follows, for there can be no tolerance of lies and deceit from one's friends. (pp. 198–199)

An important aspect of a child's personal relationships is "talking," as any parent of a budding adolescent knows only too well when the phone is tied up. Duck et al. (1991) showed that talking is *the* element in adult personal relationships that provides the constructive material from which people derive meaning in their personal relationships (Duck, 1994). Moreover, one can hardly overstate the case for "talking" as a critical relational variable in children either, as Figures 6.5 and 6.6 reveal. The decline with age in "being sociable" mirrors an age increase in "talking," indicating a transformation in the nature of "mutual activities" as development progresses. After the onset of adolescence in particular, "talking" takes a front seat to social activities of a more general sort. This is particularly evident with females and in family relationships (Figure 6.6).

"Talking" is distinguished from intimacy, since "talking" is a more neutral term, which includes less intimate, more benign forms of disclosure. Children may not openly declare their intent to tell a secret, since such telling often flows naturally out of trusting conversations with parents and friends. Thus, "talking" includes intimate and nonintimate forms of disclosure (Table 6.3). Gottman (1986) noted that early adolescents cherish confidences as a measuring stick of the integrity of relationships. But, as Bigelow and La Gaipa (1980) showed, being disloyal, such as talking about a friend behind his or her back or divulging a secret, is one of the chief ways in which friendship breaks down. Accordingly, this macrocategory groups "talking" and "being loyal and trusting" as functional counterparts.

Talking

This is essentially a family and peer rule, as revealed ($p > .42$) in the interviews (Table 3.3; Figures 6.10 and 6.11) and ratings (Figure 6.12; Tables 3.4 and 6.3). However, it is the sister relationship in particular that is rated as moderately relevant in the sibling usage of one such rule

TABLE 6.3. Means and Standard Deviations of Social Rule Ratings in the Theme "Talking"

Rule	Mother	Father	Brother	Sister	Close friend	Other friend	Other kids	Teacher
Talk with them about everyday things.	3.22** (.93)	3.05* (.99)	2.53 (1.10)	2.70 (1.07)	3.07** (.93)	2.41 (.90)	1.89 (.89)	2.02 (.96)
Tell them about your feelings and other personal things.	2.98** (1.08)	2.67* (1.15)	1.97 (1.11)	2.16 (1.15)	2.66* (1.85)	1.90 (.89)	1.48 (.77)	1.71 (.94)
Talk over problems with them.	3.21** (1.05)	2.97** (1.13)	2.17 (1.14)	2.20 (1.17)	2.81** (1.02)	2.13 (.96)	1.59 (.85)	2.12 (1.09)

Note. Nominal *N*s were 315 (Form A) and 344 (Form B), but actual sample sizes varied depending on the particular rule and relationship. Means were compared by means of Scheffé ex post facto tests. Calculations employed the multivariate within-cells error.
**$p < .01$; *$p < .05$; $p < .10$ (italics only).

(Table 6.3: "Talk over problems with them"). This makes sense in light of the gender difference (Table 3.3) favoring females on this rule and is consistent with gender differences in the theme "controlling feelings" reported in the previous chapter, and especially in regard to males' tendency not to do things that upset their sisters, also noted in the previous chapter. One can hardly have a meaningful dialogue when feelings are raw.

From research on sex differences (Bigelow, 1977; Eder & Hallinan, 1978), we expected "talking" rules to be more prevalent in older female children's peer relationships. As Table 3.3 shows, "talking" was indeed mentioned in the interviews more by females, which is also seen in Figures 6.10 and 6.11. In addition, females provided one-third more statements in the interview than males did. However, there were no gender differences in the rule-relationship ratings of this theme on the checklist, which suggested perhaps that for females "talking" is generally more central to their social relationships in general.

Perhaps also, the disappearance of gender differences in the ratings simply reflect the reality that, while females talk more, males *perceive* that they talk just as much as females do with particular people. Notwithstanding the fact that females talk more, it has proved surprisingly difficult to

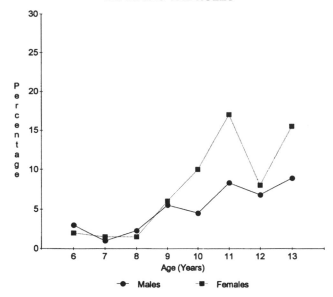

FIGURE 6.10. Percentage interview distribution of "talking" in the family domain by age and sex.

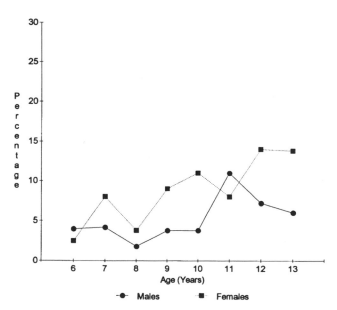

FIGURE 6.11. Percentage interview distribution of "talking" in the peer domain by age and sex.

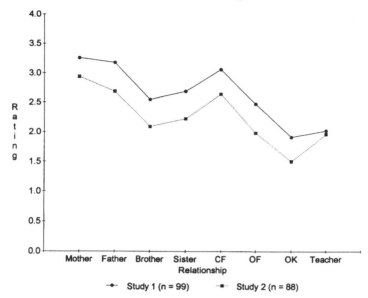

FIGURE 6.12. Ratings of "talking" by relationship.

detect consistent gender differences on intimacy or "disclosure." Even in other studies (e.g., Bigelow, 1977), intimacy potential only appeared as a mainly female aspect of close friendship at age 13. Of course, same-sex intimate exchanges do not necessarily reflect intimate information and may also take the form of feelings of attachment, giving, and sharing, as well as demonstrations of trust and loyalty (Sharabany, Gershoni, & Hofman, 1981). Therefore, while disclosure is very germane to "talking," it is important not to overemphasize its role, since intimate exchanges are also covered by a wider assortment of behaviors. Cross-gender friendships, which become more pertinent during adolescence (see, e.g., Sharabany et al., 1981), are another matter entirely.

"Talking" rules are only relevant after age 9 in relating to other adults, such as the teacher (Table 3.3), suggesting that the social distance of the student–teacher relationship narrows slightly during later childhood, as discussed below. This theme is more relevant for older children (Figures 6.10 and 6.11) because of its more abstract characteristics. (See the "being sociable" theme for a more complete age-based analysis of this rule theme.) However, all children at all ages recognized its significance in the checklist ratings. These differences in gender and age across interviews and checklist ratings illustrate the fact that interviews and questionnaires often convey different and complementary kinds of valuable information about the same sets of variables.

Specific Rules for Talking

"Talk, tell things, and discuss (general)."

Rather than a manifestation of intimacy or deeper conflict resolution, "talking" is often a general mode of social exchange that can serve to initiate relationships: for example, "Talk to [others] to get to feel comfortable together" F8 (3), or to strengthen relationships by getting to know each other more: for example, "Talk to them about things that happen, to get to know them better" F11 (2). Some children simply say they feel better when they talk about things: for example, "Discuss with others to get things off your chest and make you feel better" M13 (1), while others recognize the need to just exchange information: for example, "Tell [others] what happens at school and ask them what happens at work" M12 (1). It is clear that "talking" can cover a very wide range of different intentions depending on the content of what is discussed. Sometimes, it is just fun to talk about things: "Talk about things that have or will happen, to share excitement and good mood" F12 (2). Older children sometimes learn that their teacher is a person whom they can talk to as well (Table 3.3): "Teachers that teach you are different from most of the grown-ups that I know because you can talk to them more and you can talk to them face-to-face. But with other grown-ups, you can't really say that much because they'll say 'Well, you're young and you don't know' " F12 (3).

"Reveal your personal experiences and feelings to others."

The sharing of personal experiences is the essence of intimacy and the statements coded under this theme reflect this: "Share close things with [others], so you get to know each other better through conversations" M13 (1). Our subjects frequently used the term "sharing experiences," suggesting a mutual exchange of confidences that we take to be a key characteristic of intimacy. This rule reflects the findings of several investigators (Berndt, 1981; Bigelow, 1977; Gottman & Mettetal, 1986; Youniss & Volpe, 1978) regarding the emergence of intimacy and truth concerns during early adolescence. The rule reflects not simply a one-way transmission of information aimed at providing feedback to others about one's thoughts and feelings, but rather is a sheltered exchange built on trust. After all, the majority of talking that goes on within everyday social interactions has a rather superficial appearance, which makes this rule something special. The revealing of personal feelings and experiences is, by its very nature, not part of normal public discourse and is a special feature of close personal relationships: "Well, there's some things you tell your best friends that maybe you wouldn't tell your mother" F14 (2).

Revealing personal experiences is predominantly the preserve of close peer relationships and trusting parental ones (see, e.g., Table 6.3, "Tell them about your feelings and other personal things"). As one girl expressed it: "You hardly even talk to grown-ups as much as a friend basically because, uhm, you don't really feel comfortable sitting down and talking to them" F12 (3). Children seem to be able to reveal personal experiences to their parents if they enjoy a supportive relationship with them: "Well, like if I'm—if something happened in school, and I get in trouble, she won't really, she won't try to tease me, she'll just ask what happened and be real nice about it" M10 (1).

"Talk over problems."

As pointed out in the previous rule ("Reveal your personal experiences and feelings to others"), this rule is less an indication of intimacy than an expression of a desire to solve problems, specifically by talking to others. To "talk over problems," then, can have either a practical value: for example, "Talking through problems with others helps to solve them" M13 (1), or a therapeutic one: for example, "Talk over things that have gone wrong: it makes you feel better" M10 (1). The relevance of the closeness of a relationship to the value of this rule is clearly articulated by an 11-year-old girl: "Sometimes I just leave [others] alone if they're not really good friends of mine. Like, if they're sort of friends, I'd ask them, but then they'd say, 'Oh, just forget it, just leave me alone.' But like if I had a good friend who'd just say that, I'd probably say, 'Just talk to me, just tell me what's wrong.' " "Talking over problems" can also involve giving advice: "Like your friend is having problems with either families or people bugging them, they should be able to talk to you, you know, just give them a bit of advice. That's what I find" F12 (2).

Sometimes a parent can function much like a friend, as our mean differences of ratings illustrate (Table 6.3) and as Reid et al. (1989) found. As adolescence nears, mothers in particular can indeed be like friends (Youniss & Smollar, 1985): for example: "Well, over the years, you know, you know her [mother] better when you get older—you know her more, and that, you know, she talks just like a friend" F14 (1). Fortunately, in our view, we found both mothers and fathers to be good supports.

Being Loyal and Trusting

Curiously, the rules in this theme were mentioned (Table 3.3, Figure 6.13) primarily with respect to peer relationships during the interview phase of this project but in checklist Form B/Study 2, these rules were judged to be used significantly ($p > .41$) more within mother, father,

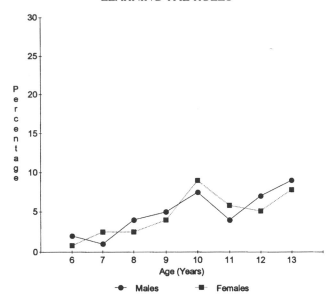

FIGURE 6.13. Percentage interview distribution of "being loyal and trusting" in the peer domain by age and sex.

brother, close friend, and teacher relationships. The interviews showed that concerns of loyalty and trustworthiness are more likely to be uppermost in children's minds in their peer relationships, since issues of fidelity, honesty, and the divulging of personally sensitive information are paramount during preteen and teenage years (see, e.g., Berndt, 1981; Bigelow & La Gaipa, 1980; Gottman & Mettetal, 1986). As we reported above, social activity ("being sociable") is also higher with close friends than in any other relationship, highlighting the powerful role that close friends play in children's lives at this time. As Gottman and Mettetal (1986) indicate, close peer relationships stand or fall on loyalty and trustworthiness. However, the presentation of a questionnaire item on the rule checklist, in a moment's reflection, forced the child to also consider loyalty and trustworthiness with respect to other types of people and produced high ratings for parents, siblings, and teachers, as well. Several other studies (e.g., Furman & Buhrmester, 1992; Reid et al., 1989) have also found such equivalencies between parents, teachers and friends with respect to informational and emotional support.

Inspection of Figure 6.14 shows clearly the sharper profile of Form B/Study 2 rules that are itemized in Table 6.4, "Trust them," "Ask them to help you out," and "Be loyal to them and be sure that they can count on you." The Form A/Study 1 rule, "Be honest with them and don't lie

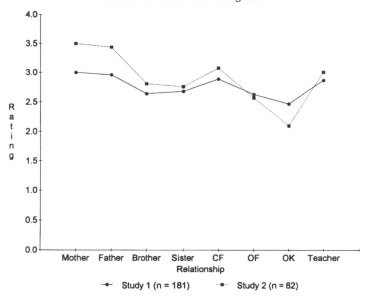

FIGURE 6.14. Ratings of "being loyal and trusting" by relationship.

TABLE 6.4. Means and Standard Deviations of Social Rule Ratings in the Theme "Being Loyal and Trusting"

	Relationships							
Rule	Mother	Father	Brother	Sister	Close friend	Other friend	Other kids	Teacher
Be honest with them, don't lie or cheat.	3.04 (.96)	3.06 (.97)	2.63 (.96)	2.67 (.44)	2.97 (.99)	2.68 (.93)	2.47 (1.00)	2.93 (1.14)
Trust them.	3.76^{**} (.68)	3.73^{**} (.74)	2.90^{*} (1.04)	2.82 (1.10)	3.28^{**} (.81)	2.71 (.79)	2.11 (.88)	3.39^{**} (.95)
Ask them to help you out.	3.31^{**} (.86)	3.15^{**} (.98)	2.55 (1.05)	2.52 (1.06)	2.83^{**} (.90)	2.37 (.80)	1.44 (.79)	2.72^{*} (.99)
Be loyal to them and be sure that they can count on you.	3.50^{**} (.72)	3.45^{**} (.78)	3.00 (1.02)	2.98 (.99)	3.29^{**} (.85)	2.85 (.85)	2.44 (1.00)	3.13 (1.02)

Note. Nominal *N*s were 315 (Form A) and 344 (Form B), but actual sample sizes varied depending on the particular rule and relationship. Means were compared by means of Scheffé ex post facto tests. Calculations employed the multivariate within-cells error.

$^{**}p < .01$; $^{*}p < .05$; $p < .10$ (italics only).

or cheat," while clearly essential in an ideal state of loyalty and trust, also appeals to a universal moral, reflecting Weston and Turiel's (1980) finding that rules of social convention (e.g., dress codes) are much more variable than moral rules (e.g., not hitting others), which are applied more universally across situations. We also saw this universality of moral rules in the "conflict management" rules in the previous chapter ("not upsetting others"). The Form B/Study 2 rules appeal directly to the stability of the relationship: "Be sure that others can count on you."

Specific Rules for Being Loyal and Trusting

"Be honest and don't lie."

While this theme echoes the sense of "Say what you really think" (Table 3.1), at times it seems more appropriate to relationships with adult authority than with peers: for example, "Don't lie to Mom and Dad so that you don't get into big trouble" F8 (1), although the theme clearly can have a peer application too: for example, "Be honest. People don't trust liars" M13 (2). What really seems to distinguish this rule from "Say what you really think" (Chapter 5) is that it assumes the form of a moral imperative. The message is clear; there is nothing morally wrong with speaking your mind, as long as it is the truth.

"Don't use or take advantage of others."

This rule was not included in the checklist. There are two related issues here, one that has to do with fairness and the other that has to do with a sense of loyalty. A sense of fairness is invoked in children's assessments as to how far they should go in pressing for things for themselves at the expense of others: for example, "Don't ask for expensive or too many things as Mom doesn't have enough money" F9 (1). Underlying this and similar statements is a judgment about what a reasonable or fair set of expectations would represent, given the other's needs; and in this sense, "Don't use or take advantage of others" social rule may be compared with "Cooperate and be fair" (Table 3.1). However, there are also considerations of loyalty and trustworthiness here: "Don't take advantage of [others], so that they will trust you and like you for sure" M13 (2). In this sense, the rule has some elements in common with "Be loyal and dependable" and "Be loyal to them and be sure that they can count on you." These two considerations of fairness and loyalty are in fact quite consistent. Fairness refers to considerations of equity in the exchange basis of a relationship, and loyalty refers to a commitment to the relationship above and beyond considerations of temporary gain. But loyalty requires that one does not overstep the bounds of fairness, as implied in the comment, "Don't use one another just to get something" M13 (2).

"Trust others."

This is another commitment rule that, more directly than "Don't use or take advantage of others," implies an investment in the relationship in question that goes beyond merely temporary concerns. It may be a way of signaling to others that they are considered as special in some manner, that a relationship with them is more intimate: "Tell [others] things you wouldn't tell other people. Trust them and they'll know it" M12 (2). By according trust to others, one may also expect some reciprocation: "Trust and tell each other everything, so you will get support" F10 (2). Undoubtedly, use of this rule can be taken as a measure of depth and intimacy within a relationship (Bigelow & La Gaipa, 1980; Gottman & Mettetal, 1986).

"Seek help."

On the surface, this appears to be a dependency rule, although it would be a mistake to see it in contrast to an autonomy-expressing rule constructed as "Be and act independent" (Table 3.1), since it is perhaps more an expression of the child's recognition that others might know better than it is an admission of failure on the child's part: for example, "Ask for help without feeling embarrassed" M12 (3). Indeed, some children are actually concerned to limit help seeking when it turns into dependency: "Try to get older kids to help you out in fights, but not to fight your battles for you" M9 (2). For some children, asking for help is a way of demonstrating trust: for example, "Go to [others] if I have a problem: [it] shows that I trust them" M12 (3); and one perceptive child recognized that asking for help can also serve as a form of flattery: "Make them feel useful by asking advice, and they'll feel more friendly to you" F12 (1). In general, this seems to be a fairly mature rule since it reflects a practical knowledge of aspects of human nature that challenge social scientists as well.

"Be loyal and dependable."

This may be seen as the other side of the coin of "Trust others," implying not only that one should trust others but that one should be trustworthy oneself: for example, "Don't tell secrets that are shared, because others won't trust you" M10 (2). In this sense, the rule may be taken as another measure of intimacy, although it stresses the safekeeping of shared information rather than its disclosure. In this important sense, this rule seems to capture something of the essence of a deeper relationship.

It is worthwhile noting that the requirements of loyalty and intimacy extend beyond the immediate relationship in question in that those requirements dictate how one should talk about the person in that person's absence: for example, "Don't talk about [others] behind their backs, or it might get back to them" F12 (3). The point might be made here, although it also applies elsewhere, that there is a certain danger in treating relationships, especially dyadic ones, in isolation from each other. What a child does in one relationship has implications for what the child does in another relationship. If children are constrained to seek some overall coherence in their social behavior between different relationships, it is not only because the children have a need for internal cognitive consistency but also because the other people with whom the children interact might draw attention to the children's inconsistencies, which may then adversely affect the children's wider group acceptance or their candidacy as someone else's friend. (See comments under "Be yourself and don't be phony," Chapter 4). Indeed, Piaget (1932/1965) stressed the role of social interaction in cognitive development, in general, on the grounds that it is only through our social exchanges with others that we become aware of our internal cognitive contradictions and, consequently, experience a pressure to surmount them, which is confirmed by recent studies on this question (Hartup et al., 1988; Nelson & Aboud, 1985). Loyalty, therefore, serves two functions: preserving the internal balance within the relationship and minimizing the need to account for one's own personal and social shortcomings.

There is another element to this rule that is best described by the word "dependability." Commitment in relationships with equals is, as we have often noted, manifested by intimacy. With those in authority, however, dependability may also take the form of showing that one can be counted on to fulfill obligations: "Be responsible: do things right away and you'll be trusted" F13 (1). This is another example of the same general rule assuming different shades of meaning in different relationships. As we have argued throughout, the meaning of social relationships can only be properly understood by examining the rules that govern them in the context of the groups and specific relationships within which they occur.

Reciprocating

The theme of "reciprocating" has assumed an important position in theoretical accounts of social development (see, e.g., Piaget, 1932/1965; Youniss, 1980). In this usage, "reciprocating" is an important element in the structure of children's relationships with other people, most notably peers, with whom children assume relatively equal roles and with whom they must learn to cooperate in order to achieve harmony. Youniss extended Piaget's notion of cooperation in peer relationships to include Sullivan's (1953) idea of preadolescent chumship (i.e., close friendship), which describes children's building relationships through a process of consensual validation, where the capacities of intimacy and mutual support, so valuable in the child's future personal life, are learned through mutual co-construction with same-sex, similar age friends. Youniss has integrated these two social processes, reciprocity and social construction, into the Sullivan–Piaget hypothesis, which predicts that children's relationships with their friends are based on reciprocity and mutuality, whereas relationships with adults, especially in the earlier childhood years, are based on a structure of unilateral authority.

"Reciprocating" as an overarching process, is not necessarily evident in the particular social rules that children use in dealing with other people in their lives. Social rules, as they are expressed by children, are verbal codifications of the behaviors they use with other people; these codes do not always take account of how other people are supposed to behave in return. It is precisely because of this fact that we cannot just rely on individuals, through their social account making (Harvey, Weber, & Orbuch, 1990; Heider, 1958), to naively articulate testable social psychological theories. Personal phenomenologies, while rich sources of social information, do not exhaustively capture the actual social processes at work in relationships with persons; these processes must often be inferred from the content of people's personal accounts. For example, the rules "Invite others over or out," and "Include others in your group or in things you do" (Table 3.1) do not explicitly mention reciprocal actions on the part of the other person (i.e., "so [others will] invite me over sometime" or "so [others will] ask me to play with them the next day"). We can only infer reciprocating here. However, rules such as "Visit each other" and "Do things together, such as playing" are explicitly reciprocal. (Much of children's accounts of the principles of social interaction, such as reciprocating, is found in Chapter 9, which focuses on social rule rationales.) The theme of "reciprocating" as it is used here is in the narrower sense, because a social rule was coded as "reciprocating" only when specific mention was made of a mutual exchange of actions that are not otherwise categorized more explicitly in other social rule themes.

As can be seen in Table 3.3 and Figure 6.15, "reciprocating" is largely a peer-only theme, which supports Youniss's (1980) Sullivan–Piaget hypothesis that reciprocal co-construction is mainly an activity that children engage in with others of equal status. However, as our checklist ratings show (Table 3.4; Figure 6.16), rules of "reciprocating" span both parents

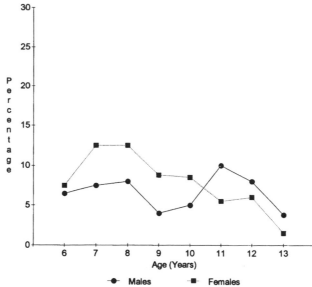

FIGURE 6.15. Percentage interview distribution of "reciprocating" in the peer domain by age and sex.

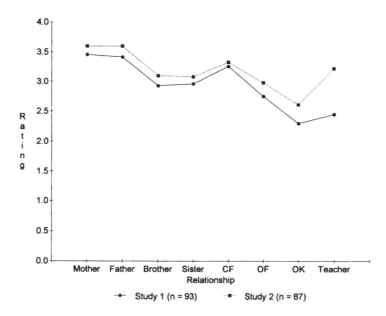

FIGURE 6.16. Ratings of "reciprocating" by relationship.

and close friend relationships as well. Again, Renshaw and Asher's (1983) work is relevant here since children's spontaneous verbalizations of social strategies are more apt to be reflected in their actual social conduct. In this sense, then, rules of "reciprocating" while equally applicable in getting along with mothers and fathers, are more apparent within the child's awareness when dealing with close friends, with whom the child is significantly more active in voluntary play, and are also evidenced by the substantially higher close friend ratings of the theme "being sociable" (Table 3.4) reported earlier.

We found, then (Table 6.5), that while the rules "Share things with them" and "Help each other out" are equally likely ($p > .44$) to occur with parents and close friends, the parent–child encounters take place within the context of parental authority where such conduct is presumably scaffolded by parental prompting. With peers, the impetus for "reciprocating" rules rests squarely with the cognitive programming of the children and their close friends.

As can be seen, the rule "Share things with others" is also used significantly more frequently with sisters as well as with parents and close friends, in spite of the finding that "being sociable," a context within which sharing is very likely, is notably low for siblings. Doubtless, an important impetus for sharing with siblings stems from parental insistence.

The other "reciprocating" rules ("Help each other out," "Be fair with them, like by taking turns") are, if anything, even more relevant ($p > .31$)

TABLE 6.5. Means and Standard Deviations of Social Rule Ratings in the Theme "Reciprocating"

	Relationships							
Rule	Mother	Father	Brother	Sister	Close friend	Other friend	Other kids	Teacher
Share things with them.	3.38^{**} (.79)	3.31^{**} (.84)	2.83 (1.04)	2.92^{*} (.90)	3.26^{**} (.70)	2.59 (.83)	2.06 (.88)	2.24 (1.05)
Help each other out.	3.46^{**} (.71)	3.44^{**} (.72)	2.99 (1.05)	3.51 (.89)	3.26^{**} (.78)	2.77 (.83)	2.24 (.89)	2.59 (1.07)
Be fair with them, like by taking turns.	3.65^{*} (.70)	3.62^{*} (.74)	3.10 (.93)	3.09 (.93)	3.39 (.76)	3.06 (.85)	2.64 (.97)	3.31 (1.02)

Note. Nominal Ns were 315 (Form A) and 344 (Form B), but actual sample sizes varied depending on the particular rule and relationship. Means were compared by means of Scheffé ex post facto tests. Calculations employed the multivariate within-cells error.

$^{**}p < .01$; $^{*}p < .05$; $p < .10$ (italics only).

within parent–child relations, further highlighting the role of parental authority in promoting reciprocal behavior beyond the family. This raises the possibility that reciprocating, which Piaget (1932/1965) assumed is the foundation of cognitive development within an egalitarian peer context, has an important foundation within the parent–child relationship. We'll have more to say about this in Chapter 7.

Specific Reciprocating Rules

"Share things."

This seems to be a genuinely prosocial category based on an underlying sense of fairness: for example, "Share things with others, like breaking a piece of chalk in two if there is only one piece" M7 (2), although it may also be motivated by an expectation of reciprocation: for example, "Sometimes you share because you want something back" M13 (1). Children seem to be aware that having something that others want can be a source of tension in a relationship: for example, "If the other person is jealous of what you have, share" F8 (2), and that sharing things is a way of improving a relationship: for example, "When [others] ask me for something, I try not to say no, then we get along better because we are happier" F8 (2). When used with adults, this strategy seems less a manifestation of a notion of fairness than it does of ingratiation: for example, "Lend the teacher things, so she won't get mad" M7 (3). As we noted above, this might account for the high ratings with parents and sisters, as well as with close friends.

"Help each other."

This, we may call a reciprocal prosocial strategy. It is quite distinct from "Offer to help others" and "Help by doing things for others" (Table 3.1) in that it stresses the bilateral character of the behavior in question: "We both help each other with things you can't do by yourself and appreciate each other for this" F9 (2). While Piagetian theory (Youniss, 1980) would lead us to hypothesize that this would be primarily a peer-oriented rule, it does have application within the family as well: "We all help each other, so things don't go so rough in our family" M9 (1).

"Cooperate and be fair."

The essence of this rule is that it invokes a criterion of fairness in social behavior, suggesting that one often has to suppress one's own desires in order to meet the other person halfway: for example, "When I'm at her house, we do what I want to do; and when she's at my house, we do what she wants to do" F6 (2). While this kind of rule clearly expresses a sense of fairness: for example, "Try to keep things fair and square, so no one has a better chance" M10 (2), some children are clearly aware that opting for fairness, taking turns, and so forth, is a way of averting conflict: "Take turns at doing what each other wants to avoid fighting" F9 (2). The fact that several children mentioned fairness in the context of conflict avoidance suggests that whatever the cognitive basis of a sense of fairness, its utilization as a criterion of child behavior is reinforced by its peacemaker effect. This is clearly a rule that one would expect to be spontaneously used with peers with whom the child has invested a relationship, although it is more important in keeping the peace with family members as well, especially when reminded.

SUMMARY

Through our contextualized analysis of "mutual activities" and "obligation," we gained valuable insights into the issues that govern children's personal relationships. For example, in the rule themes "being sociable" and "talking," we discovered that, although these themes are important for relating with parents as a whole, children tend to rate social activities as especially relevant in dealing with their close friends. Furthermore, over time, these sociability rules give way to rules of "talking," which transform the nature of social interaction into the realm of superficial and intimate exchanges with both parents and close friends. The uniqueness of these findings is the interplay between parents and close friends in the progressive unfolding of meaningful personal discourse, suggesting that close friends accentuate intimate and problem-solving relational qualities that are also characteristic of family relationships.

Since our thesis has been that relationships are rendered meaningful primarily through talk or verbal construction (Duck, 1994; Vygotsky, 1978), it appears clear that children's meaningful personal relationships indeed have their origins within early social interaction, a point originally made by Piaget (1932/1965), Gottman (1986), and Youniss and Volpe (1978) and confirmed by Zarabatany et al. (1990) with respect to children's conceptions of friendship. It is also clear, as we indicated in our previous chapter, that this cooperative function, so cherished as a peer preserve (Piaget, 1932; Sullivan, 1953; Youniss, 1980), stems from what appears to be a parallel process within both parental *and* peer interactions. Children's higher "being sociable" ratings within close friend relationships may signify less about the unique importance of those relationships in social construction than their availability. The "helping others" theme confirmed our suspicions in this regard because the reasons children have for their helping rules, which the reader will recall were rated equally for parents and close friends, had parental urging as their source. The upshot seems clear: a quality friendship may have its source in a quality parent.

Our data also clarified a particularly vexing issue raised in Chapter 2: sex differences in intimacy and disclosure, which were reflected in selected "talking" rules. From both our interviews and our questionnaires, it was clear that females mention talking more often than males do but rate it equally often in their dealings with particular persons. Even on a general basis, females communicated more rules than males did. Since we assumed that relational competency is essentially verbally governed, these findings invited the conclusion that females have more meaningful and perhaps more competent relationships than males do, particularly with respect to rules that have "talking" as their basis. In light of females' greater usage of "controlling feelings" in the previous chapter, we were inclined to agree.

The rule themes "being loyal and trusting" and "reciprocating" so often couched in friendship issues, were also more meaningful with peer relationships in our interviews. However, our relational ratings belied the incorrect notion that these rules are the sole preserve of close friendships since they are also clearly family rules as well.

In the preceding three chapters, we have discussed social rules at two levels: (1) the macrolevel, which generally addresses overarching structural issues, such as compliance and cooperation, which were addressed as rule themes and social domains; and (2) the microlevel, which examined specific rules within particular relationships. We provided detailed evidence to show that, while compliance to adult authority often "trickles down" to the microlevel of specific social rules and specific relationships, there is often a significant degree of overlap between parent–child and close friend relationships in cooperative rules. Presumably then, more than authority and compliance stem from parents. In the next chapter, we specifically illustrate at the microlevel where there is this overlap, or "fuzziness," between parent–child and close friend relationships, and we discuss its implications for socialization.

Our results in general have informed us that the meaning of a personal relationship can only be properly approximated by examining its component parts at successive levels of discourse, which in our case involved social domains, specific relationships, interviews, and rating scales. Hinde (1979, 1987) has been preaching the significance of this approach, and it is time that more of us listened.

CHAPTER 7

Social Competency and the Sorcerer's Apprentice
THE IMPORTANCE OF PARENTS

THE PARENT–CHILD, CHILD–CHILD RIDDLE

Research on parent–child and close peer relationships (see, e.g., Bigelow et al., 1992; Furman & Buhrmester, 1992; Reid et al., 1989; Weisz, 1980; Youniss, 1980) has painted a rather perplexing riddle for the student of socialization. On the one hand, parent–child relationships embody a broad pattern of parental authority and child compliance (see, e.g., Maccoby & Martin, 1983; Peterson & Rollins, 1987; Youniss, 1980); but, on the other hand, to be optimally effective the parenting process must be socially and emotionally supportive (Baumrind, 1967, 1971, 1973) and must function like a friendship. Children themselves also rate their parents highly on selected characteristics such as control, autonomy, affection, emotional support, and helping (Amato, 1990; Armentrout & Burger, 1972; Shaeffer, 1965), which our social rules data (Tables 3.3 and 3.4) reveal to be identical in most respects to children's relationships with their parents *and* close friends (e.g., Bigelow et al., 1992).

Does friendship develop intact from a supportive parent–child relationship or is it a separate relationship? How then is the parenting relationship different from friendship? These are vexing problems, since the peer literature (see, e.g., Piaget, 1932/1965; Rubin et al., 1990) asserts that peer relationships offer children unique opportunities for cooperation and negotiation not generally available with parents. The characterization of the unique quality of the parent–child relationship is an important part of the history of thinking in developmental psychology, notably with respect to Piaget (1932/1965), Sullivan (1953), and Youniss (1980), who have argued that the social worlds of parents and peers are structurally quite different: children comply with their parents and coop-erate with their friends. To take a page out of these arguments (see, e.g., Hunter & Youniss, 1982), it is not until early adolescence that children acquire more intimate versions of close friends and are capable of actually *understanding* the rules of relating, which they develop and exercise through a process of mutual construction with their peers. By default, one is then left with the unfortunate impression that unilateral parent–child relationships during early and middle childhood are bereft of mutual meaning. Our rules data suggest otherwise.

Piaget's (1932/1965) work on the morality of cooperation set the stage for our understanding of late childhood as a time of negotiated reality in which children begin to relinquish some of their egocentrism, as exemplified in relatively rigid "immutable" adult-based social rules, in favor of a social code fashioned out of a working consensus with peers. However, Piaget was not clear whether adult authority continues to dominate parent–child relationships throughout later childhood and adolescence in the face of children's capacity for decentered thought that they clearly exercise with their peers. This is an important point, since failure to make this discrimination does not allow us to separate the effects of type of relationship (e.g., parent, close friend) from develop-ment. To be specific, if the social constructs that characterize relationships are partly a function of the defining features (e.g., parental control) of the relationship itself, then perhaps children's nascent appreciation of mutual understanding may occur much earlier than Piaget envisioned. If parents are largely controlling with their children, one can hardly attribute egocentric and compliant behavior to their children's lack of develop-ment. In fact, a close reading of any modern text in child development will show that Piaget was too conservative in his age norms for decentered thought. As well, the authority and compliance features of relationships with parents continue well into the age span reserved for intimate peer relations (Hunter & Youniss, 1982; Youniss & Smollar, 1985) and can hardly then be a function of developmental abilities.

On a similar plane, Sullivan (1953) posited that during middle childhood and early adolescence, the period of "chumships" (Sullivan's term for close friendship) children begin to recognize one another as unique personalities with interpersonal sensitivities stemming from bilat-eral exchanges, where meaning is mutually constructed and validated. Like Piaget (1932/1965), Sullivan felt that older children derive their peer orientation from adult definitions of reality and, consistent with our rule findings (Table 3.3), it is the adult environment of authority that provides children with the rules of life that are not fully understood until the rules are validated through interactions with close friends. It is only when children "jointly construct norms or standards for evaluation of behavior that they can recognize the reality of the persons involved" (Youniss, 1980, p. 16). Whether we call this mutual process between equals "cooperation," "mutual engagement" (Piaget, 1932/1965), or "consensual validation" (Sullivan, 1953), the upshot is difficult to miss: adults are the source of the overall framework of rules, and thus children use many of the same social rules in dealing with both their parents and close friends. But the rules are not clearly understood until they are enacted with peers in an environment of spontaneous reciprocity. As Youniss (1980) explained it,

> Children enter the world of peers with confidence that they have mastered the rules of society. Children also believe that their understanding of the order of things, which they learned from adults, is shared by their peers. Thus, children enter interactions with peers expecting their conceptions of order to be applicable everywhere. It takes little contact with peers for children to realize that their expectation of a shared view of order is incorrect. (p. 30)

The reader is thus left with the impression that parents and peers provide distinct and necessary functions without which normal social development will not occur. Indeed, Sullivan's (1953) writings claim that close peer relationships are essential in forming a healthy personality. While we also agree that competent friendships are a vital ingredient of development, our data make us pause in looking at the relative functions served by parents and peers. Piaget (1932/1965), Sullivan (1953), and Youniss (1980), we feel, were too strong in their portrayal of social relationships with parents as being largely unilateral. As we show below, there is ample evidence with which to suggest that children actively practice their cooperative social constructing with both parents and close friends alike. While doubtless more opportunities arise for freely exchanging views with one's friends than with one's parents, as Berscheid (1986) argued, it is often the circumstances that dictate social relating. During the school years, peers are generally more available than parents are.

PARENTING REVISITED

As we show below, competent parenting is essential for competent friendship, which is reinforced by the fact revealed in the previous chapter that a child's relationships with parents and friends do not develop sequentially but in parallel. Indeed, Putallaz and Heflin (1990) and Rubin et al. (1990) have also made empirical and theoretical links between competent parenting and peer social acceptance. Thus, while friendships are important, many of the defining functions of friendships (e.g., cooperativeness, helpfulness, intimacy, and trust) are not formed exclusively within this relationship but find their roots within the crucible of parenting. For example, Rubin et al. (1990) argue that social isolation from one's "community of peers" may be rooted in the interplay of socialization (see, e.g., poverty and personal stressors) and early attachment difficulties.

We argue that effective parenting achieves its power chiefly through a combination of structure and induction (Baumrind, 1967; Becker, 1964; Hoffman, 1963; Rollins & Thomas, 1979; Shaeffer, 1965), as well as support (see, e.g., Becker, 1964; Coopersmith, 1967; Shaeffer, 1965; Weisz, 1980; Reid, 1989). Induction can be described as a democratic autocracy, in which children are invited to actively participate in the decisions that affect them, which has been most commonly referred to as authoritative parenting (see, e.g., Baumrind, 1967).

Because our social rules are verbally constructed and represented, we made specific use of the scaffolding principle (see, e.g., Bruner, 1975; Fischer & Bullock, 1984a, 1984b; Vygotsky, 1934/1962, 1978). As part of parental induction, children learn social rules by observing and listening to their parents, who demonstrate the principles of relating at a level of complexity slightly more advanced than children are capable of attaining individually, and therefore children can achieve social competency better than would be possible on their own. Because we reported a comprehensive list of social rules across a broad range of relationships, we were in an advantageous position from which to attempt to address the "parent or peer" versus "parent and peer" issue. Since our focus was on relationships and relating apart from peer interactions in general, we confined our comparisons to parent–child and close friend relations.

OUR FINDINGS: THE BIG PICTURE

In some ways, our own interview findings (Table 3.3) certainly paint a reassuring picture consistent with Youniss's (1980) Sullivan–Piaget hypothesis. Children described their relationships with their parents consistently with the way in which they described relationships with adults outside the family domain with respect to authority and compliance. Parents and adults are people to whom one shows deference and for whom one follows the rules. On the other hand, Sullivan's (1953) and Youniss's (1980) views seem to extend beyond the facts. In our study, there are several types of parent rules that are also clearly prominent within the peer domain and that are also fairly descriptive of the mutual respect and cooperation that Sullivan (1953) reserved for children's close friendship relationships. These rules include "reciprocating," "being loyalty and trusting," and "controlling feelings." The social rules elicited by nonfamily adults fall almost exclusively into the "compliance" category. "Talking," which includes superficial as well as more intimate forms of disclosure, is only slightly more prominent with peers than with family and other-adult domains. "Self-control and conflict management" and "being sociable" span both parent and peer domains. Hence, the worlds of adults and peers seem largely separate with regard to the authority themes that characterize the Sullivan–Piaget debate, but parents and peers also share many cooperative rules that Sullivan reserved for close friends.

The "parent or peer" picture begins to alter appreciably to a "parent and peer" pattern when the ratings (Table 3.4) between parent–child and close friend relationships are concerned. A much closer match is found between ratings of parent–child and close friend relations than is the case with more distant types of peer encounters. We proposed in Chapter 4 that to be effective in socialization, there should be considerable overlap, or *fuzziness,* between parent–child and peer relationships. While Table 3.3 shows such overlap, Table 3.4 reveals an almost total fusion between parent and close friend relationships, resembling the findings of other multirelational studies (e.g., Furman & Buhrmester, 1992). Here, we find the rule themes that characterize these two kinds of relationships to be almost identical. Moreover, the supportive features of personal relationships reported in the literature (see, e.g., Weiss, 1974; Weisz, 1980) have a striking resemblance to many of the social rule themes, reported in Chapters 4, 5, and 6, characteristic of social relationships with parents *and* close friends: "reliable alliance" ("being loyal and trusting": e.g., "Be sure that they can count on you"); "enhancement of worth, intimacy and affection" ("express feelings": e.g., "Show them that you really like them" and "Cheer them up when they're down"; "assertiveness": e.g., "Don't keep things inside; tell others what you really think"); and "instrumental help and nurturance" ("helping": e.g., "Help them out, like by doing things for them"). Only one rule theme (i.e., "being sociable") is rated more highly in the close friend relationship, and the other theme (i.e., "express feelings") is rated more highly for getting along with one's parents.

Contrary to Sullivan's (1953) claim, then, it would seem that children *do* in fact comprehend the "adult" social rules that they subsequently use in the world of peers, especially when these peers are close friends. It became increasingly more clear to us that the relational division between parent–child and peer relationships—especially intimate ones such as close or best friendships—is somewhat overdone. Therefore, the riddle is more precisely: "When is a parent–child relationship like a close friendship and when is a close friendship like a parenting one?" If we are to have any success in characterizing the nature of the parent–child relationship—which perhaps more than any other type of social or personal relationship lays claim to a distinct boundary separating it from other types of relationships—then how can we reconcile the paradox that during middle childhood and early adolescence the parent–child relationship seems to contain most, if not all, of the supportive features of a close friendship? In fact, Reid et al. (1989) state that "children perceive their mothers as being the best multipurpose social provider available, in contrast to friends and teachers, who are relatively specialized in their social value" (p. 907).

In light of our own checklist ratings data (Table 3.4), which show that "compliance" is shared between parents and close friends alike, even the claim of Reid et al. (1989) seems too strong. Both close friends and parents are "multipurpose social providers" (Reid et al., 1989, p. 907). While the interviews show (Table 3.3) that the worlds of peers and adults are divided along authority lines, the checklist ratings of the worlds of parent–child relationships and close friend relationships are much less so. We do not necessarily wish to be interpreted as saying that parents are dispensable when a good close friend can be substituted—hardly. Indeed, supportive parents directly provide for the child's physical and emotional needs and, by setting examples and explaining actions, help the child to learn the rules that are needed throughout life. Childhood is a period of social vulnerability and physical reliance that requires family contributions to maintain a child's sense of self-esteem (Reid et al., 1989). It is at this juncture that the notion of the parent–child relationship as a socially and relationally supportive one, resembling close peer relationships in many important respects, calls into question a nominal classification of relationships as parents, peers, close friends, and so on. In particular, the mutual construction of social meaning as evidenced in the content of the social rules themselves reveals the active social participation provided by friends and parents alike. Only by examining the functional qualities of supports—reflected in part by the social rules used—are we in a position from which to ascertain a relationship's meaning and to assess the provisions that are served by it. One of these qualities intrinsic to parenting is scaffolding.

CONTROL, SUPPORT, AND SCAFFOLDING

Since there is considerable overlap between the rules used for parent–child and close friend relationships, we propose a modification of the Sullivan–Piaget hypothesis, based on the assumption that the parent–child relationship, to be optimally adaptive, must provide the basis of all that is required for the child to be socially competent throughout the rest of life and that this basis also includes the knowledge of how to be a close friend. This view of the parenting relationship is based on two fundamental facts: (1) that with the passage of time children are relatively less involved with adults and parents than they are with their peers (Figures 6.1 and 6.2; Berndt, 1979; Csikszentmihalyi & Larson, 1984; Ellis et al., 1981; Steinberg, 1990); and (2) that children become progressively more "peerlike" in their relationships with their parents as they become older and more intellectually capable (see, e.g., Bigelow, Levin, & Cunning, 1994; Hunter & Youniss, 1982; Kuczynski, Kochanska, Radke-Yarrow, & Girnius-Brown, 1987). What sets this view apart from the Sullivan–Piaget hypothesis is that we assume that by the time children have made this "transition" from parents to peers, and especially from parents to close friends, their repertoire of social knowledge is relatively complete in most essential respects. While friendships certainly offer children new experiences and challenges, friendship essentially allows children to further and more intensely practice what they have already effectively learned through supportive exchanges with their parents.

Do children remain socially incompetent without rich exposure to peer relationships, as when they live exclusively with their parents? There is evidence (Zajonc & Markus, 1975) suggesting that for firstborn and only children, the opposite is true, although this finding assumes, questionably perhaps, that siblings can be equated with peers. Evidently, such children benefit intellectually from having more contact with the higher verbal abilities of the parents. The world of siblings is not as stimulating in this regard. As we argued in Chapter 3, intelligence is socially and verbally constructed (see, e.g., Butterworth, 1982); so perhaps the social knowledge of firstborns and only children is also superior. However, we know of no comparable studies that vary the child's exposure to peer relationships. Obviously, for ethical and practical reasons, this question is difficult to address experimentally; but, armed with our interview data, we shed light on the matter by examining how children express their social rules—and in this way we have learned something of how parents scaffold them. After all, the social context is often revealed in the articulation of the rule itself (see Chapter 3). Scaffolding may provide a bridge between parent–child and close friend relationships by preserving the inherent authority of the parent as the instrument of acquisition of social competency, while at the same time accounting for similarities between the two relationships with respect to rule use.

Since our study was based on children's phenomenologies of their personal and social relationships, we were able to identify examples of parental scaffolding of social rules by examining the verbalized content of the child's rule strategies. If we are correct in our assumption that parents effectively apprentice children to function as close friends, then we should see evidence of this teaching by examining social rule explications. Since social rules are linguistically mediated, they are acquired by the child in much the same way as many other skills and competencies by means of scaffolding (Cooper & Cooper, 1992; Rogoff, 1990).

During the middle years, Fischer and Bullock (1984b) have suggested, cognitive competency is achieved by the child through a "collaborative cycle" with the parent, wherein the child in scaffolded interaction eventually learns to complete a task, such as a puzzle, without the parent's help. In this way, the parent constantly updates his or her scaffolding to fit the child's newly developed knowledge and skill. As we suggested in Chapter 3, social rules are based on scripted episodes (see, e.g., Schank & Abelson, 1977) that themselves are acquired through social learning, and the content of these rules is presumably also scaffolded. In fact, recent data (Finnie & Russell, 1988) has linked mothers' competencies in their supervisory role to preschool children's social skill acquisition. Some of the skill codes used by these mothers in interaction with their children have an extraordinary resemblance to our social rule themes and provide a rich portrayal of the scaffolding technique. Examples of such maternal behaviors, accompanied by social rule themes in parentheses, are the following: "Helps own child join conversation with dyad" (talking), "Encourages participation with group to gain entry" (being sociable), "Encourages cooperation" (reciprocating), "Tells child to say hello" (being sociable), and "Avoids conflict by suggesting an alternative" (avoiding and ignoring).

Scaffolding is only one of a set of alternative models through which effective parenting is achieved. Putallaz and Heflin (1990) noted that modeled characteristics of parents, such as aggression (see, e.g., Bandura & Walters, 1959; Eron, 1982), altruism (see, e.g., Hoffman, 1975), and sensitive communication (Bearison & Cassel, 1975) are often reflected in their children. Scaffolding, or "coaching," however, is more inductive (Hoffman, 1963) because it encourages the give-and-take of social exchange and is therefore more appropriate to our social rules data than are other more mechanical models such as observational learning and conditioning and learning. Nevertheless, Putallaz and Heflin (1990) conclude, and we agree, that "the mother–child relationship establishes a social orientation that is likely to generalize to other relationships" (p. 197). Interestingly, Hoffman (1963) found that parents who use more power assertion were less likely to train their children to be considerate to others. Thus, parenting that is *less* unilateral is likely to be more productive in scaffolding social competency. Children's characterizations of their relationships with parents as "unilateral" (Youniss, 1980) may therefore understate the level of cooperation that does in fact take place. In the interests of accuracy though, we do not know which kinds of parenting are normative.

Consistent with our own view that social rules for dealing with parents are equally cooperative as well as authority based, Putallaz and Heflin (1990) also found in their review that infants who are securely attached are more likely to have mothers who are more responsive, cooperative, and involved (see, e.g., Ainsworth, Bell, & Stayton, 1971; Ainsworth, Blehar, Waters, & Wall, 1978; Clarke-Stewart, 1973; Londerville & Main, 1981). As the reader may recall (Chapter 3), Fogel (1993) stressed that infants are socially constructing their meaning at life's start within the intimate exchanges that occur with their mothers, which form the origins of meaningful social understanding.

If parent–child relationships are unique with respect to adult unilateral authority and child compliance, then the child's expression of specific social rules (i.e., the microlevel of analysis) should reveal the scaffolding that occurred in their construction. Thus, part of this natural authority should be mirrored in the content of the social rule strategies themselves. In this way, we can then obtain a glimpse of how parents teach their children to be socially competent. We can also examine examples of social strategies expressed within parental and close friend contexts that, by virtue of their content and how it is expressed, can also illuminate similarities and differences between these two relationships. If parent–child and close friendships are genuinely similar, then it should be evident from these examples and their rationales; however, if parent–child social strategies are based comparatively more on "compliance" than are rule strategies for dealing with a friend, we have evidence supporting the Sullivan–Piaget hypothesis. Specifically, we examined examples of peer-appropriate "cooperative" rules (Table 3.4) that spanned "self-control and conflict management," and "mutual activities" and "obligation." We did not examine the scaffolding of "compliance" rules since they were not unique to parental authority but rather reflected adult authority in general (Table 3.3).

OUR FINDINGS: THE LITTLE PICTURE

Self-control and Conflict Management

Not Upsetting Others

For this theme, there was a gradual reduction in its usage over age (Chapter 5), but it was equally relevant in dealing with any relationship. However, as indicated in Chapter 5, while children need to work things out for themselves (Shantz, 1987; Youniss, 1980), the enhanced ratings at older age levels for parents and teachers suggest that the awareness of these rules is essentially parent and adult governed (i.e., "compliance").

For example, for the rule "Don't bug or bother" the context was to avoid irritating parents "so that they will not get grouchy" F8 (3) or because "they'll just get mad" M8 (1). Similarly for "Don't argue" the appeal is to authority figures, "because they know best" M13 (1) or "to avoid fights" M11 (1). The same is true for "Don't be rude," for example, "They'll get mad" M8 (1), and "Don't interfere in adult conversations" F12 (3); "Don't fight with or physically hurt another," for example, "I have to live with [my parents]" M12 (1); and "Don't fool around," for example, "It lets [my mother] know I'm doing my work" M11 (3).

However, with peers, and with close friends in particular, the emphasis is essentially one of "reciprocating" rather than complying with adult authority: "Don't argue," for example, "or be too bossy, or they'll do the same to you" M6 (2); "Don't be rude," for example, "because you know how it feels" F13 (2); "Don't fight," for example, "or they'll stop being friends" M7 (2); "Don't fool around," for example, "then she'll want to be with me and won't get embarrassed" F9 (2); "Don't be hurtful," for example, "because you know how it feels" F13 (2). In retrospect, it is difficult to see how a child would avoid bothering her parents in order to "make sure they still want to be your parents."

As we can plainly see, the rule theme "not upsetting others" is relevant to dealing with both parents and peers, but the reasons given for not upsetting peers is one of "cooperation," whereas the avoidance of sanctions is the motivation with parents. There were relatively few prominent examples of cooperative explanations for getting along with parents, thereby offering firm support for a Piagetian (1932/1965), Sullivanian (1953), and Younissian (1980) model of parent and peer relationships. However, as Table 3.3 shows, "reciprocating" is essentially a peer theme but is especially salient for close friends and parents alike (Table 3.4). Therefore, the cooperative rules themselves may be originally *acquired* within the parent–child relationship but, as the above rationales show, are *practiced* in the peer domain—especially with close friends—in order to preserve it. This scaffolding of rule knowledge within the parent–child relationship becomes more evident in specific examples outlined below.

Controlling Feelings

The age differences in these rules reveal that it is used more widely with peers as children get older (Chapter 5) and that, on balance, it is relatively more common in dealing with peers (Table 3.3). The focus of these rules for different relationships though seems essentially one of empathy, whether in terms of parent–child relationships: for example, "Know when others need time to themselves and leave them alone" M13 (1), or peer relationship: for example, "Don't hurt others' feelings because you know how it feels" F13 (2). The lack of these rules for nonparental adults (Table 3.3) is noteworthy, since the inculcation of empathy seems to be for parents and peers alike, which supports our scaffolding hypothesis but does not necessarily restrict it to the parental role. While parents may initially have assisted in shaping the child's empathy responses, the reasons for and the practice of (Table 3.4) these kinds of social rules are not sensitive to the social worlds of parents and peers or to specific personal or social relationships, thus calling into question the need to invoke issues of authority and cooperation to account for the use of these rules. Perhaps this is just as well, for of all the rules to have a universal presence, it should be ones that reflect empathy.

Expressing Feelings

This theme was used significantly more so in dealing with parents than with other kids relationships, although close friends were very relevant as well (Table 3.4). The child evidently feels more comfortable in expressing positive feelings toward the parent (e.g., "Show them that you really like them" and "Cheer others up when they're down"), suggesting that supportive parent–child relationships generalize to the child's dealings with the close friend: for example, "Let them know you care. Say nice things" M12 (1). Although routine emotions such as releasing pent-up anger had no relational differences, we suspect that the support features of a positive parent–child relationship furnish the child with a safe, accepting environment within which such expressiveness can be exercised in all future close relationships, as with close friends, and eventually in a romantic context. These examples, while not sufficient to formally test an aspect of the Sullivan–Piaget hypothesis, do suggest that elements of reciprocity, typically associated with cooperative peer relationships, are also a key feature of the parent–child relationship.

Figuring Others Out

Even for this theme, the child seems to do some careful reconnoitering with parents as well as with friends. In fact, at times, the child seems to regard the parents as if they were strangers: for example, "Watch out for what kind of person they are so you know how to act around them" F10 (1), much the same as in getting acquainted with other children: for example, "Ask things about them to get to know them better" M11 (2). These examples simply reflect a skill central to all competent social functioning, whether with parents, friends, or people in general.

Repairing Damage

One would expect that, given the voluntary nature of peer relationships, if keeping damaged relationships matters, *reparation* would be more peer relevant, and Table 3.3 in fact supports this view, although parent–child relationships also govern the use of this rule to some extent (Table 3.4). Evidently, some care is also required in the maintenance of such "involuntary" relationships. The parental scaffolding of this rule is abundantly clear in the sorts of sample strategies that children used, and at times interactions with the parent took on a peerlike appearance. For example, making up can be scaffolded by parents through setting a good example: "Well, if she [my mom] does something bad and [then] she says 'sorry,' when she wants to play something, then I will say 'yes' " F8 (1). For this type of rule, then, it may first occur in the parent–child relationship; but, as with many other rules (Table 3.4), it is also practiced with one's close friends, so that the personal relationship is preserved. Obviously, one cannot change one's parents when there is a rift in the relationship.

However, the motivation to preserve the relationship is made in earnest when interacting with peers, especially friends: for example, "Make up after arguments because we're really good friends, and we wouldn't have anything to do if we didn't play together" M8 (2). There are also several examples where children expressed the need to make up after an offense. With parents, the issue is essentially one of accepting one's guilt, although at times this issue of guilt, such as not breaking a vase on purpose, can be seen in the reasons given for making up with the friend: for example, "If [others] know that you didn't do it on purpose, say, if you're a nice person, and then they'll probably just be your friend" F10 (2). But to claim that the motives of reciprocity and relationship preservation are seeded solely in the world of peers is simply not supported, since there are instances, as shown in the first example, where children clearly illustrate scaffolding of this kind of rule by the parent with a keen motivation that appears very peerlike.

To further illustrate, for the rule "Make up with them after a fight or an argument," we see the parent imposing authority in response to the child's misdeeds, so that the child will feel an empathy response and want to make amends: for example, "Sometimes I'll do something bad and then she, my mom, will give me a spanking, and I'll tell her that I'm sorry" F10 (1). In addition, "I don't want to get into trouble, and then we'll be even" F8 (1) appeals to a kind of equity of the sort expected within a morality of reciprocity (Piaget, 1932/1965) that, in theory, is more normative for peer relationships; but here we also see reciprocity in the context of parent–child relationships.

Mutual Activities

As indicated in Chapter 6, these kinds of rules are treated as archetypal of peer relationships. One plays with one's friends, not with one's parents. While our data (e.g., "being sociable") supports this view (Table 3.4) with respect to close friends, parents are not irrelevant (Table 3.3, Figures 6.1 and 6.2). As we have been arguing, these social rules are essentially scaffolded by parent–child interactions, either through direct participation or through get-togethers, parties, and neighborhood contacts. Then these activities are subsequently practiced in both parent and peer relationships, particularly close peer relationships, which encompass the need to preserve the relationship by means of the exercise of these rules. Subsequent use of rules in the peer relationship may reflect social competency by virtue of the freer nature of peer interactions, relative to the world of parents, but it may well be that parents simply do not usually have the time available to behave in a more peerlike manner with their children. This is a big environmental restraint. Perhaps, if parents had the time, they would engage in more playful exchanges with their children. After all, as we shall see in Chapter 9, children mention having fun as a rationale for involvement with family and peers alike.

Being Sociable

With peers, the goal clearly is to make friends: for example, "Make them laugh so that they will like you and you will be more friends" F6 (2). However, with parents, the goal is to improve or preserve the quality of the parent–child relationship: for example, "Try to make them laugh, so you won't be fighting later" F6 (1). To further illustrate: "Visit each other's houses to get to know each other" M11 (2) and "Do family activities together as a way to get to know others better" F11 (1). If we did not know the relational sources of these statements, we may well reflexively attribute them to friendship.

Helping Others

Even these kinds of altruistic rules, which are authority-bound in the home, are often exercised in the service of nurturing the harmony of the relationships that one has within the family: for example, "If I didn't, the jobs wouldn't get done" M6 (1), and with one's friends, "Help others to do things, so you can be more close and come to understand each other more" F13 (1) and "This makes us better friends" F11 (2). Consistent with our own findings (Table 3.4), Sullivan (1953) indicated that helping, along with intimacy, loyalty, and support, are cardinal features of a preadolescent chumship, but clearly (Table 3.3) helping is also a family affair. It remains to be seen whether the function of mutual helping, a vital process of knowing about oneself and one's friends, is in early evidence in supportive parent–child relationships. It is likely a scaffolded aspect of secure parenting (see Putallaz & Heflin's 1990 review). Given our previous examples for other rules, even if children at times regard their parents as relatively boring companions, children do appear to relate to parents in a peerlike manner when the opportunity arises.

OBLIGATION

Talking

Such rules are well exercised within parent–child relationships, both for routine exchanges and for communication of intimacies. Clearly then, sharing intimacies is not the sole preserve of a close friendship, although at times the specific content warrants it: for example, "Well, there's some things you tell your best friends that maybe you wouldn't tell your mother" F14 (2), since this kind of rule is at times very much in evidence in relating to parents: for example, "Share close things with them, so you get to know each other better through conversations" M13 (1).

Being Loyal and Trusting

However, with this theme, the onus is on not getting into trouble with parents: for example, "Don't lie to mom and dad so that you won't get into big trouble" F8 (1), and on preserving the relationship itself in dealing with peers: for example, "Don't take advantage of them, so that they will trust you and like you for sure" M13 (2). It is interesting to note (Table 3.4) that the child is very sensitive to issues of trust (e.g., "Be sure that they can count on you") for parents and close friends, suggesting that cooperative peerlike functions may be nascent in a simpler form within a relation with parents.

THE APPRENTICESHIP OF SOCIAL COMPETENCY

While these excerpts from the social rule interviews were preliminaries toward a more solid research foundation, they nevertheless encouraged us to reconsider our intuitive models of parents. First, are there really two main social worlds of childhood, the world of parents and the world of peers? While far from conclusive, our data suggest that this is an oversimplification. Parents do indeed perform both authority-based "Do as your are told" functions as well as more supportive functions shared with the peer domain, but in particular with the close friend relationship. In our view, it is here that the theoretically clean bifurcation between parents and peers is most troubling. While Sullivan's (1953) portrait of the preadolescent chumship is considered to be essential for proper socialization to be complete, the social rules training that the child enjoys with the parent is not appreciated for the vital role it plays. It is precisely within the close friend relationship that the social rules that children express are most like many of the rules that are used in relating to their parents. Evidently, not all social competencies emerge out of the free flow of peer relationships and can be traced to origins within the family (see Ladd, 1992). For example, Elicker, Englund, and Sroufe (1992) found that secure attachment in infancy is correlated with preadolescent social competency with peers (10 years later!). What is more, Parke, Cassidy, Burks, Carson, and Boyum (1992) view parents as educators of their children's competency in relating to peers through the advice, support, and direct teaching of social strategies that parents give to children, in particular in children's dealings with emotional understanding. It would certainly be an inviting prospect to see whether children and their parents can reliably identify which relationship a social rule statement was derived from, for the distinctive social meaning of these relationships may at times be quite subtle.

As well, as our data largely reveal, there are very few age-related changes in the frequency with which these rules are used between these two types of relationships. This has important implications for our view of parents and children in socialization. Are children trained in the family and launched into the world of peers or does social learning within these two domains occur separately but in parallel? As indicated at the start of this chapter, over time, children reduce their relationships with parents in preference for peers; but the influence of parents is still relatively large, where parents scaffold, model, and reinforce children's social competencies as a stepping-stone to children's close friend relationships and to the world at large.

Training children to relate competently with others is, in our view, a relatively intense process even when adolescence is reached; and parental influence over children's actions is more indirect, but nonetheless felt. In fact, Maccoby (1984b) posited that during preadolescence, parents actually intensify their influence over their children, so that by the time adolescence is entered in earnest, children can be more fully acculturated into the ways of the world. This period is accompanied by heightened parent–child conflict (Bigelow et al., 1994), which occurs approximately at the same developmental juncture as more intense involvements with peers. It is also a serious oversight to lump all parents together as if they compose a homogeneous species. Clearly, some parents are more supportive than others (Baumrind, 1967; Maccoby & Martin, 1983; Peterson & Rollins, 1987; Shaeffer, 1965), and future investigations would do well to make this differentiation. It would not surprise us if the worlds of parents and peers are most sharply defined where parents are not supportive; this would make the world of peers very tempting, indeed, and would make the child more vulnerable to the arena of antisocial as well as social experiences.

While our data suggest that both parents and close friends can be equally supportive in middle childhood and early adolescence, it is still apparent that parents exercise more unilateral control over children (Table 4.2). As Maccoby and Martin (1983) have stressed, in the final analysis the function of parenting is one of control. As noted above (Maccoby, 1984b), during early and middle adolescence, children heighten their challenge toward this authority and power (Furman & Buhrmester, 1992), which heralds an increase in the child's emerging competencies in the face of this parental attempt to enhance control. However, as Maccoby (1984a) has indicated, the process is one of coregulation, which is comparable to the scaffolding processes mentioned earlier (Fischer & Bullock, 1984a, 1984b) where parents continually adjust their powers of "autonomy granting" in light of the child's newly acquired skills. Naturally though, the process is perceived by the adolescent as an imposition to be endured. This period of enhanced social apprenticeship can be viewed as an attempt on the part of parents to assist the adolescent in self-regulation in preparation for complete autonomy needed in the wider, colder worlds of school and work and their attendant formal responsibilities. One is impelled to ask why it is, if supportive parents are so much like close friends, that children seek friends so much?

As Furman and Buhrmester (1992) have indicated, though, there are several plausible reasons why adolescents make this transition from parental to close friend attachments: advanced cognitive development and shared desires for self-exploration; emergent sexuality that is most comfortably discussed with close peers; interests acquired outside the family; and an emerging autonomy from the family based on biological maturation, which Blos (1967) describes as a "second individuation." While each of these reasons contains plausible elements, we were especially intrigued by Blos's accounting of this parent-to-friend transition. We were particularly interested in the issues of autonomy because they are structural rather than based on the specific provisions of a personal relationship between the newly adolescent child and the supportive parent (see Frank, Avery, & Laman, 1988). That is, Blos's theory predicts that the adolescent enters the world of peers regardless of how supportive or friendshiplike their actual relationships with their parents are.

For Blos, the adolescent's maturational task is to extract oneself from the strictures of the family. Parallel to early attempts by a toddler to gain physical separation from the parent, the adolescent attempts to shed family dependencies in the service of the emerging self, which must be validated against "objects" outside parental control, similar in the main with Sullivan's notion of children's "consensual validation" with "chums." Blos's views are also quite compatible with those of Maccoby (1984a) in her description of the coregulation hypothesis because, unless the parents are supportive and nurturing, the adolescent cannot make a smooth transition from the family to the wider world. While at times rebelling against parental authority, the adolescent at other times needs such authority desperately. After all, says Blos, there are numerous instances of regression as well as of advancement before the transition to adulthood is complete. An overly strict and confining parenting experience may entice the adolescent to make a premature rupture from the family before the social apprenticeship is complete, resulting in incomplete formation of a mature ego. In a real sense, then, supportive parents are much like close friends during this time, so that the leap from family to peers is not violent and premature but one that makes the transition relatively smooth. Presumably then, the more authoritarian or neglectful (Baumrind, 1967; Shaeffer, 1965) parents are toward their children, the less structure and support is offered to their children in their personal relationships and the more likely adolescent children are to seek from their peers the emotional and social supports that are so lacking in their parents.

A very illuminating short-term longitudinal study connecting parental support and children's orientations toward their peers during early adolescence was done by Fuligni and Eccles (1993). Armed with a thorough literature review, they reasoned that early adolescents orient themselves more toward peers than parents because of their emergent needs for practicing newly acquired intellectually complex reasoning, independent thinking, and formation of a personal identity (see, e.g., Youniss, 1980) which are met more by peer relationships. Since the parent–child relationship is inherently more asymmetrical, it is difficult for the child to meet these independence needs within this relationship because it has an unequal balance of power. There is typically a waxing and waning of the child's closeness toward the parent as adolescence progresses in earnest (see, e.g., Bigelow et al., 1994; Blos, 1967; Maccoby, 1984a), eventually resulting in a more friendlike *rapprochement* with parents during later adolescence (Youniss & Smollar, 1985). However, Fuligni and Eccles realized that some parents are more likely than others to relinquish unilateral control over their children during early adolescence, while still effectively monitoring their activities; some children's needs for a closer, more mutual relationship can then still be satisfied to some extent with their parents. Other parents have difficulty relinquishing control and in so doing encourage their children to be overinvolved with their peers.

As predicted, fewer perceived decision-making opportunities with parents are related to a higher frequency of turning to peers for advice, which might be better obtained from more informed parents, "When I want to talk about my future job plans, or educational plans, I talk to my friends. When I want to talk about a personal problem, I talk to my friends." In addition, parental strictness and lower scores on decision-making opportunities with parents are both related to extreme peer orientation. However, children who perceive their parents as having high levels of monitoring are less likely to show extreme peer orientation. Fuligni and Eccles's (1993) measure of extreme peer orientation includes the following items:

- How much does the amount of time you spend with your friends keep you away from doing things you ought to do?
- Would you act dumber or less talented than you really are in order to make someone like you?
- It's okay to let your school work slip or get a lower grade in order to be popular with your friends.
- It's okay to break some of your parents' rules in order to keep your friends. (pp. 631–632)

These authors also found that as the parent–child relationship changed from sixth to seventh grades, children whose parents were less likely to involve their children in decision making were more likely to seek the advice of their peers over their parents and to have an extreme peer orientation; in addition, children whose parents were relatively more strict were more likely to have an extreme peer orientation.

Clearly, then, children within overly autocratic relationships with their parents during this sensitive time are at risk for becoming "sorcerer's apprentices," whereby the embrace of friends is purchased at the price of incipient social and personal competencies. Thus ill equipped for the sophistication of the world at large, such adolescents suffer from social and occupational failures that for the most part are preventable. While our data (Table 3.4) show that social rule knowledge is fairly developed even during middle childhood, as Sullivan (1953) indicated, it needs to be practiced or "apprenticed" (Rogoff, 1990) before fuller mastery is attained. It may well be that supportive parents as well as close friends provide the preadolescent with just such an environment. The risks to the child of deviant behavior and impaired educational progress stemming from excessive attachment to peers are legion (e.g., Kandel & Lesser, 1972). Poor parental monitoring, along with little parental involvement of a positive nature, as well as harsh, inconsistent discipline are serious risk factors for delinquent behavior (Patterson, DeBaryshe, & Ramsey, 1989). We, therefore, reason that a significant function of parenting during early adolescence is to show children the "social ropes" of being a close friend so that the transition to adolescent relationships and beyond is a relatively smooth one.

Certainly, one of the most serious questions remaining in this rich field is to determine the social knowledge that is transmitted from different types of parent–child relationships to adolescents' close peer relationships and to determine whether there is a unique form of social knowledge that can only be acquired between friends. Perhaps, it is not *what* is learned but *how* it is learned that distinguishes parental and peer relationships. It is likely that without the overarching authority that parents provide in the early years, children would not be the attentive pupils that they need to be. Perhaps also, we should, as informed investigators of social and personal relationships, be less inclined to typify the social content and functions of a relationship on the basis of its nominal status. In our view, while there are indeed overall rule differences characterizing different social domains and relationships (Tables 3.3 and 3.4), it may well be more accurate to describe and classify relationships by their individual qualities (e.g., supportive, strict, democratic, distant) and the social knowledge that transpires within and between them. A differential approach such as this would very likely transform the way in which relationships are investigated. The question "When is a parent a friend and when is a friend a parent?" is then resolved by addressing the supportive functions that parents provide for their children. Where these functions converge, the riddle all but dissolves.

In this chapter, our examination of parent–child and close friend relationships has been grounded in an essentially descriptive and phenomenological methodology. Much of the parenting literature just reviewed is essentially behavioral. Criticisms of children's descriptions of their social relationships, such as Berndt's (1986) study of children's friendships, and presumably also the studies reported in this book, stress an inherent lack of predictive validity. For example, Berscheid (1986) noted that Berndt's self-report data, which are similar to those of Bigelow (1977), overlook the causal environmental determinants of relationships, such as their availability. She noted that such contextual factors are the raison d'etre of any relationship and that a child's "insider" views of a relationship are no substitute for "objective" accounts. While we do not debate the importance of "outsider" accounts in predicting the course of a relationship, we nevertheless erect the importance of description and personal account making as a necessary and indispensable window on the *meaning* of relationships. What is more, when one deliberately records the scripted behaviors crucial to the child's construction of a social rule, as we have done, we then have a rare opportunity to bridge external and internal models of representation within a genuinely contextual one. It remains to be seen how predictive social rules are.

CHAPTER 8

Siblings

THE RELATIONSHIP YOU DON'T HAVE TO EARN TO KEEP

While our findings heralded the prominence of social rules within parent and close friend relationships, we did not wish to neglect siblings. Sibling relationships have a unique quality, largely because their existence is governed in part by parental authority and because the relationship itself is nonvoluntary—one cannot typically break up with one's sibling. To illustrate this unique quality, one of our young subjects related an incident that happened when he and his elder sister had gone to a movie. During what must have been a love scene, his sister had put her hand over his eyes to stop him from seeing what was on the screen. Clearly aggrieved at this act of censorship, he complained: "Why did she have to do that? She's not my mother or anything." The incident illustrates an important ambiguity that lies at the very heart of sibling relationships. On the one hand, they are somewhat like friendships in that they embody selected aspects of "talking," "being loyal and trusting," and "reciprocating" (Table 3.4), a moderate degree of companionship and common activities (Table 6.1); and, on the other hand, they also contain an element of obligation and authority (Table 4.1, "Do the work that they ask you to do"), reflecting the hierarchy of parent–child relationships.

Most rules were used at a moderate level (Table 3.4) in sibling relationships, which underscores their saliency. Moreover, simply because children rated many kinds of social rules as less frequently used with siblings than with any other salient relationship, this does not permit us to conclude that they are less important or that they do not serve a unique function. When one examines the content of specific social rule statements within the sibling relationship, one is often impressed by their

175

unique "siblinglike character", especially in regard to the handling of conflict. As we show below, there are qualities to sibling relationships that are really quite distinct and that merit separate treatment. As Bryant and De Morris (1992) claimed, sibling relationships are part of a cooperatively organized family group. Hence, the sibling relationship is affected directly by the parent–child relationship; that is, how children behave with each other depends also on how they are treated by their parents. Our social rule analyses permitted us to develop a portrait of the texture of the relationship as well as some understanding of how it is situated within the framework of other relationships.

Historically, the first thing to note as a general characteristic of sibling relationships is that, with decreasing family size, such relationships are actually becoming less prevalent. Hernandez (1993) reports that the median number of siblings per family in the United States has dropped from 7.29 in 1865 to an estimated 1.86 in 1994. While it is still uncommon for children to have no siblings at all (Hernandez projects 5.7% as only children in 1994), large families, within which a child might experience a range of different sibling relationships of different ages and genders, are largely a thing of the past, at least in the developed world. Most children (51.2%) have only one other sibling. In our own study, we found that only about one-third of our participants had both brothers and sisters.

With the introduction of compulsory schooling, all children are brought into daily contact with large numbers of their age-mate peers, and the impact of peers has come to overshadow that of siblings, a fact that is clearly acknowledged in the much greater attention that has been accorded by developmentalists to peers (see, e.g., Shantz & Hobart, 1989). Nevertheless, as we indicated in Chapter 2, the sibling relationship has not disappeared and its dynamic is deserving of detailed attention. One can even consider the sibling relationship as a naturalistic relationship experiment, in that siblings are like peers in almost any outward manifestation; after all, they are children. For example, we cannot assume that age differences discriminate siblings from peers. With the exception of twins, siblings are usually separated, sometimes widely, in years. But it would be a mistake to claim, as Shantz and Hobart have, that peer relationships are between age-mates since children commonly play with others who are separated from them by 2 or more years (Ellis et al., 1981). As a result, the function of siblings seems to rest in part on the ubiquitousness of the relationship within the ever-constant umbrella of parental authority. However, the notion that siblings are defined by rivalry for parental attention is only part of a larger supportive picture (Furman & Buhrmester, 1985a, 1985b). What is more important to our study is *how* siblings and peers provide each other with support and resolve their conflicts, a problem on which the literature is largely silent (Shantz &

Hobart, 1989). In this way, the meaning of the sibling relationship can be observed.

SIBLINGS: THE "INVISIBLE" COMPANIONS

Even when siblings are physically available, they often seem to be "just there," even though they spend a great deal of time with each other (Csikszentmihalyi & Larson, 1984), perhaps even more than with their parents (Bank & Kahn, 1975). As we elaborate below, even a cursory inspection of the rule-relationship matrix in Table 3.4 illustrates this fact. Siblings are not like peers and do not attract the kind of attention that peers do but still serve an important function in the child's socialization, which lasts enduringly into adulthood and old age (Connidis & Davies, 1992).

This "invisible" quality of sibling relationships is clearly reflected in our rules checklist data. In general (Table 3.4) and on a number of important rule groupings, "following rules" (Figure 4.3), "showing deference" (Figure 4.6), "pleasing others" (Form A/Study 1, Figure 4.7), "repairing damage" (Figure 5.10), "talking" (for brothers, Figure 6.12), and "being loyal and trusting" (Form A/Study 1, Figure 6.14), the level of usage as rated by the rule checklist appears significantly less for siblings than for either parents or close friends. For none of the rule groupings did the subjects rate the sibling relationship as the locus of greatest usage. It would appear therefore that the sibling relationship is, in the minds of children at least, less salient than relationships with parents and friends. At the very least, a conscious preoccupation with strategies of conduct is less apparent in the sibling relationship than in relationships with either peers or parents. It would be wrong to conclude from this, however, that sibling relationships are necessarily of less developmental significance than parent or peer relationships. What distinguishes the sibling relationship, especially in comparison with the peer relationship, is its relatively nonvoluntary character.

That siblings rate one another so relatively low in their social rule usage in the face of such high levels of actual interaction is clearly deserving of some explanation. While interviewing preteen children for another study, one of us had occasion to ask the subjects to provide detail on how they spent their time on a typical day. Their answers were remarkable in that, while they provided ample detail of their morning routines and what they did when they returned from school, many children simply did not describe what they were doing while they were at school, leaving the period from 9:00 A.M. to 3:30 P.M. as if it were blank (see also Larson et al., 1989). Even with probing, children seemed reluctant to see themselves as having done anything worth mentioning. During the time that children spend in school, they do not perceive themselves as active agents; rather, the patterns of the school day are established by others and do not allow much scope for individual initiative.

In a similar vein, when compared with peer relationships, sibling relationships also have an involuntary character that has the potential for a merely passive participation. Friendships only exist because children actively do things to maintain them. Friendships are not normally defined by some external authority or body, nor are they established through a kinship tie; they are maintained solely by the conscious activity of the participants. Without that activity, the relationship cannot be said to exist. Peer relationships necessarily call for agency on the part of the participants, and, as a consequence, they call for a more conscious elaboration of social strategies. On the other hand, as parts of the family unit, sibling relationships seem to have an existence and a continuity largely independent of the actions of their participants; they do not require much conscious enactment in order to exist. While parent–child relationships are also nonvoluntary, as indicated in Chapter 7, the activities that children engage in with their parents are largely scaffolded ones designed to implant in the child a sense of agency that often simulates the texture of a close friend relationship. However, as the example at the beginning of this chapter suggests, sibling relationships often share some of the compliance and authority features otherwise reserved for parents (i.e., "She's not my mother or anything"); and as we show below, there may be some evidence of this scaffolding in the sibling relationship as well.

Sibling relationships have their own unique character; they are not mirror images of parent–child relationships. For example, the quality of arguments, at least in preschoolers, is quite different between these two relationships (e.g., Slomkowski & Dunn, 1992) and in our view reflects the vital scaffolding process. To illustrate, Brown and Dunn (1992) found that, over time, preschool siblings are more likely to refer to their own feelings (e.g., "You like Barbie dolls!") with each other than with their mothers, who refer to their feelings for them (e.g., "You don't like that, do you?"). Moreover, the positive (i.e., supportive) and negative (i.e., conflictual) features of sibling interactions are quite stable from preschool to adolescence (see, e.g., Dunn, Slomkowski, & Beardsall, 1994), so it is likely that siblings continue to be unique throughout the lifespan.

SIBLINGS AND SUPPORT

As indicated in Chapter 2, compared with peers, siblings have been characterized by the literature as relatively harsh and controlling (Furman

& Buhrmester, 1985a, 1985b; Stoneman et al., 1984). On the basis of our study, we found that rather than being more *conflictual*, siblings are relatively *indifferent* toward each other compared to relationships with friends, parents, and teachers. It would be incorrect then to claim that sibling relationships are inevitably more hostile or abrasive. In our study, sibling relationships were no higher than any other relationship with respect to "conflict management." In preschoolers at least, conflict is the same or lower between siblings (see, e.g., Dunn & Munn, 1985) as it is with peers (see, e.g., Eisenberg & Garvey, 1981), although Shantz and Hobart (1989) alerted us to the methodological deficiencies (e.g., observations versus self reports) in making such comparisons. The advantage of our rule-by-relationship matrix is that several relationships are examined by a common method.

There is some basis for claiming that siblings offer a unique supportive function that bears some resemblance to peers. According to Abramovitch, Corter, Pepler, and Stanhope (1986), in spite of commonly heard parental exhortations that their children are always "at each others' throats," friendly interactions outnumber hostile ones. According to these authors, the elder sibling, who is most often the dominant one, not only gives more affection but also expresses more hostility; however, there is no evidence that this finding necessarily has any negative implications for either sibling, dominant or submissive, within the world of peers. Because sibling relationships are characterized by early reciprocity and play, they may well help to compensate for any lack of peer companionship and closeness.

Although some of the above literature portrays sibling interactions in a relatively harsh light, we must be careful not to attribute hostility to the sibling relationship itself. By focusing on children's social rules instead of observing their behavioral interactions, we managed to isolate the sibling relationship from the situational determinants that affect sibling behavior. For example, Singer and Singer (1981) have linked excessive television viewing to preschool siblings' aggressiveness with each other. By virtue of their common residence, siblings watch more television with each other than with their peers. Presumably, these effects continue to some extent in middle and later childhood. As Shantz and Hobart (1989) have illustrated, the structured nature of family life places a great deal of constraint on the kinds of activity choice of the participants.

One theme, reminiscent of a peer experience that emerged in our interviews, was that common activities shared between siblings serve to cement the relationship: "We play games together—it helps us find out what each of us is like" M12 (1). Another subject mentioned doing things together "so that we can feel more comfortable with each other" F12 (1), suggesting that there is an intrinsic feeling of distance or discomfort that needs to be overcome. Certainly, siblings sometimes see each other as a substitute for friends: for example, "We play together and feel like real friends" F9 (1), and as an alternative to loneliness: for example, "We have a good time when we do things together, and this way we each know that we care about each other, and no one feels alone" F11 (1). As indicated by Singer and Singer (1981), when preschool children have no siblings, they have more of a tendency to make up fantasy playmates or imaginary brothers and sisters, attesting to the unique functions that these activities serve.

Perhaps then, siblings may well provide children with a socially supportive "bridge" to the world of peers. There is good empirical support (McCoy, Brody, & Stoneman, 1994) for this claim, which contrasts with compensatory models (see, e.g., Kramer & Gottman, 1992; Stocker, 1994). McCoy et al. (1994) describe siblings as a blend of behaviors that characterize adult *and* peer relationships. This blend helps to connect interactional styles used with parents to those used with friends. These investigations found an inverse relationship between sibling conflict and friendship quality. The quality of the sibling relationship was in turn related to lack of parental conflict, which predicted qualitatively superior best friend relationships 5 years later. However, this "bridge" can be crossed in both directions. Kramer and Gottman showed that for pre-schoolers, the quality of peer play, fantasy play, and conflict management were good predictors of children's interactions with their younger siblings. Indeed, as we argued in the previous chapter, parents provide a large part of the scaffolding function, but a case for siblings (and peers) can also be made.

Compared with parent–child relationships, the world of child–child relationships, which of course includes siblings, is inherently more symmetrical and may therefore afford children more opportunities for mutual interaction (see Youniss, 1980), but we must be careful not to overstate this argument since the comparison seems to end there: siblings are not substitute peers. As Abramovitch et al. (1986) found, there is no basis to conclude that patterns of sibling interactions carry over directly into peer relationships, even though older siblings are, like peers (Youniss, 1980), more reciprocal with one another. Older siblings seem to initiate activities more, which may include aggressive as well as helpful behaviors (Azmitia & Hesser, 1993).

Examples of this "bridging" function were reported in Chapters 5 and 6, where it was important not to upset one's brother at ages 9 and 10, which progressively extended to other friends and close friends from ages 10 to 13. We made the distinction between "Talk over problems with them," which is a more disclosive and salient feature of close friend relationships during early adolescence (see, e.g., Bigelow & La Gaipa,

1980; Sullivan, 1953) and "Talk with them about everyday things," which showed no discernible difference in usage between siblings and the more casual levels of friendship and peer relationships (Table 6.3), but may well set the stage for more intimate peer involvements later on.

Of particular interest to us was the observation (Table 6.4) that children rated their siblings almost as highly as their parents and close friends with respect to the rule "Be loyal to them and be sure that they can count on you," one of the few rules where the sibling pattern followed that for close peers, thus reflecting the supportive features of siblingship within the larger structure of family obligation. We suspected that because the relationship with siblings is not really a negotiated one, it provides the child with a relatively safe practice arena for testing out social-relational knowledge and specific behavioral skills that would be more costly to do with one's friends. Signs of this closeness and mutual support were apparent in the interview responses. Older siblings, for example, can sometimes pave the way for their juniors: for example, "Help [your brother] to figure out problems that you've already dealt with" F13 (1), or can smooth things out with parents: for example, "I feel sorry for my brother when he gets blamed for something he didn't do, and I try to help him deal with it" M9 (1). But sometimes these strategies can simply lead to more trouble: "Sometimes I try to help out my sister when she gets into trouble, and sometimes it works, but other times it gets me into trouble too" M8 (1), a clear example of the complicated and ambiguous nature of the sibling relationship.

The sibling relationship certainly holds some potential for mutual disclosure and a common sharing of experiences, partly as an alliance against the power of parents: for example, "We talk about getting back at Mom" M10 (1), but partly also out of genuine friendship: for example, "I have special talks with one brother because I'm the only one he talks to [and] we both feel like someone" F11 (1), which Sullivan (1953) could easily have used to describe a chumship. This potential for sharing experiences can override and even inhibit the seemingly more natural tendency for conflict: "We get together and talk to tell each other what has been happening to each of us. Usually we do not fight after this" F11 (1). One young girl expressed an almost unwilling empathy with her brother: "I will cry for my brother if he is getting heck from my Dad. I don't know why I do this" F9 (1). This insulation of "siblingship" from disruption owing to antagonistic behaviors has also been reported by Abramovitch et al. (1986).

While siblings are like peers in many respects, they are structurally different on at least one dimension: gender. With siblings, the likelihood of having to play with another child of the opposite sex is comparatively high, which is quite unique compared to the relatively sex-segregated world of peer relationships (Maccoby & Jacklin, 1987). In our work with adolescents (Tesson et al., 1990), we found that boys really need such practice since they are, relative to girls, rather clumsy in their social rule usage in dealing with the opposite sex. For example, boys are more often apt to act silly when they are with girls, displaying an awkwardness not generally seen in girls of the same age.

Boys' skills in dealing with cross-sex peer relationships may be acquired within the family through interaction with their sisters (Dunn, 1984; Stoneman et al., 1984). After all, boys cannot very well ignore their sisters since they are forced by dint of family membership and all the daily routines that this entails to interact with them. To support this claim, boys rated their use of the rule "Talk over problems with them" (Table 6.3) almost as highly for sisters as for close friends, suggesting that for boys who have sisters the sibling relationship may help bridge social competencies of this nature from the family context to the world of friends.

The supportive features of siblingship are also illustrated by Azmitia and Hesser (1993) who found that older same-gender children are more likely than friends to be effective teachers in helping their siblings in a toy construction task. While there were many similarities between the teaching efforts of siblings and peers, sibling-teachers produced superior performance; they gave more spontaneous teaching episodes, explanations, and feedback than peer-teachers did, which reflects some of the supportive functions one might otherwise reserve for relationships with parents (see Chapter 7). Regrettably, the quality of the peer relationship, or "friend," was not addressed. However, the main finding was that sibling-learners were more likely than peer-learners to spontaneously pressure their sibling-teachers than their peer-teachers. This pressure took the form of blocking and correcting the sibling-teacher's efforts and asking for feedback. Evidently, one cannot push one's friend this far. As we have been arguing, the relationship between the child and the other person is more important in determining what is learned than what was taught and also shows that siblings feel relatively safe within a sibling relationship, safe enough to challenge the expertise of the older brother or sister. Accordingly, some of the harshness of sibling relationships may have an adaptive purpose.

This feeling of security within the sibling relationship also has its parallels within peer relationships, since Hartup, French, Laursen, Johnston, and Ogawa (1993) found that children were more conflictual with friends than nonfriends in playing a board game, presumably because, within a friendship, children are more free and secure. This perception of greater liberty within a closer relationship such as a friendship has also been linked to superior performance on a comprehension task (see, e.g., Nelson & Aboud, 1985), where friends were more critical of one another and explained themselves more. However, these studies did not distinguish between levels of friendship, distinctions that we found to be quite indispensable. Perhaps close friends are more supportive than siblings, as Table 3.4 suggests. In the wider contexts of relationship types though, while sibling relationships can be construed as effective forced training for adaptive friendships (Ainsworth et al., 1974; Hartup, 1979; McCoy et al., 1994; Parsons, 1955), we feel that this function is overstressed. As we argued elsewhere (Bigelow et al., 1992) and in the previous chapter, the generalization gradient is better from parents to close friends. It would be very revealing to compare the social knowledge of children without siblings with those children with siblings, since this kind of study, if properly controlled with respect to levels of friendship involvement, would help to put the issue to rest.

SIBLINGS AND CONFLICT

Notwithstanding the elements of mutual support that we found in the sibling relationship, there were also clear signs of conflict. What is most intriguing though is how siblings resolve their conflicts, not how much conflict they have. As we illustrate below through children's own comments, while most peer conflicts are settled by the children themselves without the intervention of adults (see, e.g., Hay & Ross, 1982), adults are either explicitly or implicitly used as referees in solving sibling conflicts. While maternal intervention does not necessarily reduce siblings' future hostility (Kendrick & Dunn, 1983), routine failure of parents to intervene is irresponsible and may contribute to learned helplessness (Bennett, 1990).

We argue that sibling relationships are distinct from peer relationships because the former occur within the watchful purview of parents, whose authority over time is internalized in siblings' relationships with one another, as illustrated in our opening example. This parental presence imposes structure (e.g., loyalty) without the fuller cooperation and resolution so necessary in close peer relationships (see, e.g., Genishi & Di Paolo, 1982), but such information in childhood and early adolescence is sparse (Shantz & Hobart, 1989).

Consistent with our view that the resolution of sibling disagreements is generally scaffolded by reference to unilateral adult authority, Montemayor and Hanson (1985) found that siblings used withdrawal or authoritarian tactics rather than peerlike negotiation (see, e.g., Piaget, 1932/1965; Sullivan, 1953; Youniss, 1980). Indeed, in a study of adults' recollections of sibling conflict, those reporting high levels of conflict (20% of the sample) also reported having parents who themselves engaged in more severe, and therefore less cooperative, forms of violence (Graham-Bernmann, Cutler, Litzenberger, & Schwartz, 1994), although violence among peers is a problem as well (Olweus, 1978). Conflict management for siblings is less negotiated than with peers because disputes from the beginning have been policed by the parents.

Many, but not more, of the children's responses in the interviews to questions about their sibling relationships showed a preoccupation with conflict and its resolution. While conflict management rules dealing with "not upsetting others" and "controlling feelings" were not rated (Table 3.4) as any more frequently used in siblings relationships, compared with parents and close friends, siblings were far less inclined to want to repair the relationship after a disagreement. Because the relationship is formally defined, it is not governed only by its quality, and there is not as pressing a need to actively manage it. As we show below, the quality of sibling conflict is subtly different from that of a peer conflict and is marked by appeals to parental authority, distancing strategies, and efforts to keep the peace because the relationship cannot simply be broken off. As Kendrick and Dunn (1983) observed, parents intervene in their children's arguments when those arguments get out of hand, insisting that the children make up with each other. More than any other relationship, the sibling relationship is very much affected by the family network of which it is an integral part.

It was apparent from the interviews that whether parents are present or not, they are always an element to be reckoned with in dealing with siblings and are most frequently invoked in the settlement of conflicts: "If I get mad at my brother for something pretty bad, I will tell Mom because she can deal with him better" F9 (1). It is because parents are always potential parties to sibling conflicts—perhaps, not always impartial ones—that siblings might be seen as rivals or competitors for their parents' attention. It seems evident to us that peer relationships seldom invite such parental intervention. A useful avenue for further research on the "bridging" question is to compare the origins of conflict resolution strategies between siblings and friends since we need to address the hypothesis that the scaffolding of conflict resolution strategies by parents (see Chapter 7) during children's interactions with their siblings may penetrate children's social rule understanding so that children can then deploy such strategies independently with their peers. Such comments from children themselves would shed valuable light on whether the social fabric of sibling and close friend relationships is cut from a common social cloth.

In the social rules interviews, children's commentaries were full of the "don'ts" of dealing with brothers and sisters, such as the following: "Don't bug or bother," for example, "Stay out of the way when my brother has his friends over so I won't get in the way and he won't get rough with me" F6 (1); "Don't argue," for example, "Don't try to make him do something he doesn't want to do" F10 (1); and, above all, "Don't fight," for example, "Don't push him down or hurt him because he will do the same when he is bigger" F7 (1). One of the central features of the sibling relationship is that it is defined by circumstances that are quite beyond the control of its participants. It may not be that conflict is any more intrinsic to this relationship than it is to any other, but its significance is different because, whether they like each other or not, siblings are obliged to deal with each other on a day-to-day basis.

Distancing strategies, such as ignoring insults and limiting the extent and the intensity of conflict are therefore important for siblings: "When [my brother] calls me names, I ignore him, and he gets tired. It helps him realize what he's done wrong" M12 (1). An alternative to just ignoring is to put some distance between oneself and the situation. Often this is difficult in family conflicts, but for many children the privacy of their own room, if they have one, is an important refuge from arguments or simple harassment: "When [family members] bug me, I ignore them and go into my room and play with my cat to calm my nerves" M10 (1). Children often do not have easy ways of dealing with their own anger, and the privacy of a room offers an opportunity for both escape and reflection: "If I've had a fight, then I go to my room where it's quiet, and I think things over" M10 (1). Friends also provide an alternative to the pressure of conflictual family relationships: "If my older sister ignores me, I ignore her back and go do something else, like call a friend" F9 (1).

Perhaps the real value of the sibling relationship, then, is that even though participants can find temporary refuge from each other, in their rooms or with their friends, they are nevertheless locked into the relationship; therefore, the pressure to compromise to keep the peace is more than in a relationship that can be merely broken off if it is a source of social discomfort. For the same reason, there is less pressure to nurture the relationship itself. It is a question of minimizing the negatives rather than accentuating the positives. We found children quite cognizant of the advantages of meeting their siblings halfway in order to resolve differences: "When we disagree over what to play, we think of new games, and then we decide together—this way we end up spending time together" F8 (1). Sometimes, our subjects showed themselves to be quite pragmatic about the advantages of making deals: "Sometimes I will strike a bargain with my sister, and she will give me something in turn for me keeping quiet about something she did wrong" F12 (1).

We also found considerable recognition of the need for fairness in such things as taking turns or deciding what gets watched on television, but the motivation for fairness again seems more pragmatic than moral: "Plan to trade chores if you can't take your turn or if you have something better to do" F10 (1). Quite often it is driven simply by the need to avoid conflict: "Take turns: it's fair, and people won't get mad" M9 (1). In fact, the need to avoid conflict seems to underlie a great deal of social interaction between siblings. What marks the sibling relationship from the peer relationship, then, is the feeling of obligation that the former contains. We found frequent reference to the need for acquiescence to the demands of brothers or sisters, a kind of *deference* that did not assume the form of the obedience owed to parents but more simply a giving in to the wishes of the other merely to keep the peace: "I try to go along with what she wants even if I don't want to. It helps to avoid fights, but it doesn't make you closer" M12 (1). Interestingly enough, such acquiescence does not always reflect power differentials because of age superiority. In fact, we found frequent cases where older siblings gave in to the whims of their juniors: for example, "Give in and don't argue because the younger ones always get their own way" F12 (1), reminiscent of young children's conflict resolution strategies recorded by Sutton-Smith and Rosenberg (1968), who found that younger siblings often cry, sulk, or appeal to others outside the dyad (e.g., complaining to a parent).

As others (Dunn, 1984) have argued, the ubiquity of sibling conflict should not be taken as an indicator that its influence on the developmental process is, in some way, largely negative or even inert. On the contrary, the very obligatory nature of the relationship, which makes it so prone to conflict in the first place, also drives children to find ways to manage and contain the conflict it gives rise to. This was apparent in the way our subjects expressed the need for making up after fights. Sometimes the making up appears as a reluctant recognition of the inevitable: "If I do something bad, like hit my sister, then I get sent to my room. After an hour I can come out and have to say sorry" M8 (1). But in other cases there seems a genuine acknowledgment of the benefits of peaceful coexistence: "We try to settle problems ourselves if there was a fight. We know that we can have arguments but not stay mad at each other and be as close as before" F12 (1).

The conflict inherent in sibling relationships should not be taken simply as an unfortunate consequence of the ascribed nature of kinship links. Its importance lies in the fact that it necessarily calls for the development of strategies of conflict resolution. As we argued above, it is because siblings cannot escape each other that they are driven to find ways to accommodate their differences. Conflict and its resolution is seen as playing a key role in the development of theories as central as those of Piaget (1985) and Erikson (1950) and, although children may often show a preference for the friendlier nature of their peer relationships, it is perhaps in their dealings with their siblings that they really get to hone key aspects of social competency, which will serve them well in their later lives. However, as we discussed briefly in the previous chapter, children without siblings are not at any obvious disadvantage, but clearly more sensitive examinations of this problem are in order.

As we argued in the previous chapter, there is no evidence accumulated to date that suggests that it is the nominal status of a relationship that is more important than the supportive features it provides. For example, does it matter whether the child has access to a supportive parent, sibling, or close friend when trying to learn how to be socially or academically competent? While our data suggest that siblings may offer children a relational bridge to effective peer relationships, parents can and do offer some of these functions as well; but it is not certain whether the functions served are similar. Perhaps though, this issue is better prepared by appealing to the social learning environment as a living system. As we argued in Chapter 4, in any living system there are built-in redundancies that safeguard the functioning of the organism in the presence of adverse circumstances. Perhaps siblings provide such a role as children straddle the worlds of parents and peers; although their presence is not vital, it is nevertheless helpful.

In this, as well as in the preceding chapter, we often made reference to the explanations appended to children's comments mentioned in the interviews. While at times such explanations were an integral part of the social rules themselves (e.g., "Try and make them laugh, *so you won't be fighting later*"), we also structured part of the interview (see Appendix 1) to deliberately elicit responses that, when coded, resulted in a distinct and separate set of interview data. These more formal explanations, which we termed "rationales," provided a rich tapestry for explaining the motives that govern children's relationships, and it is to these rationales that we shall now turn.

CHAPTER 9

Social Rule Rationales

THE CHILD AS A
RELATIONSHIP PHILOSOPHER

As we argued in our opening chapters, children actively construct their personal relationships, and social rules form a large part of these constructions. It is this active construction that provides the contextualized meaning within and between the different kinds of relationships in children's lives. As our data in Chapters 4, 5, and 6 illustrate, this meaning is revealed in the overarching (i.e., "macro") social principles of classes of relationships, such as peer cooperation and compliance to parent and adult authority (Youniss, 1980), and, perhaps more important, in the very detailed ("micro") level of specific kinds of rules within particular relationships, such as close friends and siblings. It is at this detailed level of analysis that the conditions of children's relationships, such as "scaffolding," (Chapter 7) are revealed in their full color.

As we explained in Chapter 2, though, determining what is meaningful about relationships is no easy task. Social scientists (e.g., Duck, 1990; Sullivan, 1953) have been trying to chip away at this problem for a long time. As Hinde (1979) has indicated, it is very difficult to come to grips with the scientific meaning of a personal or social relationship since its boundaries are often difficult to define. Consequently, on the surface at least, this "shadowy" world of social relationships appears to have a good deal of arbitrariness about it. For instance, much of our work reported in Chapters 4, 5, and 6 suggests that part of the child's social understanding (e.g., "not upsetting others" and "controlling feelings") seems to lack relational boundaries. This finding, however, does not necessarily reflect an undue woolliness on the child's part since the specific social rule statements obtained in the interviews, together with ratings of specific rules, were often quite sensitive to the nominal relationships to which they applied. Indeed, the thrust of our arguments in Chapters 1, 2, and 3 was that relational meaning is to be found by examining rules within specific relationships and the circumstances giving rise to them. In other words, the seemingly great similarities observed between selected relationships at a macrolevel often belied some sharper qualitative distinctions when our psychometric microscope was adjusted to the microlevel of individual rules and their examples.

SOCIAL RULES AND GOALS

While our search for meaning was largely fulfilled by foraging in the field of the particular, the logic contained in our phenomenological approach to personal relationships drew us inexorably to the possibility that children may be their own best analysts in this regard. As a consequence, our attention now comes full circle, by addressing the overarching structures of classes of relationships by formally accessing children's *own* explanations for the rules they use within relationships.

The subtleties of particular rule strategies illustrated in Chapters 4, 5, and 6 reveal the overlapping functions between these overarching macrostructures: for example, between parent–child and close friend relationships (see Chapter 7). Notwithstanding this *fuzziness* (see Chapter 4), these strategies often also illustrate how these macrostructures "trickle down" to the world of the particular. What the specific examples recorded during the social rule interviews taught us was that children themselves are frequently aware of the social forces that influence their behavior. Obviously then, what was also needed was to extend our phenomenological approach to its logical extreme by according children the ability to offer their own naive explanations of why rules are useful within particular classes of relationships. These explanations could be organized into conceptually meaningful categories. No matter how social rules are distributed across relationships and domains, children have their own interpretations of what they do, and these interpretations form a separate datum in their own right. As we shall see below, theorists are not the only ones who can conceptualize relationships as overarching issues; children can process rule rationales at this more general level too. What is more, as we shall see, there are a number of these broader issues that theorists have not yet identified and brought center stage to the world of children's relationships.

Aside from the limitations of a social skills approach to examining personal relationships (see Chapters 1 and 3), some social skills studies (e.g., Asher & Renshaw, 1981; Renshaw & Asher, 1982, 1983) have the advantage of addressing the *goals* that initiate, maintain, or improve children's interactions with their peers. As we shall see below, children are quite cognizant of these goals in their application of social rules. As we shall also demonstrate, our phenomenological approach to social relationships revealed a richer array of social goals than would otherwise have been evident on some a priori basis. A strictly behavioral approach deliberately avoids what has become known as "mentalistic" content, yet a phenomenological approach to personal and social relationships deals directly with this kind of subject matter—and, if anything, subjective accounts are its main source of data for understanding social behavior (Duck, 1990; Harré & Secord, 1973). Indeed, as Bandura (1977) and Hinde (1979) so clearly illustrated, as children develop, their symbolic representation of events increasingly outweighs the importance of the overt characteristics of their behavior.

To be socially meaningful, relationship exchanges and their personal constructions must be goal oriented, and many of these goals exist in symbolic form. People perceive intent, have expectancies, construct rules, and choose between goals. The meaning of social and personal relationships, then, must reside in the process of interacting as an end in itself as well as in the goals attached to them. We sought access to these interactional goals through the rationales or explanations that children appended to the social rule strategies they provided in response to interview probes (see Appendix 1, e.g., rule probe "Tell me some of the ways you use to help you get along with your mother" and rationale probe "How does doing chores help you to get along with your mother?"). Of course, not all significant social interactions and goals can be identified through even the most carefully conducted interviewing since some elements of interpersonal exchanges, such as tone of voice and posture, are rarely, if ever, consciously processed. However, as with the rules themselves, there are a lot of social goals that are consciously processed and form the material out of which meaningful relationships are constructed, and it is to these that we shall now turn.

Hinde (1979) cautioned that if we indulge too much in the subjective, affective aspects of personal and social relationships, we are at risk of losing scientific rigor: "If we are too generous in introducing them we shall find ourselves swimming in a mush with nothing firm to stand on" (p. 22). For example, Hinde probed the shape and substance of relationships by correctly insisting that they have *content* and *meaning*, which derive from the participant's embeddedness within the social group or culture. To address these concerns with the rule rationales, we content analyzed them and distributed this content across the three social domains (i.e., family, peers, other adults) to help reveal the impact that these contexts have on their social interactions. (For illustrations of rule explanations for specific relationships, e.g., for a close friend, the reader is encouraged to inspect Chapters 4, 5, and 6, within which explanations are often an integral part of the rules themselves rather than a separate part of the interview content.)

SOCIAL RULE RATIONALES

Classifying social rule explanations, or "rationales," was in itself an informative lesson in understanding the meaning of social relationships since we learned through trial and error that only by carefully examining social rules and their rationales within the contexts of the three social domains (i.e., family, peers, other adults) were we able to make useful distinctions. Because the rules were heavily intercorrelated, matching rules to rationales by using statistical procedures was an exercise in futility. It was also difficult to match rationales that were typically appropriate to more than one rule! Content analyzing rationales within relational domains was much more revealing. We also considered using a priori classifications of rule rationales, such as attempting contact, entering play, dealing with jealousy in friendship, and handling conflict (Renshaw & Asher, 1983). However, no matter how sensible such a classification may at first have appeared, it would have violated our phenomenological approach. In the end though, through careful content analysis and by heeding Hinde's (1979) contention that the meaning of social relationships is known through its embeddedness within the social structure, we achieved a measure of success and were able to categorize the rationale statements.

As specified in more detail in Appendix 1, the rationales were detached from their social rule statements and coded by consensus into 32 categories. The incidence of each of these rule rationales was then converted to a percentage by using the highest frequency within the relational domain as a ceiling. Using z-tests for proportions ($p < .01$), it was discovered that only 12 of the 32 rationale categories occurred with above chance expectation. Because of insufficient incidence, formal age and gender analyses were not practicable; however, females uttered significantly more rationales (1,557) than did males (940), perhaps indicating higher female levels of meaningful verbalization. Age patterns were indicated through inspection. We arranged the rule rationales by domain (Table 9.1) and, as one can readily see, there is a natural distribution in so doing that is conceptually meaningful.

PEER RELATIONSHIPS
AND THE "ROBINSON CRUSOE SYNDROME"

Because peer relationships stand or fall on their own merits, peer rationales deal more with issues that only voluntary social interactions require: initiating a relationship, maintaining a relationship, and improving a relationship, each resting entirely on the social skills that the child brings into the relationship. Exiting a relationship is theoretically relevant also, but the interview required children to tell us how they got along with other people, not how they failed to do so. However, as Table 9.1 shows, peers also deal explicitly with an understanding of each other and the other person. These data speak directly to the need to appreciate the child's personal accounting of relationships to more fully

TABLE 9.1. Frequency and Percentage Incidence of Social Rule Rationales by Domain

	Incidence		
Domain	Family (n = 282)	Peers (n = 264)	Other adults (n = 196)
All domains			
To make others feel good	20 (56)	16 (41)	16 (31)
To make oneself feel good	16 (45)	*19* (49)	10 (19)
To avoid trouble and fights	*40* (114)	36 (76)	30 (59)
Family and other adults			
To avoid making other persons angry	*30* (86)	3 (9)	*35* (68)
To gain personal advantage	*19* (54)	4 (10)	*16* (31)
To show consideration	*29* (82)	5 (14)	*13* (26)
Family and peers			
To have fun and enjoyment	*20* (57)	*22* (58)	6 (12)
Peers			
To initiate a relationship	2 (7)	*27* (71)	*11* (21)
To maintain a relationship	10 (29)	*24* (63)	4 (7)
To improve a relationship	11 (30)	*22* (57)	7 (13)
To better understand the other person	7 (21)	*20* (54)	12 (23)
To better understand each other	8 (24)	*14* (37)	5 (9)

Note. Rationales were classified in a domain when percentage incidence was 10% or greater (z-test for proportions, p < .01). Significant percentage differences between domains are italicized. Subject frequencies are in parentheses.

understand their meaning, since children are obviously capable of articulating their purpose. It is also worthy of note that if we had formulated an arbitrary set of rationale categories instead of closely examining what the children themselves communicated about their relationships, significant material such as this would have been lost.

To Initiate a Relationship

Sample rationales in this category (Table 9.1) often stressed engaging in an activity with other children in order to "be their friend" or "do stuff and see each other." Obviously, aside from having fun and enjoyment, which occurs in families and peer groups alike, an important goal for peer interaction is to establish a friendship. Such relationship goals are obviously less relevant within family or other adult (i.e., teacher) contexts since these relationships are formally defined. That such rationales usually stem from social facilitation rules (Table 3.1), which are very prominent in close friend relationships (Table 3.4), suggests a good fit here with the social skills literature reviewed in Chapter 1. To "do things together, such as playing" reflects useful ways to behave with other children, and such actions are indispensable in the beginning stages of a peer relationship. It makes sense, then, that these skills also become construed as social rules.

To Maintain a Relationship

This rationale (Table 9.1) most clearly demonstrates the division between voluntary peer relationships and formal, involuntary ones, as in the family. When a child does annoying or offensive things in the family, people get upset or angry, but the relationship as such is rarely at issue. However, in the peer group, the relationship itself is always potentially at stake. Sample rationales in relation to offensive behaviors (rule theme "not upsetting others") are "so that you'll get along"; or "so that you can still be friends." It is also clear (Table 9.1) that such rationales can also apply to some degree to permanent (i.e., family) relationships because even in a permanent relationship, there are degrees of relatedness that are earned.

To Improve a Relationship

These kinds of rationales (Table 9.1) are attached largely to "repairing damage" rules (e.g., "Talk and make up after fighting") and rules that foster increased understanding of self and other, such as "figuring others out" and "talking": for example, "Making up can strengthen a relationship," "Get to know [others] better . . . so then you can be closer," and "Discuss things with [others] . . . so that you have a really good relationship." It is intriguing to note that making up with someone does not simply restore the relationship to its former level of closeness but actually serves the function, at least as children perceive it, of improving the relationship. This raises the interesting possibility that creating offenses in a relationship may have a hidden motive: to improve the relationship through *reparation*. As we explained in Chapter 5 though, testing the relationship in this way is a risky enterprise not to be undertaken lightly.

To Better Understand Each Other

Peer relationships (Table 9.1) focus predominantly on understanding the self and the other person (ages 11 to 13), which, although pertinent in other domains, is not a chief feature of those relationships. Rationales in this category could have been written in by Sullivan (1953) himself. Perhaps, then, the large social rule theme of social facilitation (Table 3.1), which is the clear preserve of close friend relationships (Table 3.4), has as its principal function helping children achieve mutual understanding. Evidently, the old saying "We only know ourselves through others" is amply illustrated here. "To better understand each other" applies mostly to the rule theme "talking": for example, "We talk about things . . . to understand more about each other" and "It lets me know [others] and for them to know me." No wonder Robinson Crusoe nearly went mad until Man Friday made his appearance. Self-knowledge is clearly a vital source of meaning in personal relationships.

Harvey et al. (1990), in their fascinating treatise of personal accounts, elaborated on several aspects of self-understanding that are served by "relationship talk" in adults, but especially the need to establish a sense of control and understanding that provides one ultimately with a sense of closure. Relationship talk, as Duck (1994) also explained, is the material out of which adult personal relationships are constructed. Evidently, the motive behind people's evolving discussions is to provide a continuously edited sense of self and other. Herein, we see this process is well under way in childhood.

To Better Understand the Other Person

Rules giving rise to rationales under this heading (Table 9.1) spanned several themes, such as "being sociable," "figuring others out," and "talking," producing rationales such as "so you can understand them more," "in order to get to know them better," and "...so you can find out what they are like." Unlike the family domain, where persons are not new discoveries, the peer domain makes this category particularly germane. This rationale stresses children's curiosity about others. Moreover, by actively socializing with and analyzing others, one has the material out of which to integrate the self within the relationship.

From the foregoing, it becomes clear that one of the principal functions of a close friendship is to provide participants with an ongoing and unfolding narrative (McAdams, 1993) within which participants can account for the occurrence of events and can know each other better. The narrative of course is in constant need of editing since social behavior, and how people account for it, is not inherently stable (Duck, 1994). This is perhaps why mutual understanding has such a high profile, for it is not a static thing but must continually be updated and reworked. This is especially true, in our view, within children's peer relationships, since development, and all the different abilities and experiences that accrue to it, is occurring at an inherently quicker pace than in adulthood, although this claim begs empirical clarification.

FAMILY AND OTHER ADULT RELATIONSHIPS

The rationales for family and other adults clearly speak to the authority dimension of adult–child encounters, which forms a pervasive structure for children's social relationships (Youniss, 1980) with adults. In Chapter 4, we showed that adult–child authority was in evidence both at the macro- and microlevels of analysis. It is also at play within this group of rationales.

To Avoid Making the Other Person Angry

Rule themes such as "not upsetting others," "following rules" (especially "Do what you are told and obey" and "Do obligatory work") and "controlling feelings" (e.g., "Don't be hurtful by calling names or criticizing") are likely to give rise to rationales such as "to avoid making the other mad," "so others won't get mad at you," "so we won't get yelled at," and "so there will not be arguments or anger" (Table 9.1). The respect for or fear of the adult's superior power and authority is very evident here.

To Show Consideration

Rationales involving "to show consideration" (Table 9.1) (e.g., "so that mother has time to relax," "to save the other person doing it," and "so [others] don't have so much to do") are typically attached to rule themes such as "following rules" (e.g., "Do what you are told and obey" and "Do obligatory work" and "helping others" (e.g., "Offer to help others," "Help by doing things for others," "Teach and show others how to do things"). Respect for authority rather than pure empathic concern is believed to be at the root of these remarks since the incidence of this kind of rationale within the peer group was not very high, although as we argued in Chapter 7, such rules help to scaffold empathy, which is a necessary link to the world of mutual friendships.

To Gain Personal Advantage

This kind of rationale (Table 9.1) addresses the bald fact that children are socially and materially dependent on the adults in their lives. Rules producing such rationales span themes of "being assertive" (e.g., "Be manipulative to get what you want") and "following rules" (e.g., "Do obligatory work"). Sample rationales are "so [others] will give us money," "so I can get to play hockey," and "so that you can make a deal to be allowed to do something." These rationales should not be regarded with too much cynicism since, if handled properly, the occasions that give rise to such understandings encourage children to engage in socially adaptive actions that please both themselves and others.

FAMILY AND PEER RELATIONSHIPS

To Have Fun and Enjoyment

In spite of their differences with respect to self and mutual understanding and relationship management, family and peer relationships are obviously alike in their equivalent goal of having fun and enjoyment (Table 9.1). Numerous kinds of rules have pleasure as their aim, deriving mainly from "being sociable" rules, such as "Be nice and pleasant and say "Hi."" "Joke and fool around or be humorous and funny," "Invite others over or out," "Visit each other," "Do things together, such as playing," and "Include others in your group or in things you do." The goal for these rules is to have fun: for example, "because it's fun," "to laugh and have fun," and "so you can have fun and enjoy each other." The suggestion is that some forms of social interaction have no other goal than that they are intrinsically satisfying or pleasurable.

In our view, the *fun* aspects of personal relationships have not been given nearly enough limelight, since the *flow* of relationships that provides such enjoyment is a rich source of learning and entertainment; and when relationships are in this happy state, clearly they are working as they were designed to do. It was left for the children to inform us of this vital aspect of relationships. It is now up to us to determine the qualities of relationships that are associated with this goal.

ALL DOMAINS

To Make Oneself and Others Feel Good

Two of these rationales (Table 9.1), "to make others feel good" and "to make oneself feel good," as with the "fun and enjoyment" goal above, address the affective aspects of relationships. Again, a phenomenological approach to relationships revealed important features of relationships that would otherwise go unnoticed. While "feeling good" may seem to be a rather unarticulated reason for relating, what are more interesting are the various strategies that can be used to achieve this. Unlike having fun, "feeling good" rationales stem from several kinds of rule themes, such as "expressing (positive) feelings" (e.g., "Demonstrate affection" and "Cheer others up and be nice to them") and include preventing others from feeling bad. Sample rationales for making others feel good are that "it makes [others] happy" and "because [others] might be sad."

"Being assertive" rules are also pertinent here with respect to one's parents, such as "Be and act independent" "so that they don't worry." "Being assertive" is also useful in helping the self feel good. For example, a response to "Let others know when they've upset you or made you mad" was "to get feelings out, and you won't feel like punching." Rule themes dealing with altruism, like "reciprocating" and "helping others," produced rationales such as, "It makes you feel good inside"; and the rule theme "being sociable" (e.g., "Do things together") gave rise to the response that it "makes me feel less lonely."

These appetitive aspects of personal relationships address what may be termed the "natural opiates" of close, supportive family and friendship ties. In fact, we often describe love relationships, which are obviously more relevant in adolescence and adulthood, as "intoxicating." Close relationships that work simply make people feel good. Interestingly, there is a connection between illicit drug use, which provides a chemical substitute for these "good feelings," and dysfunctional family relationships (see, e.g., Loeber, 1990; Shedler & Block, 1990). Such studies suggest that it may not be the use of drugs per se that leads to adolescent delinquency and antisocial behavior but rather that early problems with parent–child relationships set the stage for drug abuse later on. While we don't wish to discount the direct disruptive effects of drugs on interpersonal relationships, perhaps these children are simply trying, in the only way they know, to fill a powerful chemical need, normally satisfied by loving relationships, by any means at their disposal. In interviews with children and youth, Coombs and Landsverk (1988) found that those who abstained or infrequently used drugs expressed their closeness to the parents, the importance of getting along with parents, wanting to be like the parent, having a trusting mother, receiving praise from their parents, and feeling that they can talk over problems with fathers. The relevance of supportive social rules to drug abstinence is difficult to miss. The children in our study seem to be telling us in direct language that relationships that work (i.e., feel good) are very important to them. Perhaps more updated scales of relationships, based on measures of mutuality and trust like those used by Mannarino (1980) and McGuire and Weisz (1982), would do well to include these additional appetitive features.

To Avoid Trouble and Fights

"To avoid trouble" (Table 9.1) is not only a rationale for doing things but by itself is also a universal social rule ("Don't fight with or physically hurt another" Table 3.4), reminding us that social reasoning is intrinsically a recursive process (see Appendix 1). Indeed, several rationales look like social rules, and one social rule may be used as an explanation for another. Conflict prevention is such a pervasive aspect of dealing with people in all walks of life that children speak of it directly as self-restraint (e.g., "Don't fight!") or learning to deal with people in more indirect ways in order to avoid conflict. For example, "avoiding and ignoring" rules, such as "Don't take notice of bothersome people," "Leave bothersome situations and find something else to do," and "Avoid people or situations that are troublesome," elicited rationales such as "so you don't get into trouble," "to stay away from fights," and "or they'll beat me up." What is interesting to note in examining the examples that children append to their prosocial forms of behavior (e.g., "helping others" and sharing rules in Chapters 4 and 6) is that such altruistic acts are quite often motivated by the need to avoid conflict. The presence of such rationales shows that conflict avoidance may be an important factor underlying seemingly altruistic acts. These data may also dishearten the purists among us who believe in the utter selflessness of altruistic acts, but we stress that social relationships are inherently very pragmatic.

COMMENTARY

The above rationales that children gave for applying the rules provided us with a portrait of relationship goals that brought us back to the first principles of social interaction and relationship building so eloquently elaborated by Sullivan (1953) in his theory of chumship in preadolescents and extended by Youniss (1980) in his Sullivan–Piaget hypothesis.

Sullivan (1953) argued quite persuasively that social knowledge, much as Hinde (1979) observed, is inherently arbitrary and vague, making attempts to render it into an ordered body of knowledge very difficult indeed. However, the clear distinctions that children made in their rationales for relating permitted us to better discern the boundaries separating one type of relationship from another. Only by developing, maintaining, and improving a relationship on equal terms with another person (i.e., a "chum" or a close friend) can children understand themselves and others. It is precisely by means of this mutual shaping of personal and social perception that the boundaries of self and other are forged.

We caution, though, that rule rationales by themselves tell only half the story, since relationship goals without rule content are empty. As discussed more fully in Chapter 7, there are aspects of parent–child relationships that actively scaffold children's peerlike social rules and can therefore assume functions otherwise available only in a close peer relationship. This function is only revealed in its fullness of form when specific rules are examined within particular relationships. Indeed, if it were not for this built-in redundancy, the transition from family to friends would be abrupt and disorderly. It is also true that unless we have half an eye on the overarching structures of relationships, whether these structures are of authority and compliance, on the one hand, or cooperation and mutual understanding, on the other, we are at some risk of becoming lost in the forest of the particular. Children's relationships exist and thrive at several levels of complexity (Hinde, 1979) and should be understood in that light.

As Sullivan (1953) suggested, it is only through the exchanges between ourselves in relation to others that we can achieve a sense of who we are, how we appear to others, and how others appear in relation to ourselves. Only through this day-to-day struggle can we have, as Harvey et al. (1990) suggested, a sense of control and closure over our social lives. Without this sense of order, there is a diminished sense of who we are as people. Since we worked with children, we saw only the leading edge of this voyage toward personal and mutual understanding. Perhaps, as we continue to document the phenomenological rules and rationales of personal and social relationships through adolescence and adulthood, we may then be able to determine whether the ultimate meaning of social relationships is indeed personal and mutual understanding. We believe that it is.

CHAPTER 10

Concluding Remarks

The principle purpose of our enterprise was to determine what relationships mean to children and how children manage those relationships. Driven by Wohlwill's (1973) maxim that description is the first principle of good science, we set out to record an exhaustive content of children's social rules as children themselves construct them. Complete description was necessary in our view because we reasoned that the pursuit of any particular social-relational issue (e.g., compliance versus cooperation) is not really possible without addressing the full array of strategies that children themselves feel are meaningful in the governance of their various relationships. Only in this way can the true characteristics of a particular relationship be ascertained. In this respect, our work has been successful.

The whole corpus of children's social rules is replete with social issues, ranging from compliance and autonomy, to self-assertiveness and conflict management, to mutual activities and the governance of obligation, intimacy, and trust. The sheer volume of social rules and their sensitivity to particular social relationships validated our use of the rule-by-relationship matrix in our examination of their usage. It was often only through the careful examination of specific rule content and how it was expressed that the true nature of a relationship was revealed. As we have just seen, relationship differences ranged from the very blunt (e.g., "Do as you're told!") to the very subtle (e.g., "Help [others] out because you know how it feels"). Duck's (1994) argument that personal relationships are exercises in construed meanings and Fogel's (1993) point that children co-construct their relationships with their environment and the people within it were amply supported in the coherent patterns of social rules that the children communicated to us and in the way in which the children applied those rules in their complex social lives.

A strong undercurrent of our investigation concerned the belief that social cognition is structured: mainly, that children organize their relationships with other people in a coherent and accessible manner. Such a belief extended social constructive principles expressed by many investigators (e.g., Butterworth & Light, 1982; Sullivan, 1953) by showing that there are categorically organized "social rules" that form the building blocks of meaningful social interaction. If social cognition does not have the anchoring features of physical cognition (e.g., conservation tasks), it does not mean that social cognition cannot be investigated as a coherent body of knowledge. Our participants clearly informed us that it can. The connections between social rules and other domains of cognition, such as mathematical and moral reasoning, may help to determine whether social cognition is a separate or integral aspect of thinking and relating.

Our contextualisitic approach was also a genuine effort to seriously address the deficiencies in developmental research originally uncovered by Bronfenbrenner (1979). While we think that much of Bronfenbrenner's original recipe for valid developmental research has been followed more in the breach than in the observance, there are hopeful signs of change. For example, Wozniak and Fischer (1993) are cautiously optimistic that the examination of human behavior is starting to leave the simpler and often less accurate pattern of pursuing reductionistic Newtonian-like principles to one of recognizing that thinking is relational and co-constructive (see Fogel, 1993) with the environment. The social environment in particular is a complex one (Hinde, 1992), and valid answers cannot be found without considering the characteristics of the person and the environment jointly. After all, we are not just doing science, we are doing social science. Perhaps Bronfenbrenner (1993) said it best with his adaptation of Kurt Lewin's (1935) equation, namely, $D = f(PE)$, that is, "Development is a joint function of person and environment" (p. 7).

We also feel, along with Wozniak and Fischer (1993), that it is not wise for social scientists to be linear slaves to the contexless physical sciences, but for an additional reason: the content of our social subject matter is often not sufficiently described to warrant its more parametric treatment. It is precisely for this reason that our approach, along with Wosniak's (1993), to contextual research has been primarily phenomenological and descriptive. If we are going to properly understand how children create and govern their behaviors meaningfully within the relationships that compose their environment, we must be prepared to examine each specific social issue within the larger developmental and relational matrix in which it occurs. Lest we make our castles out of sand, we must also be prepared to investigate relationships by using the content that children (and adults) themselves use. One of the most important general messages of our research is that children themselves have a rich tapestry of meanings that they coherently structure and through which they order their social lives.

We began our book by asserting the need to examine relationships from a verbal rather than a purely behavioral perspective as we reasoned that what is often missing in social developmental work is the fuller appreciation of participants' relational meaning system, which is a cognitively constructed and verbally communicated affair. As Youniss (1978) claimed, a disadvantage with past cognitive-developmental approaches to social relationships has been their appeal to vague stages and their distance from behavior (Berscheid, 1986). Our methodology for recursive interviewing, however, took pains to incorporate children's representations of the interpersonal behaviors that they say they use as integral parts of their social rules. In this way, social rules are anchored to actual events that children experience. Interestingly enough, since we began our project, there has been a recognition among some developmental psychologists (see Dodge, 1986; Rubin & Krasnor, 1986) that it is helpful to understand how children's social behaviors are scripted in order to better understand how children interpret situations and to predict how children respond to those situations. Dodge is quite right in alerting us to the fact that overlearned, routinized social strategies become fairly automatic and nonconscious. However, our recursive interviewing technique showed us that much of this overlearned material is accessible. A problem for future research certainly will be to determine the limits of verbal discourse in accessing social meaning. Such issues notwithstanding, perhaps what we are witnessing is the beginning of a rapprochement between cognitive and behavioral perspectives.

Our methodology was unique in another way, since it used both verbal accounts as well as ratings of children's social rules and relationships. While other social developmentalists (e.g., Bigelow, 1983; Furman & Bierman, 1984) have also used multiple methods, our effort was unique in that it attempted to integrate those methods in the service of meaning. For example, because children mentioned reciprocity rules mostly in dealing with their peers, these rules have more meaning in peer relationships, even though children's rule ratings showed that reciprocity rules are used for both parents and close friends. The developmental origins of social rules within the parent–child relationship could therefore be addressed.

We viewed this multimethod approach as indispensable from an intuitive basis, but in retrospect this is how information is actually stored. Kandel (1991) reminds us that elementary operations are brought together into a coherent general representation (e.g., social rules), but we know from a strictly neurological basis that information is not stored in this way but rather as distinct verbal and visual categories. Thus, when we ask children to read a social rule and to imagine its behavioral roots, we are accessing, albeit indirectly, the rule's imaginative origins. On the other hand, the constructed meaning of the rule as accessed through recursive interviewing addresses how children manufacture a sense of the rule's coherency and hence its social meaning. The use of several methods within the same investigation is cumbersome but essential in our view, since the methods serve as valuable counterpoints in attempting to explain rule usage.

Our examination of children's social rules and relationships did not have a single preconceived "top-down" theory about how relationships work that was then subjected to empirical testing. Our methodology used a "bottom-up" approach that recorded the rules that are actually used. The issues that surfaced from the latent organization of our data then allowed us to create informed theoretical statements about how relationships of different kinds are actually managed. This was an especially necessary approach in a contextualistic endeavor such as ours, since the resolution of some of the problems that plague the literature on children's relationships was only really addressable in this way and at a level of detail not possible with preconceived "top-down" approaches.

Our work has gleaned social information from almost a thousand children in an attempt to understand how they apply rules across the different domains and types of relationships that govern their lives. Although each type of relationship has its defining features, the relationships embracing the richest fund of social knowledge were those of parent–child and of close friend (peer) relationships.

One of the more pronounced implications from our findings was that the sharp distinctions between parents and peers that are so prominent (see, e.g., Piaget, 1932/1965; Sullivan, 1953; Youniss, 1980) in the developmental literature are much more blurred when a fully contextualized examination such as ours is undertaken. Parents carefully scaffold essentially all the elements of social understanding that children also use with their peers, especially their close friends. While we certainly are in no position from which to diminish the value of peer relationships—indeed, those relationships compete with parental ones for the lion's share of social-relational content—our data drove home the point also made by Putallaz and Heflin (1990) and Rubin et al. (1990) that children's peer competencies have their roots within competent parent–child relationships that are crucial to long-term adjustment. (Our inclusion of relationships with other adults clearly revealed that children recognize adult authority and the compliance it implies. Parents, however, were not simply regarded as "adults.") We look forward to longitudinal studies of children's social rules and the origins of those rules in infancy and preschool periods in order to further illuminate the prepotent developmental scaffolding processes that we feel are the foundation of those rules. This should be a fruitful avenue of inquiry. For example, Fogel (1993) has alerted us to the rich social experiences of infants and young children that form the foundation for later development.

Our data also allowed us to conclude that peer relationships are not in themselves meaningful without making clear distinctions between close friends and other less intimate forms of peers. In our data, it was very evident that close friends are a unique and rich source of social experience for children, confirming the early notions of Sullivan (1953) that close friends, or "chums," provide a very active source of social practice. Perhaps equally important, we were in a position from which to detect how close friends are similar to parents in almost every sense, including a similarity in the rules of compliance normally reserved for getting along with parents. However, upon very close inspection, the specific kinds of rules and strategies used with close friends at times revealed the more cooperative quality of peer encounters (e.g., "Go along with") touted by children in other studies (e.g., Youniss, 1980) as providing a clear dividing line between these two types of relationships.

We think that this parent–child versus child–child issue is at least partly resolved by appealing to the verbal meaning that children constructed in the interviews, which were much more consistent with the parent–child, child–child division that forms the basis of the Sullivan–Piaget hypothesis (Youniss, 1980). The rule rationales were even more clearly supportive of this division. Evidently, children create these two worlds for themselves, which no doubt are functionally important to them; but the fact remains that the specifics of social understanding have more in common when close friends are compared with parents. The distinction between parents and peers is a real one, but the social competencies acquired within each relationship are often quite similar. In hindsight, this state of affairs is what one would have expected if socialization is to be at all efficient.

The upshot of these findings was that without a fully contextualized examination of children's personal and social relationships, investigators are risking less than clear portrayals of specific relationships that would otherwise be corrected. We are careful, though, to reserve judgment on this issue of the alleged uniqueness of close friends since methodological limitations make it difficult to separate experiences from one relationship to another: the experiences are inextricably intertwined.

With few exceptions, siblings were less involved than all other active relationships, including relationships with teachers. We therefore termed "invisible" the sibling relationship. However, the contextual approach that we used also allowed us to characterize sibling relationships from a much more informed basis than was otherwise possible, especially in the way in which support is provided and conflicts are resolved. Although siblings were not as frequently interactive with each other as with close friends (e.g., "Stay out of the way when my brother has his friends over"), there were numerous instances of siblings' offering each other meaningful peerlike support (e.g., "We play together and feel like real friends").

We concluded that relationships between siblings are not inherently any more conflictual than are other relationships and that our level of detail allowed us to show that the quality of conflict resolution within the sibling relationship is unique in that children are driven by the binding character of family relationships to find ways to deal with each other. At other times, siblings simply learn to live with each other without resolving things. One seldom enjoys this kind of liberty with peers. For example, sibling conflicts were often resolved in a unique way that was in part scaffolded by their closeness to parents (e.g., "If I get mad at my brother for something pretty bad, I will tell mom because she can deal with him better") but was not a simple parroting of parent–child relationships. Because there is not as much negotiation between siblings as in other relationships, conflicts are often quite different between siblings because their compulsory social context encourages siblings to resolve differences that a friend may not endure (e.g., "When [my brother] calls me names, I ignore him, and he gets tired"; "I try to go along with what [my sister] wants even if I don't want to").

Given the high profile that parents assumed in our study, we were impelled to speculate on the wider significance of this fact for practitioners. We were reminded of the hoary past that psychoanalytic theory and practice has had with respect to the ubiquity of the parent–child bond and its utility on the psychiatrist's couch. The current resurgence in the interest of investigators in attachment (see, e.g., Ainsworth et al., 1978; Ladd, 1992) and its import to subsequent social development we think is timely. We now know more of the fuller texture of the parent–child relationship and the importance of a loving, supportive family environment in creating an environment within which social and personal competency is achieved. Our social rules data is an important additional data set in an altogether intricate puzzle of socialization.

Practically speaking, we now need to examine the social rule differences and deficiencies of children, adolescents, and adults who are experiencing relational failures or simply seem to lack relational meaning. Armed with social rules data, therapists may then begin to intervene in an informed and constructive way to attempt to help clients to recoup and reconstruct some of what has not been learned or what has been lost. After all, our participants clearly indicated in their rule rationales that the understanding of self is intimately linked with mutual understanding. Our own mental health is therefore deeply embedded within the history of our personal relationships. Certainly for children, the task of interpersonal understanding must be, if anything, even more demanding, since children pay the full price for failure: long-term social rejection, loneliness, and lack of personal fulfillment. We are deeply indebted to the children for the privilege of being invited into their personal world of people and how they deal with them. We also look forward to investigating social-relational understanding with respect to different parenting styles and cultural contexts. The road from theory to practice is extensive but worth taking.

Extracting Social Rules from Interviewing

RECURSIVE INTERVIEWING

Social rules are linguistically embedded in children's phenomenologies of their personal and social relationships. In order to be theoretically neutral in extracting these rules from children's memories of their relationships, we embraced an information-processing approach, assuming only that social rules are encoded into memory and retrieved when social circumstances occur that bear resemblance to those situations that gave rise to the original rules. We considered that the child's social rule understanding is a set of working hypotheses (i.e., behavioral expectancies or strategies) of interpersonal interactions that are encoded within an "open program" (Mayr, 1974). The elaboration of this program can be viewed as an essential aspect of socialization, the ultimate end of which is to acquire a competent working program for relating to significant others. Accordingly, our task was essentially to access these social strategies by means of a thorough and theoretically neutral interviewing format. Once these strategies have been identified, they then can be readily grouped into classes of social rules.

We used an adapted form of George Kiss's (1972) recursive concept analysis (RCA). Recursive concept analysis was originally designed by Kiss as a lexical program for subjective meaning that was to be used in clinical settings. Interestingly, Kiss's ultimate and ambitious goal was to generate a computer program that would eventually produce a subjective dictionary. It is a highly structured interviewing technique that elicits information about the organization of knowledge in the individual's mind by explicating meaning in relation to particular target concepts. Meaning is operationally defined here as the conceptual components underlying a stimulus word or term. For example, the term "friend" can be explicated by the patient/subject to determine its idiopathic conceptual roots (e.g., "do no harm"). Kiss assumed that the meaning of words, and in our study the meaning of social harmony (i.e., getting along with others or maintaining a relationship with them), consists of concepts that successive questioning resolves into their respective components. The concepts triggered by this interviewing are naturally embedded in one another.

In principle, the structure of these concepts can be analyzed to an arbitrary degree of detail on successive levels of inquiry. In practice, however, this recursive process incurs increasingly more redundant loops, that is, when the subject is repetitive and when content becomes, according to Kiss, "atomic." In our own work, we found that social rule explication was repetitive at the third level. As with Kiss's work, we noted that considerable encouragement was often needed to keep children going since they at times got discouraged when they found it necessary to loop back to strategies used at earlier stages in the interview. This circularity is an inevitable feature of recursive interviewing. Of course, we did not proceed further when it was clear that new information was not forthcoming or when signs of acute distress were noticed.

Rules and Rationales

Concretely, at the first level of recursion, the subject was asked to explicate the meaning of one particular target phrase (i.e., "What are the ways you use in order to deal with your family/peers/other grown-ups?"), and the interviewer took notes of the numerous concepts generated (i.e., the social strategies), which were then subsequently abstracted on-line by the interviewer into a provisional set of social rules. The social rules were then read back to the child and modified if the meaning was not properly understood (see Appendix 2). At the second level of recursion, the interviewer then asked the child to explicate each of the concepts (i.e., the rules) in turn. For example, after several responses referring to the theme "talking," the interviewer would say, "You said that you talk with your friends. Could you tell me a bit more? What does it mean to talk?" At the second (and sometimes third) level of recursion, these responses were then grouped in turn into their component rule strategies (e.g., "Tell one another about our troubles," "Tell each other about everyday things"). Naturally, the deeper the interviewing progressed, the more the redundancy that occurred in the rules generated. The interview stopped at the third level of explication or when full redundancy was reached, which was usually at the second level. Finally, obscurities and ambiguities in the complete social rule list were resolved by further questioning, which typically took the form of reading the strategy back to the child and asking him or her if that was what he or she meant to say.

Relational Content

We kept the interview anchored in concrete relational behaviors, representing focused exchanges between the subject and two or more persons. Unlike a general content analysis, which usually attempts to categorize all interview responses, a relational content analysis focuses only on comments that embody social rules governing expectancies of behavior between the child and the other person(s). The emphasis here is on interpersonal transactions. Comments of a purely descriptive, vague, or one-sided nature were excluded in the relational coding and social rule category construction. One-sided comments may refer to physical appearances or to attributed personality traits such as "honesty," "sincerity" or "understandingness," and vague responses are devoid of behavioral referents such as "He likes me, and I like him." These do not contain social rule strategies. Relational comments, on the other hand, reveal an interpersonal code or program: for example, "When others bug me, I ignore them and go into my room, play with my cat to calm my nerves" [rule = when bothered, leave the situation]; "If there is a disagreement over what you are going to do, try to compromise" [rule = compromise and don't disagree]. As one can see, social rules define the boundaries of our behavior within social relationships.

To further anchor the children's interview responses in behavioral social rules, we routinely asked children how a particular strategy helped them to get along with a particular person. While this aspect of the interview did not deal with social rules per se, we thought that a fuller appreciation of the meaning of the social rule was to be found in its explanation. The reader should note that while we couched the meaning of social relationships primarily in terms of the classes of social rules that govern given personal and social relationships, we also surmised that the meaning built directly into the interview schedule itself (i.e., "Tell me the ways in which you get along with your brother") contained a number of its own explicative components as well (e.g., "to get to know him better," "to avoid further fights," etc.).

Specifically then, each target rule statement was followed up by an explanatory probe to verify the utility of the social strategy involved: "You said that you deal with your friends by playing games with them. How does playing games help you deal with your friends?" Content stemming from this part of the interview was referred to as the "rationales," which were analyzed separately. In subsequent coding described below, we

separated any rule rationales from the social strategies so that explanations were not confused with the rules themselves. For example, "Be sure
of yourself and know what you are doing so you can be trusted" consists
of two parts: "Be sure of yourself and know what you are doing" and "so
you can be trusted." The following is another example: "After a fight, we
say sorry and make up so that we can be friends." The strategy is "we say
sorry and make up," and the rationale is "so that we can be friends." We
dealt with rules and rationales separately, not only because they are
intrinsically different types of social responses but also because, after
careful analysis, it became evident that in most instances there were no
good fits between particular kinds of social rules and types of rationales;
in fact, rules and rationales seemed largely interchangeable. The specifics
of the entire interview procedure and the pilot study can be found in
Appendix 2.

PEER INVESTIGATORS

Elkind and Weiner (1978) aptly indicated that in any investigation of
children's thinking, we must be aware of the fact that children may well
have different frames of reference from our own. If we have learned
anything of substance in developmental psychology, it is that children
often, if not typically, think differently from adults. They classify things
differently according to their age and maturity (see, e.g., Flavell, 1963,
1985). To help guard against adult bias in interviewing, we recruited the
help of a group of six children, consisting of three males of ages 7, 10,
and 13 and three females of ages 7, 10, and 13.

Each peer investigator initially served as a pilot interview subject and
was interviewed on three successive occasions. In both individual and
group discussions, the peers provided feedback about the specifics of the
interview protocol and suggested various ways in which the procedure
could be modified to appeal to other children. Some of their suggestions
incorporated into the interviewing procedure were as follows. They said
that most kids don't think about "getting along with others," which was
our initial probe. Instead, they suggested "dealing with people" or simply
"keeping things smooth." We used these openers interchangeably. They
also felt that kids found it difficult to open up at the start of the interview,
especially since they didn't know the interviewer and because they hardly
ever got a chance to think and talk openly about such matters. A 5- to
7-minute lead-in was suggested, which allowed for rapport building and
which gave the children time to gather their thoughts. The peers who
provided feedback were unanimous in recommending that each subject
be totally informed about the purpose of the project and the nature of

the interview procedure. Real experiences, rather than hypothetical ones, were stressed since pretend situations tended to lead kids away from what really happens in a relationship. The peers were particularly helpful in providing us with child-appropriate terms, such as "other grown-ups" for nonfamily adults. Finally, they were clear that interview probing of private areas of interaction would be difficult, so we didn't press such areas. In the words of one peer investigator, "If a kid does something wrong that is personal, they just want to bury it, not to talk about it."

SUBJECTS

Twenty males and twenty females each of ages 6 through 13 were individually interviewed by five same-sex adults: the three investigators and two female graduate assistants. These subjects were randomly selected from children enrolled in the public and separate school systems in the Region of Sudbury. School officials who were familiar with the school population assisted in identifying schools that would reflect the economic and geographic mix of the region. Most subjects (95%) were from intact families consisting of their original members. Parental permission varied between 70% to 90% per classroom.

CATEGORY CONSTRUCTION

Given that the focus of the investigation was to generate social rule categories and only secondarily to identify the justifications or rationales for them, we split each grid statement into two parts: the social rule strategy and the rationale. The social rule strategies were generally composed of behavioral actions, as well as some statement of the goal or an elaboration of the strategy. We included any explanation that was essential in understanding the strategy. The remainder of the grid statement was treated as a rationale. The following is an example: (Part 1) "If I really want something bad, I just keep asking her over and over again, except if she's in a bad mood"; (Part 2) "If I keep on asking, she caves in and I get what I want." The following is another example: (Part 1) "Be sure of yourself and know what you are doing" (Part 2) "so you can be trusted."

For both the social rule strategy statements (i.e., the Part 1's) and the rationales (i.e., the Part 2's), construction of category coding schemes was accomplished by gathering similar statements in an iterative way by inspecting each one and going down the lists of statements and matching similar ones into groups, which then formed the provisional categories. This process started with grid statements of the 13-year-olds, followed by those of the 10- and 7-year-olds. At each step, the proposed categories were verified with the peer investigators. A set of 63 Part 1 and 32 Part 2 categories was generated and cross-checked with a sample of 6- and 12-year-old grid statements to ensure that content was being fully captured. Working from grid sheets, which included grid statements in their entirety, each statement was split into its two parts, and each part was coded by two adult coders, with disagreements resolved by a third coder, thereby coding all statements to consensus. The 63 interview categories are listed in Table 3.1, the rationales in Table 9.1. Reliability procedures and calculations can be found in Appendix 2.

SOCIAL RULES CHECKLIST

We also decided to use social rule ratings to supplement the interviews-derived social rules. It was very obvious from Furman and Bierman's (1984) research on children's conceptions of friendship that interviews and rating scales provide very different kinds of data regarding the child's sensitivity to the information. Furman and Bierman (1984) found that questionnaires are significantly more likely to reveal conceptual competency than interviews are, which is a variation on the perceptual truism that recognition is easier than recall. Rating scales are more readily responded to, of course, and portray the child's level of social sophistication in higher, more advanced terms than do interviews, which require the child to actively process social information and if anything underestimate competence (see Chapter 1: "Measurement Concerns").

However, the issue is not simply one of using the measurement device that yields the best psychometrics, since interview-based data may well have higher external validity. Renshaw and Asher's (1983) work, as cited in Chapters 1 and 3, is particularly relevant here as a meaningful way to account for differences between interviews and questionnaires. Although children who are popular and rejected have the same social goals in dealing with peer problems, it was only through in-depth interviewing that the conceptual differences were detectable between popular and rejected groups. Renshaw and Asher also found that children who spontaneously report (i.e., encode) social skills rather than simply check them off on a questionnaire instrument are more likely to act in socially appropriate ways. Given these findings, we viewed our interview data, which after all are composed of spontaneous social rule comments, as inherently more powerful in their connection to the child's actual conduct. The checklist data also tap social knowledge, but on a more passive (i.e., decoded) level, perhaps indicative of initial levels of social learning. However, rather than worry the point of which kind of data (interview or questionnaire) best reflects a child's social rule knowledge, questionnaire data as a common metric served primarily to identify specific relationship differences for each social rule theme and category within each social domain.

In order to obtain a common metric with which to examine social rules within specific social relationships, a questionnaire or "checklist" was used that allowed the child to rate how frequently the rule was used within each of eight social relationships (i.e., mother, father, brother(s), sister(s), close friend(s), other friend(s), other kids, and teachers). There were 56 rules in the checklist, which were represented by exemplary social rule statements (i.e., "strategies") uncovered in the previous interview phase of the study. The participants had to circle how often they used the particular rule within each relationship.

The interview rules (Table 3.1) and the checklist items (Table 3.2) were phrased differently because the ratings were phrased in more specific social strategies representing the social rules, which would then become more meaningful as questionnaire items. These strategies were taken directly from interview content. For example, the rule "Don't bug or bother" (Table 3.1) became "Don't bug or bother them" (Table 3.2), and "Talk, tell things, and discuss" (Table 3.1) became "Talk with them about everyday things" (Table 3.2). Due to low frequencies (%), there were seven social rules that were not incorporated into the checklist. These will become obvious as each theme is presented in the book.

With the aid of the "peer investigators" in selecting child-relevant terms, we had 659 children of both sexes from ages 9 to 13 rate the 56 strategies with respect to mother, father, brother, sister, close friends (i.e., kids you think of as your best friends), other friends (i.e., kids you count as friends but who are not close friends), other kids (i.e., kids you have to deal with on a regular basis, as in the schoolyard, but whom you don't really consider as friends), and teacher. Participants had to circle how often they used the particular rule within each of the eight relationships. Note that step-parents were given as alternatives; and if the children had more than one person in a given relationship (e.g., two brothers, two friends), they had to treat the multiple-person relationship as one. Ratings were 1 (always), 2 (most of the time), 3 (sometimes), or 4 (never).

Peer investigators felt that children could not make more than a 4-point discrimination. In addition, pilot testing with the peer investigators showed that it was too difficult to rate all 56 rules in one sitting. Accordingly, we administered the checklist in two forms. Approximately half (*n* = 344) the participants responded to Form A (Study 1) and the other half (*n* = 315) responded to Form B (Study 2). These rules were then grouped into 15 conceptually defined rule themes, 11 of which were common to each form of the checklist.

APPENDIX 2

The Recursive Interview Protocol

RULE-BY-RELATIONSHIPS GRID SHEETS

The conventional approach to data reduction when using an interview procedure is to transcribe or tape-record content for later transcription and then subject the printed material to content analysis. During the course of our pilot testing, we learned that it was easier and more accurate to have the child provide an ongoing verification of the recursively derived social rule summary statements: for example, "You said you watch T.V., play games and go for walks with your parents. It sounds like 'doing things together' is important for you in getting along with your parents. Is this correct?" In this way, an important initial step in the coding process was achieved without having to laboriously record everything that the child said. This technique also short-circuited the tendencies of some children to give a lengthy list of concrete behaviors within the same category of response, such as, "We play ball, checkers, baseball, play with our toys, play games, play hockey, play outside, in his room, in the backyard," and so forth.

A form was eventually developed that enabled the interviewer to write down each of the discrete recursively derived statements that emerged for each individual (e.g., mother, father, sister, brother) within each of the three domains (i.e., family, peers, nonfamily adults). Thus, the interviewer could record the social rule strategies that occurred for each domain while verbally verifying them with the subject as to their accuracy. This was an efficient method for capturing relevant interview content.

THE PEER INVESTIGATORS

The peer investigators were identified by school personnel as talented individuals who would readily respond to working on a research project. The teachers selected 6 peer investigators out of a pool of 30 candidates. Telephone contact was made with parents and children, followed by a visit in the home, during which the entire project and expected work involved was outlined. Parents were also provided with a written description of the project and were asked to sign forms permitting their children's involvement in the project. Children also endorsed a contract stipulating what was expected of them as well as what was expected of the project coordinators. At completion of the project, the children were paid $100.00 each for their efforts.

PILOT STUDY

A pilot sample of 36 children, two males and two females from each of grades 6 through 14 years, was used to refine the interview protocol and finalize the training of the adult interviewers. Interview tapes were analyzed by one senior investigator who was adept at recursive interviewing. Points of departure from standard procedure were noted and discussed in group sessions with the peer investigators, who offered suggestions (see above) about subjects' reactions to the interview procedure. The actual interview instructions to subjects appears below.

THE INTERVIEW PROCEDURE

Interviews were conducted in the school setting, but we were careful not to take the children out of class when there was a favorite activity or free time period, such as recess. Each interview was from 45 to 70 minutes in length, with older children requiring longer time spans. Children's permission for tape-recording was obtained prior to interviewing, and confidentiality was assured by telling the children that we used coded numbers, not names, to keep track of different tapes. They were also told that they could discontinue the interview at any time. There were no refusals. In order to expose interviewers to a constant mix of interview length and complexity, the interviews were done in three waves: 7-, 10-, and 13-year olds; 6-, 9-, and 12-year-olds; and 8- and 11-year-olds. The order of the social domains (i.e., family, peers, other adults) was counterbalanced so that half the interviews began with family and the other half with peers. Through pilot testing, we learned that beginning an interview with the other-adults domain was very awkward for children since they had to go back and correct answers to this domain after encountering the family domain.

Specific instructions to subjects were as follows:

This research project was designed to find out about kids' getting along with other people. The project is funded by the federal government, and we work at Laurentian University. This project is going on in a lot of schools all over Sudbury; it will take a couple of years to do and more than 1,000 kids will be involved.

Each of us has to deal with many different people on a regular basis, such as people in our families, people our own ages, and others. It is important to know how to deal with these different people. We are particularly interested in how kids just like yourself deal with different people. We really don't know much about how kids deal with people in their families, kids their own age, and other grown-ups. We want to learn as much as we can about this, and the best way to do this is to talk to kids directly. Everything you tell me will be very useful. Your thoughts and opinions are very important. There are no right or wrong things to say.

During the interview, there may be times when neither of us will be talking. That's all right. You may need time to think. It's okay for you to take your time and pause so you can tell me what you really think.

We will start the interview by my asking you to tell me all you can about getting along with people. I will listen to your ideas and perhaps makes some notes. Then we will go back, and I will ask you to talk more about them. We will do this for getting along with people in the family, getting along with kids your own age, and getting along with other adults.

It might help to explain more of what we are going to be talking about. Everybody has to deal with a number of different people regularly, and we are interested in how they do this. Sometimes getting along with a person can be pretty smooth, and other times it can be a bit rough. In any case, we try somehow or another to get along with others as best we can. We want to know how *you get along with people (deal with people) and keep things smooth.*

We are going to have you talk about your getting along with your family. Who is in your family? Okay, tell me about your dealing with these people. Let's start with how you deal with _____? How does "strategy" help you get along with _____?

We are going to have you talk about getting along with other kids. Most kids know other kids who may be really close friends, other kids who are friends, and then just kids that they have to deal with regularly. I want you to think about some kids your own age who are really close friends, some kids your own age who are just friends, and some kids your own age whom you wouldn't call friends but you still have to deal with them. Okay, tell me about your dealing with kids your own age. How does "strategy" help you get along with _____?

We are going to have you talk about your getting along with other grown-ups. There are other grown-ups that you have to deal with besides your parents. Tell me about your dealing with other grown-ups. (If no reference is made to teachers, introduce "How about your dealing with teachers?"). How does "strategy" help you deal with _____?

All responses were probed in a nondirective way, such as allowing the subjects to take their time, giving them permission to say whatever comes into their head, and reminding them that there are lots of things that go on between them and others in their family/peer group or with other grown-ups. Responses were encouraged by prompts such as "Go on," "Tell me more," and "That's interesting, go on," "Yes," "Anything else?," "Is that all?" and so forth. Responses were periodically updated, rephrased, and generalized.

RELIABILITY

Interview consistency was checked by assigning the first 30 transcripts to two of the five interviewers, other than the person who was responsible for generating the transcript. Each interview was then carefully checked for completeness of recursive procedure, and slippages were discussed in group meetings.

The second type of reliability check involved the rule-by-relationship grid statements generated from the interview. Using 50 interviews drawn at random, an independent rater read each transcript and compiled a list of social rule statements for each of the three domains, using the grid sheets as if he or she were actually conducting the interview firsthand. Comparisons were then made between the content of the interviewer's grid sheets and those of the reliability coder. Percentage agreement between the two sets of grid statements was 87.

SOCIAL RULES CHECKLIST

Subjects

The 659 participants ranged from ages 9 to 13 years (grades 3 to 8); 344 responded to Form A, and 315 to Form B of the checklist. Because of missing values on particular relationships (e.g., no father, no sister), effective sample sizes varied between 83 and 100, depending on the particular rule theme entered into analysis. Participants were obtained from public and separate schools within the local districts of Sudbury, Ontario, and included a blend of blue-collar and middle-class families. Permission was obtained from both parents and children prior to testing, and they had the right to withdraw at any time. The participation rate was 95%.

Procedure

All checklist testing was done in each participant's respective classroom. A brief background was provided to the earlier interview phase of the project so that the relevancy of the checklist items could be known. Checklist instructions read: "How often I use 'the strategy' with them. Circle either 1, 2, 3, or 4: 1. Always, 2. Most of the time, 3. Sometimes, 4. Never." The research assistant selected a strategy (e.g., "Share things with others") and illustrated that the participants had to decide how often they used this strategy in "getting along" with each of the eight persons on the checklist, showing how to make a decision: for example, "If you always share things with your mother, you would circle the 1." (Ratings were subsequently transformed from 1 to 4 to 4 to 1 to reflect "always" to "never" for statistical analyses.) Participants were also instructed not to guess but to leave an item blank if they didn't understand it or if they didn't have such a person to cite (e.g., no father).

Pilot testing, as well as feedback from our peer investigators, furnished us with the specific terms (e.g., "mom" and "dad" instead of "mother" and "father") and relationships (e.g., "close friends", "other friends", "other kids") that we incorporated into the checklist. Such feedback also informed us that it was necessary to split the checklist into two parts (Study 1 and Study 2) because children couldn't respond to 56 rules in one sitting.

APPENDIX 3

Data Analyses

The interview material was content analyzed into 63 social rule categories (Table 3.1) that were distributed among 15 themes. Percentage of usage of individual themes was then distributed by domain (family, peers, other adults), age (6 to 13) and sex and was analyzed descriptively. In the interests of having a common metric, percentage comparisons for each of these themes was analyzed on the basis of calculating the difference between the higher percentage and the lower percentage, treating the lower percentage as zero. Based on z-scores for proportions, it was determined that a particular theme was significantly ($p < .05$) above zero at a given age level or that it was significantly different between genders if it had a percentage difference of 6.6 or more.

Each of the 15 (domain × age × sex) figures for the interview social rule themes was accompanied by corresponding checklist-rating data. The social rule theme ratings were analyzed by means of 15 separate multivariate 8 × 5 × 2 (relation x age (9 to 13) × sex) analyses of variance, with repeated measures on relationship (mother, father, brother(s), sister(s), close friends, other friends, other kids, teacher). F-tests were performed by means of Wilks Lamba; significant univariate F-tests were reported only when the multivariate effect for the given rule theme was significant, and multivariate results were reported only when the overall MANOVA for that variable was significant.

Checklist figures show the relationship and sex distributions of the particular social rule themes. For explanatory purposes, there was also a table of mean relationship ratings for each social rule contained in the theme. Significant relationship differences on particular rules were only reported where the multivariate relationship effect for the rule theme was significant. An examination of specific relationship mean differences was accomplished by means of Sheffé ex post facto analyses (in Ferguson,

1976) using the multivariate within-cells standard deviation as a basis for calculation. The multivariate within-cells standard deviation for the particular rule theme was also used to calculate Sheffe's for relationship mean differences on particular component social rules. Because children were asked to leave an item blank rather then guess, cases were deleted where there were missing values. As a result, there was usually a larger sample size when a rule was analyzed by itself than when it was included with other rules within a theme. However, mean ratings on specific rules were generally comparable to mean ratings within themes because there were negligible differences in mean ratings owing to fluctuations in sample size. (See Bigelow et al., 1992, for more specific comparisons on a related set of analyses.) Age × relation and sex × relation ex post facto tests on social rule themes were calculated as orthonormalized transformations of mean differences, which uses a system of weights to identify the source of significant mean differences. Missing values did not permit aggregate MANOVAs.

References

Abramovitch, R., Corter, C., Pepler, D. J., & Stanhope, L. (1986). Sibling and peer interactions: A final follow-up and a comparison. *Child Development, 57,* 217–229.

Ainsworth, M. D. S., Bell, S. M., & Stayton, D. J. (1971). Individual differences in strange-situation behavior of one-year-olds. In H. R. Schaffer (Ed.), *The origins of human social relations.* London: Academic Press.

Ainsworth, M. D. S., Bell, S. M., & Stayton, D. J. (1974). Infant–mother attachment and social development: "Socialization" as a product of reciprocal responsiveness to signals. In M. Richards (Ed.), *The integration of a child into a social world.* New York: Cambridge University Press.

Ainsworth, M. D. S., Blehar, M., Waters, E., & Wall, S. (1978). *Patterns of attachment.* Hillsdale, NJ: Erlbaum.

Alessandri, S. M., & Wozniak, R. H. (1987). The child's awareness of parental beliefs concerning the child: A developmental study. *Child Development, 58,* 316–323.

Amato, P. (1990). Dimensions of the family environment as perceived by children: A multidimensional scaling analysis. *Journal of Marriage and the Family, 52,* 613–620.

Argyle, M., & Henderson, M. (1985). *The anatomy of relationships and the rules and skills needed to manage them successfully.* London: Heinemann.

Armentrout, J. A., & Burger, G. K. (1972). Children's reports of parental childrearing behavior at five grade levels. *Developmental Psychology, 7,* 44–68.

Asarnow, J. (1983). Children with peer adjustment problems: Sequential and nonsequential analysis of school behaviors. *Journal of Consulting and Clinical Psychology, 51,* 709–717.

Asher, S. R. (1978). Children's peer relations. In M. E. Lamb (Ed.), *Socio-personality development.* New York: Holt.

Asher, S. R., & Coie, J. D. (1990). *Peer rejection in childhood.* New York: Cambridge University Press.

Asher, S. R., & Gottman, J. M. (Eds.). (1981). *The development of children's friendships.* New York: Cambridge University Press.

Asher, S. R., & Renshaw, P. D. (1981). Children without friends: Social knowledge and social skill training. In S. R. Asher & J. M. Gottman (Eds.), *The development of children's friendships.* New York: Cambridge University Press.

Asher, S. R., & Williams, G. A. (1987). Helping children without friends in home and school. In *Children's social development: Information for teachers and parents.* Urbana, IL: ERIC, Clearing House on Elementary and Early Childhood Education.

Azmitia, M., & Hesser, J. (1993). Why siblings are important agents of cognitive development: A comparison of siblings and peers. *Child Development, 64,* 430–444.

Bandura, A. (1977). *Social learning theory.* Englewood Cliffs, NJ: Prentice-Hall.

Bandura, A. (1978). The self-system in reciprocal determinism. *American Psychologist, 33,* 344–358.

Bandura, A., Grusec, J. E., & Menlove, F. L. (1966). Observational learning as a function of symbolization and incentive set. *Child Development, 37,* 499–506.

Bandura, A., & Menlove, F. L. (1968). Factors determining vicarious extinction of avoidance behavior through vicarious modeling. *Journal of Personality and Social Psychology, 8,* 99–108.

Bandura, A., & Walters, R. H. (1959). *Adolescent aggression.* New York: Ronald.

Bandura, A., & Walters, R. H. (1963). *Social learning and personality development.* New York: Holt, Rinehart & Winston.

Bank, S. P., & Kahn, M. D. (1975). Sisterhood–brotherhood is powerful: Sibling sub-systems and family therapy. *Family Process, 14,* 311–337.

Bank, S. P., & Kahn, M. D. (1982). *The sibling bond.* New York: Basic Books.

Baumrind, D. (1967). Child care practices anteceding three patterns of preschool behavior. *Genetic Psychology Monographs, 75,* 43–88.

Baumrind, D. (1971). Current patterns of parental authority. *Developmental Psychology Monographs, 4* (1, Pt. 2).

Baumrind, D. (1973). The development of instrumental competence through socialization. In A. D. Pick (Ed.), *Minnesota Symposia on Child Psychology* (Vol. 7). Minneapolis: University of Minnesota Press.

Bearison, D. J., & Cassel, T. Z. (1975). Cognitive decentration and social codes: Communication effectiveness in young children from differing family contexts. *Developmental Psychology, 11,* 29–36.

Becker, W. C. (1964). Consequences of different kinds of parental discipline. In M. L. Hoffman & L. W. Hoffman (Eds.), *Review of child management research* (Vol. 1). New York: Russell Sage Foundation.

Bennett, J. C. (1990). Nonintervention into siblings' fighting as a catalyst for learned helplessness. *Psychological Reports, 66,* 139–145.

Berger, P. L., & Luckmann, T. (1966). *The social construction of reality.* New York: Doubleday.

Berndt, T. J. (1979). Developmental changes in conformity to peers and parents. *Developmental Psychology, 15,* 608–616.

Berndt, T. J. (1981). Age changes over time in prosocial intentions and behavior between friends. *Developmental Psychology, 17,* 408–416.

Berndt, T. J. (1983). Correlates and causes of sociometric status in childhood: A commentary on six current studies of popular, rejected, and neglected children. *Merrill-Palmer Quarterly, 29,* 439–448.

Berndt, T. J. (1986). Children's comments about their friendships. In M. Perlmutter (Ed.), *Minnesota Symposia on Child Psychology* (Vol. 18). Hillsdale, NJ: Erlbaum.

Berndt, T. J., & Hoyle, S. G. (1985). Stability and change in childhood and adolescent friendships. *Developmental Psychology, 21,* 1007–1015.

Berscheid, E. (1986). Comments on Berndt: Children's comments about their friendships. In M. Perlmutter (Ed.), *Minnesota Symposia on Child Psychology* (Vol. 18). Hillsdale, NJ: Erlbaum.

Bichard, S. L., Alden, L., Walker, L. J., & McMahon, R. J. (1988). Friendship understanding in socially accepted, rejected, and neglected children. *Merrill-Palmer Quarterly, 34,* 33–46.

Bierman, K. L. (1986). Process of change during social skills training with preadolescents and its relation to treatment outcome. *Child Development, 57,* 230–240.

Bigelow, B. J. (1977). Children's friendship expectations: A cognitive-developmental study. *Child Development, 48,* 246–253.

Bigelow, B. J. (1983). Assessing children's friendship expectations: Supplementing the semistructured interview with picture sequence tasks. *Human Relations, 36,* 285–308.

Bigelow, B. J., & Deck, T. (1996). *A content analysis of peer play in a daycare centre.* Unpublished manuscript, Laurentian University, Sudbury, Ontario.

Bigelow, B. J., & La Gaipa, J. J. (1975). Children's written descriptions of friendship: A multidimensional analysis. *Developmental Psychology, 11,* 857–858.

Bigelow, B. J., & La Gaipa, J. J. (1980). The development of friendship values and choice. In H. C. Foot, A. J. Chapman, & J. R. Smith (Eds.), *Friendship and social relations in children.* New York: Wiley.

Bigelow, B. J., Levin, E., & Cunning, S. (1994). Support and control in parent–child relations from childhood to early adolescence: The Maccoby–Minuchin hypothesis. In E. Porter, G. Tesson, & J. H. Lewko (Eds.), *Sociological studies of child development* (Vol. 7). Greenwich, CT: JAI Press.

Bigelow, B. J., Lewko, J. H., & Salhani, L. (1989). Sport-involved children's friendship expectations. *Journal of Sport and Exercise Psychology, 11,* 152–160.

Bigelow, B. J., & Pellarin, S. M. (1989). *Popularity and friendship conceptions in middle childhood: An analysis in terms of sociometric status, social impact and friendship reciprocity.* Unpublished manuscript, Laurentian University, Sudbury, Ontario.

Bigelow, B. J., Tesson, G., & Lewko, J. H. (1992). The social rules that children use: Close friends, other friends, and "other kids" compared to parents, teachers, and siblings. *International Journal of Behavioral Development, 15,* 315–335.

Blos, P. (1967). The second individuation process of adolescence. *Psychoanalytic Study of the Child, 22,* 162–186.

Bohm, D. (1973). Quantum theory as an indication of a new order in physics.

Part B. Implicate and explicate order in physical law. *Foundations of Physics, 3,* 139–168.

Bohm, D. (1980). *Wholeness and the implicate order.* London: Routledge & Kegan Paul.

Bourdieu, P. (1990). *The logic of practice* (R. Nice, Trans.). Cambridge: Polity Press.

Bower, E. (1969). *Early identification of emotionally handicapped children in school.* Springfield, IL: Charles C. Thomas.

Brainerd, C. J. (1973a). Neo-Piagetian training experiments revisited: Is there any support for the cognitive-developmental stage hypothesis? *Cognition, 2,* 349–370.

Brainerd, C. J. (1973b). Order of acquisition of transitivity, conservation, and class inclusion of length and weight. *Developmental Psychology, 8,* 105–116.

Brainerd, C. J. (1978). The stage question in cognitive-developmental theory. *Behavioral and Brain Sciences, 1,* 173–213.

Bretherton, I., Fritz, J., Zahn-Waxler, C., & Ridgeway, D. (1986). Learning to talk about emotions: A functionalist perspective. *Child Development, 57,* 529–548.

Bronfenbrenner, U. (1979). *The ecology of human development.* Cambridge: Harvard University Press.

Bronfenbrenner, U. (1993). The ecology of cognitive development: Research models and fugitive findings. In R. H. Wozniak & K. W. Fischer (Eds.), *Development in context: Acting and thinking in specific environments.* Hillsdale, NJ: Erlbaum.

Brown, J. R., & Dunn, J. (1992). Talk with your mother or your sibling? Developmental changes in early family conversations about feelings. *Child Development, 63,* 336–349.

Bruner, J. S. (1975). The ontogenesis of speech acts. *Journal of Child Language, 2,* 1–19.

Bryant, B. K., & De Morris, K. A. (1992). Beyond parent–child relationships: Potential links between family environments and peer relations. In R. D. Parke & G. W. Ladd (Eds.), *Family peer relationships: Modes of linkage.* Hillsdale, NJ: Erlbaum.

Buhrmester, D., & Furman, W. (1987). The development of companionship and intimacy. *Child Development, 58,* 1101–1113.

Bukowski, W. M., & Hoza, B. (1989). Popularity and friendship: Issues in theory, measurement, and outcome. In T. J. Berndt & G. W. Ladd (Eds.), *Peer relationships in child development.* New York: Wiley.

Butterworth, G. (1982). A brief account of the conflict between the individual and the social in models of cognitive growth. In G. Butterworth & P. Light (Eds.), *Social cognition: Studies of the development of understanding.* Chicago: University of Chicago Press.

Butterworth, G., & Light, P. (1982). *Social cognition: Studies of the development of understanding.* Chicago: University of Chicago Press.

Byrne, D., & Griffitt, W. (1966). A developmental investigation of the law of attraction. *Journal of Personality and Social Psychology, 4,* 699–702.

Canfield, F. E., & La Gaipa, J. J. (1970, April). *Friendship expectations at different stages in the development of friendship.* Paper presented at the meeting of the Southeastern Psychological Association, Louisville, KY.

Carr, E. H. (1961). *What is history?* Harmondsworth, England: Penguin.

Chalmers, J. B., & Townsend, M. A. R. (1990). The effects of training in social perspective taking on socially maladjusted girls. *Child Development, 61,* 178–190.

Chandler, M. J. (1982). Social cognition and social structure. In F. C. Serafica (Ed.), *Social-cognitive development in context.* New York: Guilford Press.

Chandler, M. J., & Greenspan, D. (1972). Ersatz egocentrism: A reply to H. Borke, *Developmental Psychology, 7,* 104–106.

Clarke-Stewart, K. A. (1973). Interactions between mothers and their young children: Characteristics and consequences. *Monographs of the Society for Research in Child Development, 38* (Serial No. 153).

Coie, J. D. (1990). Toward a theory of peer rejection. In S. R. Asher & J. D. Coie (Eds.), *Peer rejection in childhood.* Cambridge: Cambridge University Press.

Coie, J. D., & Dodge, K. A. (1983). Continuities and change in children's social status: A five-year longitudinal study. *Merrill-Palmer Quarterly, 29,* 261–282.

Coie, J. D., Dodge, K. A., Terry, R., & Wright, V. (1991). The role of aggression in peer relations: An analysis of aggression episodes in boys' play groups. *Child Development, 62,* 812–826.

Coie, J. D., & Kupersmidt, J. B. (1983). A behavioral analysis of emerging social status in boys' groups. *Child Development, 54,* 1400–1416.

Collingwood, R. G. (1956). *The idea of history.* New York: Oxford University Press.

Collins, R. (1985). *The sociological traditions.* New York: Oxford University Press.

Collins, R. (1988). *Theoretical sociology.* San Diego: Harcourt Brace Jovanovich.

Combs, M. L., & Slaby, D. A. (1977). Social skills training with children. In B. B. Lahey & A. E. Kazdin (Eds.), *Advances in clinical child psychology.* New York: Plenum.

Connidis, I. A., & Davies, L. (1992). Confidants and companions: Choices in later life. *Journal of Gerontology, 47,* 115–122.

Connolly, J., & Doyle, A. (1981). Assessment of social competence in preschoolers: Teachers versus peers. *Developmental Psychology, 17,* 454–462.

Cooley, C. H. (1902). *Human nature and the social order.* New York: Scribner's.

Coombs, R. H., & Landsverk, I. (1988). Parenting styles and substance abuse during childhood and adolescence. *Journal of Marriage and the Family, 50,* 473–482.

Cooper, C. R., & Cooper, R. G., Jr. (1992). Links between adolescents' relationships with their parents and peers: Models, evidence, and mechanisms. In R. D. Parke & G. W. Ladd (Eds.), *Family–peer relationships: Modes of linkage.* Hillsdale, NJ: Erlbaum.

Coopersmith, S. (1967). *The antecedents of self-esteem.* San Francisco: Freeman.

Corsaro, W. A. (1981). Friendship in the nursery school: Social organization in a peer environment. In S. R. Asher & J. M. Gottman (Eds.), *The development of children's friendships.* Cambridge: Cambridge University Press.

Corsaro, W. A., & Rizzo, T. A. (1988). Discussione and friendship: Socialization processes in the peer culture of Italian nursery school children. *American Sociological Review, 53,* 879–894.

Cowen, E. L., Pederson, A., Babigian, H., Izzo, L. D., & Trost, M. (1973).

Long-term follow-up of early detected vulnerable children. *Journal of Consulting and Clinical Psychology, 41,* 154–161.

Csikszentmihalyi, M., & Larson, R. (1984). *Being adolescent: Conflict and growth in the teenage years.* New York: Basic Books.

Damon, W. (1977). *The social world of the child.* San Francisco: Jossey-Bass.

Damon, W., & Hart, D. (1988). The development of self-understanding from infancy through adolescence. *Child Development, 53,* 841–864.

Dannefer, D., & Perlmutter, M. (1990). Development as a multi-dimensional process: Individual and social constituents. *Human Development, 33,* 108–137.

Denzin, N. (1977). *Childhood socialization.* San Francisco: Jossey-Bass.

DiPietro, J. (1981). Rough-and-tumble play: A function of gender. *Developmental Psychology, 17,* 50–58.

Dodge, K. A. (1980). Social cognition and children's aggressive behavior. *Child Development, 51,* 162–170.

Dodge, K. A. (1983). Behavioral antecedents of peer social status. *Child Development, 54,* 1386–1399.

Dodge, K. A. (1986). A social information processing model of social competence in children. In M. Perlmutter (Ed.), *Minnesota Symposia on Child Psychology* (Vol. 18). Hillsdale, NJ: Erlbaum.

Dodge, K. A., & Coie, J. D. (1982). Behavior patterns of socially rejected and neglected preadolescents: The roles of social approach and aggression. *Journal of Abnormal Child Psychology, 10,* 389–409.

Dodge, K. A., & Feldman, E. (1990). Issues in social cognition and sociometric status. In S. R. Asher, & J. D. Coie (Eds.), *Peer rejection in childhood.* Cambridge: Cambridge University Press.

Dodge, K. A., & Frame, C. L. (1982). Social cognitive biases and deficits in aggressive boys. *Child Development, 53,* 620–635.

Dodge, K. A., Price, J. A., & Coie, J. D. (1990). On the development of aggressive dyadic relationships in boys' peer groups. *Human Development, 33,* 260–270.

Dowd, J. (1990). Ever since Durkheim: The socialization of human development. *Human Development, 33,* 138–159.

Duck, S. W. (1973). *Personal relationships and personal constructs: A study of friendship formation.* London: Wiley.

Duck, S. W. (1990). Relationships as unfinished business: Out of the frying pan and into the 1990's. *Journal of Social and Personal Relationships, 7,* 5–28.

Duck, S. W. (1991a, May). *New lamps for old: A new theory of relationships and a fresh look at some old research.* Paper presented to the Third Conference of the International Network on Personal Relationships, Normal/Bloomington, IL.

Duck, S. W. (1991b). *Understanding relationships.* New York: Guilford Press.

Duck, S. W. (1994). *Meaningful relationships.* London: Sage.

Duck, S. W., & Miell, D. E. (1986). Charting the development of relationships. In R. Gilmour & S. W. Duck (Eds.), *The emerging field of personal relationships.* Hillsdale, NJ: Erlbaum.

Duck, S. W., Rutt, D. J., Hurst, M., & Strejc, H. (1991). Some evident truths about conversations in everyday relationships: All communications are not created equal. *Human Communication Research, 18,* 228–267.

Dunn, J. (1984). *Sisters and brothers.* London: Fontana.

Dunn, J., & Kendrick, C. (1982). *Siblings.* Cambridge: Harvard University Press.

Dunn, J., & Munn, P. (1985). Becoming a family member: Family conflict and the development of social understanding. *Child Development, 56,* 480–492.

Dunn, J., Slomkowski, C., & Beardsall, L. (1994). Sibling relationships from the preschool period through middle childhood and early adolescence. *Developmental Psychology, 30,* 315–324.

Dweck, C. S. (1981). Social-cognitive processes in children's friendships. In S. R. Asher & J. M. Gottman (Eds.), *The development of children's friendships.* Cambridge: Cambridge University Press.

Eder, D., & Hallinan, M. T. (1978). Sex differences in children's friendships. *American Sociological Review, 43,* 237–250.

Edwards, D., & Middleton, D. (1988). Conversational remembering and family relationships: How children learn to remember. *Journal of Social and Personal Relations, 5,* 3–25.

Eisenberg, A. R., & Garvey, C. (1981). Children's use of verbal strategies in resolving conflicts. *Discourse Processes, 4,* 149–170.

Elder, G. (1984). Families, kin and the life course: A sociological perspective. In R. D. Parke (Ed.), *Review of child development research: Vol. 7. The family.* Chicago: University of Chicago Press.

Elicker, J., Englund, M., & Scroufe, L. A. (1992). Predicting peer competence and peer relationships in children from early parent–child relationships. In R. D. Parke & G. W. Ladd (Eds.), *Family–peer relationships: Modes of linkage.* Hillsdale, NJ: Erlbaum.

Elkind, D. (1981). *Children and adolescents: Interpretive essays on Jean Piaget* (3rd ed.). New York: Oxford University Press.

Elkind, D., & Weiner, I. B. (1978). *The development of the child.* New York: Wiley.

Ellis, S., Rogoff, B., & Cromer, C. (1981). Age segregation in children's social interactions. *Developmental Psychology, 17,* 399–407.

Emde, R. (1994). Individuality, context, and the search for meaning. *Child Development, 65,* 719–737.

Ericsson, K. A., & Simon, H. A. (1980). Verbal reports as data. *Psychological Review, 87,* 215–251.

Erikson, E. (1950). *Childhood and society.* New York: Norton.

Eron, L. D. (1982). Parent–child interaction, television violence, and aggression of children. *American Psychologist, 37,* 197–211.

Erwin, P. (1985). Similarity of attitudes and constructs in children's friendships. *Journal of Experimental Child Psychology, 40,* 470–485.

Featherman, D. L., & Lerner, R. M. (1985). Ontogenesis and sociogenesis: Problematics for theory and research about development and socialization across the lifespan. *American Sociological Review, 50,* 659–676.

Ferguson, G. A. (1976). *Statistical analysis in psychology and education* (4th ed.). New York: McGraw-Hill.

Finnie, V., & Russell, A. (1988). Preschool children's social status and their mothers' behavior and knowledge in the supervisory role. *Developmental Psychology, 24,* 789–801.

Fischer, K. W., & Bullock, D. (1984a). Cognitive development in middle childhood: Conclusions and new directions. In W. A. Collins & K. Heller (Eds.), *The elementary school years: Understanding development during middle childhood.* Washington, DC: National Academy Press.

Fischer, K. W., & Bullock, D. (1984b). Cognitive development in school-age children: Conclusions and new directions. In W. A. Collins (Ed.), *Development during middle childhood: The years from six to twelve.* Washington, DC: National Academy Press.

Flavell, J. H. (1963). *The developmental psychology of Jean Piaget.* New York: Van Nostrand Reinhold.

Flavell, J. H. (1981). On cognitive development: Presidential address, Society for Research in Child Development, Boston, Massachusetts, April 2–5, 1981. *Child Development, 53,* 1–10.

Flavell, J. H. (1985). *Cognitive development* (2nd ed.). Englewood Cliffs, NJ: Prentice-Hall.

Fogel, A. (1993). *Developing through relationships: Origins of communication, self, and culture.* New York: Harvester.

Foster, S. L., DeLawyer, D. D., & Guevremont, D. C. (1986). A critical incidents analysis of liked and disliked peer behaviors and their situational parameters in childhood and adolescence. *Behavioral Assessment, 8,* 115–133.

Frank, S. J., Avery, C. B., & Laman, M. S. (1988). Young adults' perceptions of their relationships with their parents: Individual differences in connectedness, competence, and emotional autonomy. *Developmental Psychology, 24,* 729–737.

Fuligni, A., & Eccles, J. S. (1993). Perceived parent–child relationships and early adolescents' orientation toward peers. *Developmental Psychology, 29,* 622–632.

Furman, W., & Bierman, K. L. (1984). Children's conceptions of friendship: A multimethod study of developmental changes. *Developmental Psychology, 20,* 925–931.

Furman, W., & Buhrmester, D. (1985a). Children's perceptions of the personal relationships in their social networks. *Developmental Psychology, 21,* 1016–1024.

Furman, W., & Buhrmester, D. (1985b). Children's perceptions of the qualities of sibling relationships. *Child Development, 56,* 448–461.

Furman, W., & Buhrmester, D. (1992). Age and sex differences in perceptions of networks of personal relationships. *Child Development, 63,* 103–115.

Furstenburg, F. S. (1985). Sociological ventures in child development. *Child Development, 56,* 281–288.

Furth, H. G. (1980). *The world of grown-ups: Children's conceptions of society.* New York: Elsevier.

Garfinkel, H. (1967). *Studies in ethnomethodology.* Englewood Cliffs, NJ: Prentice-Hall.

Gaskins, S., Miller, P. J., & Corsaro, W. A. (1992). Theoretical and methodological perspectives in the interpretive study of children. In W. A. Corsaro & P. J. Miller (Eds.), *Interpretive approaches to children's socialization*. San Francisco: Jossey-Bass.

Genishi, C., & Di Paolo, M. (1982). Learning through argument in a preschool. In L. C. Wilkinson (Ed.), *Communicating in the classroom*. New York: Academic Press.

Gibson, E. J. (1969). *Principles of perceptual learning and development*. New York: Appleton-Century-Crofts.

Gibson, J. J. (1979). *The ecological approach to visual perception*. London: Houghton-Mifflin.

Giddens, A. (1984). *The constitution of society*. Cambridge: Polity Press.

Ginsberg, D., Gottman, J. M., & Parker, J. G. (1986). The importance of friendship. In J. M. Gottman and J. G. Parker (Eds.), *Conversations of friends*. Cambridge: Cambridge University Press.

Glick, J. G. (1978). Cognition and social cognition: An introduction. In J. G. Glick & A. Clarke-Stewart (Eds.), *The development of social understanding*. New York: Gardner Press.

Gnepp, J., & Gould, M. E. (1985). The development of personalized inferences: Understanding other people's emotional reactions in light of their prior experiences. *Child Development, 56,* 1455–1464.

Goffman, E. (1959). *The presentation of self in everyday life*. New York: Doubleday.

Goffman, E. (1967). *Interaction ritual*. New York: Doubleday.

Goffman, E. (1983). The interaction order. *American Sociological Review, 18,* 1–17.

Golding, W. (1954). *Lord of the flies*. London: Faber & Faber.

Gottman, J. E. (1983). How children become friends. *Monographs of the Society for Research in Child Development, 48* (3, Serial No. 201).

Gottman, J. M. (1986). The world of coordinated play: Same and cross-sex friendship in young children. In J. M. Gottman & J. G. Parker (Eds.), *Conversations of friends: Speculations on effective development*. Cambridge: Cambridge University Press.

Gottman, J. M., Gonso, J., & Rasmussen, B. (1975). Social interaction, social competence, and friendship in children. *Child Development, 46,* 709–718.

Gottman, J. M., & Mettetal, G. (1986). Speculations about social and affective development: Friendship and acquaintanceship through adolescence. In J. M. Gottman & J. G. Parker (Eds.), *Conversations of friends: Speculations on affective development*. Cambridge: Cambridge University Press.

Gottman, J. M., & Parkhurst, J. (1980). A developmental theory of friendship and acquaintanceship processes. In W. A. Collins (Ed.), *Minnesota Symposia on Child Psychology* (Vol. 13). Hillsdale, NJ: Erlbaum.

Graham-Bernmann, S. A., Cutler, S. E., Litzenberger, B. W., & Schwartz, W. E. (1994). Perceived conflict and violence in childhood sibling relationships and later emotional adjustment. *Journal of Family Psychology, 8,* 85–97.

Gresham, F. M. (1981). Validity of social skills measures for assessing social competence in low-status children: A multivariate investigation. *Developmental Psychology, 17,* 390–398.

Gresham, F. M. (1986). Conceptual issues in the assessment of social competence in children. In P. S. Strain, M. J. Guralnick & H. M. Walker (Eds.), *Children's social behavior development, assessment, and modification*. Orlando, FL: Academic Press.

Gronlund, N. W. (1955). The relative stability of classroom social status with unweighted and weighted sociometric choice. *Journal of Educational Psychology, 46*, 345–354.

Hallinan, M. (1981). Recent advances in sociometry. In S. Asher & J. Gottman (Eds.), *The development of children's friendships*. New York: Cambridge University press.

Hamlyn, D. (1982). What exactly is social about the origins of understanding? In G. Butterworth & P. Light (Eds.), *Social cognition: Studies in the development of social understanding*. Chicago: University of Chicago Press.

Harré, R. (1977). Friendship as an accomplishment: An ethnographic approach to social relationships. In S. Duck (Ed.), *Theory and practice in interpersonal attraction*. London: Academic Press.

Harré, R., & Secord, P. F. (1973). *The explanation of social behavior*. Totowa, NJ: Littlefield, Adams & Co.

Harris, P., & Olthof, T. (1982). The child's conception of emotion. In G. Butterworth & P. Light (Eds.), *Social cognition: Studies of the development of understanding*. Brighton, England: Harvester.

Hartup, W. W. (1974). Aggression in childhood: Developmental perspectives. *American Psychologist, 29*, 336–341.

Hartup, W. W. (1978). Children and their friends. In H. McGurk (Ed.), *Child social development*. London: Methuen.

Hartup, W. W. (1979). The social worlds of childhood. *American Psychologist, 34*, 944–950.

Hartup, W. W. (1983). Peer relations. In E. M. Hetherington (Ed.), P. H. Mussen (Series Ed.), *Handbook of child psychology: Vol. 4. Socialization, personality, and social development*. New York: Wiley.

Hartup, W. W., French, D. C., Laursen, B., Johnston, M. K., & Ogawa, J. R. (1993). Conflict and friendship relations in middle childhood: Behavior in a closed-field situation. *Child Development, 64*, 445–454.

Hartup, W. W., Laursen, B., Stewart, M. I., & Eastensen, B. (1988). Conflict and the friendship relations of young children. *Child Development, 59*, 1590–1600.

Harvey, J. H., Weber, A. L., & Orbuch, T. L. (1990). *Interpersonal accounts: A social psychological perspective*. Oxford: Basil Blackwell.

Haste, H. (1987). Growing into rules. In J. Bruner & H. Haste (Eds.), *Making sense: The child's construction of the world*. London: Methuen.

Hay, D. F., & Ross, H. S. (1982). The social nature of early conflict. *Child Development, 53*, 105–113.

Heider, F. (1958). *The psychology of interpersonal relations*. New York: Wiley.

Hernandez, D. J. (1993). *America's children: Resources from family, government and the economy*. New York: Russell Sage Foundation.

Hinde, R. A. (1979). *Towards understanding relationships*. London: Academic Press.

Hinde, R. A. (1987). *Individuals. relationships and culture: Links between ethology and the social sciences.* Cambridge: Cambridge University Press.

Hinde, R. A. (1992). Developmental psychology in the context of older behavioral sciences. *Developmental Psychology, 28,* 1018–1029.

Hoffman, M. L. (1963). Child-rearing practices and moral development: Generalizations for empirical research. *Child Development, 34,* 295–318.

Hoffman, M. L. (1975). Altruistic behavior and the parent–child relationship. *Journal of Personality and Social Psychology, 31,* 937–943.

Hoffman, M. L. (1983). Empathy, guilt and social cognition. In W. F. Overton (Ed.), *The relationship between social and cognitive development.* Hillsdale, NJ: Erlbaum.

Howes, C. (1990). Social status and friendship from kindergarten to third grade. *Journal of Applied Developmental Psychology, 11,* 321–330.

Humphrey, N. (1976). The social function of intellect. In P. Bateson, & R. A. Hinde (Eds.), *Growing points in ethology.* Cambridge: Cambridge University Press.

Hunter, F., & Youniss, J. (1982). Changes in functions of three relations during adolescence. *Developmental Psychology, 18,* 806–811.

Jones, G. P., & Dembo, M. H. (1989). Age and sex role differences in intimate friendships during childhood and adolescence. *Merrill-Palmer Quarterly, 35,* 445–462.

Kandel, E. R. (1991). Brain and behavior. In E. R. Kandel, J. H. Schwartz, & T. M. Lessell (Eds.), *Principles of neural science* (3rd ed.). Norwalk, CT: Appleton and Lange.

Kandel, D. B., & Lesser, G. S. (1972). *Youth in two worlds.* San Francisco: Jossey-Bass.

Kassin, S. M., & Pryor, J. B. (1985). The development of attribution processes. In J. B. Pryor & J. D. Day (Eds.), *The development of social cognition.* New York: Springer-Verlag.

Kelly, G. A. (1955). *The psychology of personal constructs.* New York: Norton.

Kendrick, C., & Dunn, J. (1983). Sibling quarrels and maternal responses. *Developmental Psychology, 19,* 62–70.

King, C. A., & Young, D. (1981). Peer popularity and peer communication patterns: Hyperactive versus active but normal boys. *Journal of Child Psychology, 9,* 465–482.

Kiss, G. R. (1972). *Recursive concept analysis.* Unpublished manuscript, University of Edinburgh, Scotland. MRC Speech and Communication Unit, Edinburgh, Scotland.

Kohlberg, L. (1969). Stage and sequence: The cognitive developmental approach to socialization. In D. A. Goslin (Ed.), *The handbook of socialization theory and research.* Chicago: Rand McNally.

Kohn, M., & Clausen, J. (1955). Social isolation and schizophrenia. *American Sociological Review, 20,* 265–273.

Kramer, L., & Gottman, J. M. (1992). Becoming a sibling: "with a little help from my friends." *Developmental Psychology, 28,* 685–699.

Kuczynski, L., Kochanska, G., Radke-Yarrow, M., & Girnius-Brown, O. (1987). A developmental interpretation of young children's noncompliance. *Developmental Psychology, 23,* 799–806.

Ladd, G. W. (1983). Social networks of popular, average, and rejected children in school settings. *Merrill-Palmer Quarterly, 29,* 283–307.

Ladd, G. W. (1992). Themes and theories: Perspectives on processes in family-peer relationships. In R. D. Parke & G. W. Ladd (Eds.), *Family–peer relationships: Modes of linkage.* Hillsdale, NJ: Erlbaum.

Ladd, G. W., & Crick, N. R. (1989). Probing the psychological environment: Children's cognitions, perceptions, and feelings in the peer culture. In M. L. Maehr & C. Ames (Eds.), *Advances in motivation and achievement: Motivation enhancing environments* (Vol. 6). Greenwich, CT: JAI Press.

La Gaipa, J. J., & Wood, H. D. (1985). An Eriksonian approach to conceptions of friendship of aggressive and withdrawn preadolescent girls. *Journal of Early Adolescence, 5,* 357–369.

La Greca, A. M. (1990). *Through the eyes of the child.* Needham Heights, MA: Allyn & Bacon.

Larson, R., Ham, M., & Raffaelli, M. (1989). The nurturance of motivated attention in the daily experience of children and adolescence. In M. L. Maehr & C. Ames (Eds.), *Advances in motivation and achievement: Motivation enhancing environments* (Vol. 6). Greenwich, CT: JAI Press.

Laucht, M., & Schmidt, M. H. (1987). Psychiatric disorders at age 13: Results and problems of a long-term study. In B. Cooper (Ed.), *Psychiatric epidemiology.* London: Cooper Helm.

Lerner, R. M. (1992). Dialectics, developmental contextualism, and the further enhancement of theory about puberty and psychosocial development. *Journal of Early Adolescence, 12,* 366–388.

Lever, J. (1976). Sex differences in the games children play. *Social Problems, 23,* 479–487.

Lewin, K. (1935). *A dynamic theory of personality.* New York: McGraw-Hill.

Lewin, K. (1943). Defining the field at a given time. *Psychological Review, 50,* 292–310.

Liddle, G. P. (1962). Psychological factors involved in dropping out of school. *The High School Journal, 45,* 276–280.

Light, P. (1979). *The development of social sensitivity: A study of social aspects of role-taking in young children.* Cambridge: Cambridge University Press.

Livesley, W. J., & Bromley, D. B. (1973). *Person perception in childhood and adolescence.* London: Wiley.

Loeber, R. (1990). Development and risk factors of juvenile antisocial behavior and delinquency. *Clinical Psychology Review, 10,* 1–41.

Londerville, S., & Main, M. (1981). Security of attachment, compliance, and maternal training methods in the second year of life. *Developmental Psychology, 17,* 289–299.

Maccoby, E. E. (1984a). Middle childhood in the context of the family. In A. Collins (Ed.), *Development during childhood: The years from six to twelve.* Washington DC: National Academy Press.

Maccoby, E. E. (1984b). Socialization and developmental change. *Child Development, 55,* 317–328.

Maccoby, E. E. (1990). Gender and relationships: A developmental account. *American Psychologist, 45,* 513–520.

Maccoby, E. E., & Jacklin, C. N. (1987). Gender segregation in childhood. In H. W. Reese (Ed.), *Advances in child development and behavior* (Vol. 20). Orlando, FL: Academic Press.

Maccoby, E. E., & Martin, J. A. (1983). Socialization in the context of the family: Parent–child interaction. In E. M. Hetherington (Ed.), P. H. Mussen (Series Ed.), *Handbook of child psychology: Vol. 4. Socialization, personality, and social development* (4th ed.). New York: Wiley.

Mannarino, A. P. (1976). Friendship patterns and altruistic behavior in preadolescent males. *Developmental Psychology, 12,* 555–556.

Mannarino, A. P. (1980). The development of children's friendships. In H. C. Foot, A. J. Chapman, & J. R. Smith (Eds.), *Friendship and social relations in children.* Chichester, England: Wiley.

Masters, J. C., & Furman, W. (1981). Popularity, individual friendship selection and specific peer interaction. *Developmental Psychology, 17,* 344–350.

Mayr, E. (1974). Behavior programs and evolutionary strategies. *American Scientist, 62,* 650–659.

McAdams, D. P. (1993). *The stories we live by: Personal myths and the making of the self.* New York: Morrow.

McCall, G. (1982). Becoming unrelated: The management of bond dissolution. In S. W. Duck (Ed.), *Personal relationships 4: Dissolving personal relationships.* London: Academic Press.

McCoy, C. L., & Masters, J. C. (1985). The development of children's strategies for the social control of emotion. *Child Development, 56,* 1214–1222.

McCoy, J. K., Brody, G. H., & Stoneman, Z. (1994). A longitudinal analysis of sibling relationships as mediators of the link between family processes and youths' best friendships. *Family Relations, 43,* 400–408.

McDavid, J. W., & Harari, H. (1966). Stereotyping of names and popularity in grade-school children. *Child Development, 37,* 453–459.

McGuire, K. D., & Weisz, J. R. (1982). Social cognition and behavior correlates of preadolescent chumship. *Child Development, 53,* 1478–1484.

Mead, G. H. (1934). *Mind, self and society.* Chicago: University of Chicago Press.

Miell, D. E. (1987). Remembering relationship development: Constructing a context for interactions. In R. Burnett, P. McGee, & D. Clarke (Eds.), *Accounting for relationships.* London: Methuen.

Minuchin, P. (1985). Families and individual development: Provocations from the field of family therapy. *Child Development, 56,* 289–302.

Montemayor, R., & Hanson, E. (1985). A naturalistic view of conflict between adolescents and their parents and siblings. *Journal of Early Adolescence, 5,* 23–30.

Morrison, P., & Masten, A. S. (1991). Peer reputation in middle childhood as a predictor of adaptation in adolescence: A seven-year follow-up. *Child Development, 62,* 991–1007.

Myers, J. L., & Well, A. D. (1991). *Research design and statistical analysis.* New York: Harper Collins.

Nelson, J., & Aboud, F. E. (1985). The resolution of social conflict between friends. *Child Development, 56,* 1009–1017.

Nelson, K., & Gruendel, J. (1981). Generalized event representation: Building blocks of cognitive development. In M. Lamb & A. L. Brown (Eds.), *Advances in developmental psychology* (Vol. 1). Hillsdale, NJ: Erlbaum.

Newcomb, A. F., & Bagwell, C. L. (1995). Children's friendship relations: A meta-analytic review. *Psychological Bulletin, 117,* 306–347.

Newcomb, A. F., & Brady, J. E. (1982). Mutuality in boys' friendship relations. *Child Development, 53,* 392–395.

Newman, D. (1986). The role of mutual knowledge in the development of perspective taking. *Developmental Review, 6,* 122–145.

Newson, J., & Newson, E. (1976). *Seven years old in the home environment.* New York: Wiley.

Oden, S., & Asher, S. R. (1977). Coaching children in social skills for friendship making. *Child Development, 48,* 495–506.

Oden, S., Herzberger, S., Mangione, P. L., & Wheeler, V. A. (1984). Children's peer relationships: An examination of social processes. In J. C. Masters & K. Yarkin-Levin (Eds.), *Boundary areas in social and developmental psychology.* New York: Academic Press.

Olweus, D. (1978). *Aggression in the schools: Bullies and whipping boys.* Washington, DC: Hemisphere.

Palazzoli, M. S., Cecchin, G., Prata, G., & Boscolo, L. (1978). *Paradox and counterparadox: A new model in the therapy of the family in schizophrenic transaction.* New York: Jason Aronson.

Parke, R. D., Cassidy, J., Burks, V. M., Carson, J. L., & Boyum, L. (1992). Familial contribution to peer competence among young children: The role of interactive and affective processes. In R. D. Parke & G. W. Ladd (Eds.), *Family–peer relationships: Modes of linkage.* Hillsdale, NJ: Erlbaum.

Parker, J. G., & Asher, S. R. (1993). Friendship and friendship quality in middle childhood: Links with peer group acceptance and feelings of loneliness and social dissatisfaction. *Developmental Psychology, 29,* 611–621.

Parsons, T. (1937). *The structure of social action.* New York: McGraw-Hill.

Parsons, T. (1955). Family structure and the socialization of the child. In T. Parsons & R. Bales (Eds.), *Family, socialization and interaction process.* New York: Free Press.

Patterson, G. L., DeBaryshe, B. D., & Ramsey, E. (1989). A developmental perspective on antisocial behavior. *American Psychologist, 44,* 329–335.

Peery, J. C. (1979). Popular, amiable, isolated, rejected: A reconceptualization of sociometric status in preschool children. *Child Development, 50,* 1231–1234.

Peevers, H. B., & Secord, P. F. (1973). Developmental changes in attribution of descriptive concepts to persons. *Journal of Personality and social Psychology, 27,* 120–128.

Pellarin, S. M. (1988). *Popularity and friendship in middle childhood: A conceptual approach.* Unpublished masters thesis, Laurentian University, Sudbury, Ontario.

Pellegrini, D. (1985). Social cognition and competence in middle childhood. *Child Development, 56,* 253–264.

Perry, D. G., & Bussey, K. (1984). *Social development.* Englewood Cliffs, NJ: Prentice-Hall.

Peterson, G. W., & Rollins, B. R. (1987). Parent–child socialization, In M. B. Sussman & S. K. Steinmetz (Eds.), *Handbook of marriage and the family.* New York: Plenum.

Pettit, G. S., Bakshi, A., Dodge, K. A., & Coie, J. D. (1990). The emergence of school dominance in young boys' play groups: Developmental differences and behavioral correlates. *Developmental Psychology, 26,* 1017–1025.

Piaget, J. (1965). *The moral judgement of the child.* London: Routledge & Kegan Paul. (Original work published 1932)

Piaget, J. (1970). *Genetic epistemology* (E. Duckworth, Trans.). New York: Columbia University Press.

Piaget, J. (1985). *The equilibrium of cognitive structures.* Chicago: University of Chicago Press.

Piaget, J., & Inhelder, B. (1956). *The child's conception of space* (F. J. Langdon & E. L. Lunzer, Trans.). London: Routledge & Kegan Paul.

Planalp, S., & Benson, A. (1992). Friends' and acquaintances' conversations 1: Perceived differences. *Journal of Social and Personal Relationships, 9,* 483–506.

Pope, A., Bierman, K. L., & Mumma, G. H. (1991). Aggression, hyperactivity, and inattention–immaturity: Behavior dimensions associated with peer rejection in elementary school boys. *Developmental Psychology, 27,* 663–671.

Price, M. J., & Ladd, G. W. (1986). Assessment of children's friendships: Implications for social competence and social adjustment. In P. J. Prinz (Ed.), *Advances in behavioral assessment of children and families* (Vol. 2). Greenwich, CT: JAI Press.

Putallaz, J. M., & Gottman, J. M. (1981a). An interactional model of children's entry in peer groups. *Child Development, 52,* 986–994.

Putallaz, J. M., & Gottman, J. M. (1981b). Social skills and group acceptance. In S. R. Asher & J. M. Gottman (Eds.), *The development of children's friendships.* New York: Cambridge University Press.

Putallaz, J. M., & Heflin, A. H. (1990). Parent–child interaction. In S. R. Asher & J. D. Coie (Eds.), *Peer rejection in childhood.* Cambridge: Cambridge University Press.

Register, L. M., & Henley, T. B. (1992). The phenomenology of intimacy. *Journal of Social and Personal Relationships, 9,* 467–481.

Reid, M., Landesman, S., Treder, R., & Jaccard, J. (1989). "My family and friends": Six- to twelve-year-old children's perceptions of social support. *Child Development, 60,* 896–910.

Reisman, J. M., & Shorr, S. I. (1978). Friendship claims and expectations among children and adults. *Child Development, 49,* 913–916.

Renshaw, P. D., & Asher, S. R. (1982). Social competence and peer status: The distinction between goals and strategies. In K. Rubin & H. Ross (Eds.), *Peer relationships and social skills in childhood.* New York: Springer-Verlag.

Renshaw, P. D., & Asher, S. R. (1983). Children's goals and strategies for social interaction. *Merrill-Palmer Quarterly, 29,* 353–374.

Robbins, L. C. (1982). Parental recall of child-rearing practices. In U. Neisser (Ed.), *Memory observed: Remembering in natural contexts.* San Francisco: Freeman.

Roff, M. (1961). Childhood social interactions and young adult bad conduct. *Journal of Abnormal Child psychology, 63,* 333–337.

Roff, M., Sells, S. B., & Golden, M. M. (1972). *Social adjustment and personality development in children.* Minneapolis: University of Minnesota Press.

Rogoff, B. (1990). *Apprenticeship in thinking: Cognitive development in social context.* New York: Oxford University Press.

Rolf, J. E. (1976). Peer status and the directionality of symptomatic behavior: Prime social competence predictors of outcome for vulnerable children. *American Journal of Orthopsychiatry, 46,* 74–88.

Rollins, B. C., & Thomas, D. L. (1979). Parental support, power, and control techniques in the socialization of children. In W. R. Burr, R. Hill, F. I. Nye, & I. L. Reiss (Eds.), *Contemporary theories about the family: Vol. 2. General theories/theoretical orientations.* New York: Free Press.

Rubin, K. H., & Krasnor, L. R. (1986). Social-cognitive and social behavioral perspectives on problem solving. In M. Perlmutter (Ed.), *Minnesota Symposia on Child Psychology* (Vol. 18). Hillsdale, NJ: Erlbaum.

Rubin, K. H., LeMare, L. J., & Lollis, S. (1990). Social withdrawal in childhood: Developmental pathways to peer rejection. In S. R. Asher & J. D. Coie (Eds.), *Peer rejection in childhood.* Cambridge: Cambridge University Press.

Rubin, Z. (1973). *Liking and loving: An invitation to social psychology.* New York: Holt, Rinehart & Winston.

Saarni, C. (1977). Children's understanding of display rules for expressive behavior. *Developmental Psychology, 13,* 3–10.

Scarlett, H., Press, A., & Crockett, W. (1971). Children's descriptions of peers: A Wernerian developmental analysis. *Child Development, 44,* 439–453.

Schank, R. C., & Abelson, R. P. (1977). *Scripts, plans, goals, and understanding.* Hillsdale, NJ: Erlbaum.

Schneider, B. H., Wiener, J., & Murphy, K. (1994). Children's friendships: The giant step beyond peer acceptance. *Journal of Social and Personal Relationships, 11,* 323–340.

Schwartz, D., Dodge, K. A., & Coie, J. D. (1993). The emergence of chronic peer victimization in boys' play groups. *Child Development, 64,* 1755–1772.

Selman, R. (1976). Toward a structural analysis of developing interpersonal relations concepts: Research with normal and disturbed preadolescent boys. In A. Pick (Ed.), *Minnesota Symposia on Child Psychology* (Vol. 10). Minneapolis: University of Minnesota Press.

Selman, R. (1980). *The growth of interpersonal understanding: Developmental and clinical analysis.* New York: Academic Press.

Selman, R. (1981). The child as a relationship philosopher. In S. R. Asher & J. M. Gottman (Eds.), *The development of children's friendships.* New York: Cambridge University Press.

Selman, R. L., & Byrne, D. F. (1974). A structural–developmental analysis of levels of role-taking in middle childhood. *Child Development, 45,* 803–806.

Selman, R. L., & Jacquette, D. (1978). Stability and oscillation in interpersonal awareness: A clinical–developmental analysis. In C. B. Keasey (Ed.), *Nebraska Symposium on Motivation* (Vol. 25). Lincoln: University of Nebraska Press.

Shaeffer, E. S. (1965). Children's reports of parental behavior: An inventory. *Child Development, 36,* 413–424.

Shantz, C. U. (1987). Conflicts between children. *Child Development, 58,* 283–305.

Shantz, C. U., & Hobart, C. J. (1989). In T. J. Berndt & G. W. Ladd (Eds.), *Peer relationships in child development.* New York: Wiley.

Sharabany, R., Gershoni, R., & Hofman, J. E. (1981). Girlfriend, boyfriend: Age and sex differences in intimate friendships. *Developmental Psychology, 17,* 809–815.

Shedler, J., & Block, J. (1990). Adolescent drug use and psychological health: A longitudinal inquiry. *American Psychologist, 45,* 612–630.

Sheingold, K., & Tenney, Y. J. (1982). Memory for a salient childhood event. In U. Neisser (Ed.), *Memory observed: Remembering in natural contexts.* San Francisco: Freeman.

Sherif, M., Harvey, O. J., White, B. J., Hood, W. R., & Sherif, C. W. (1961). *Intergroup cooperation and competition: The Robbers Cave experiment.* Norman: University of Oklahoma Press.

Shotter, J., & Newson, J. (1982). An ecological approach to cognitive development: Implicate orders, joint action and intentionality. In G. Butterworth & P. Light (Eds.), *Social cognition: Studies of the development of understanding.* Brighton, England: Harvester.

Shuart, V., & Lewko, J. (1988). Children as coders of social data: A pilot study. *Merrill-Palmer Quarterly, 34,* 89–103.

Singer, J. L., & Singer, D. G. (1981). *Television, imagination, and aggression: A study of preschoolers.* Hillsdale, NJ: Erlbaum.

Slomkowski, C. L., & Dunn, J. (1992). Arguments and relationships within the family: Differences in young children's disputes with mother and sibling. *Developmental Psychology, 28,* 919–924.

Sroufe, L. A., & Rutter, M. (1984). The domain of developmental Psychopathology. *Child Development, 55,* 17–29.

Stein, C. H. (1992). Ties that bind: Three studies of obligation in adult relationships with family. *Journal of Social and Personal Relationships, 9,* 525–547.

Steinberg, L. (1990). Interdependence in the family: Autonomy, conflict and harmony in the parent–adolescent relationship. In S. S. Feldman & G. L. Elliot (Eds.), *At the threshold: The developing adolescent.* Cambridge: Harvard University Press.

Stocker, C. M. (1994). Children's perceptions of relationships with siblings, friends, and mothers: Compensating processes and links with adjustment. *Journal of Child Psychology and Psychiatry, 35,* 1447–1459.

Stoneman, Z., Brody, G. H., & MacKinnon, C. (1984). Naturalistic observations of children's activities and roles while playing with their siblings and friends. *Child Development, 55,* 617–627.

Strayhorn, J. M. (1988). *The competent child: An approach to psychotherapy and preventive mental health.* New York: Guilford Press.

Sullivan, H. S. (1953). *The interpersonal theory of psychiatry.* New York: Norton.

Sutton-Smith, B., & Rosenberg, B. G. (1968). Sibling consensus on power tactics. *Journal of Genetic Psychology, 112,* 63–72.

Tesson, G., Lewko, J. H., & Bigelow, B. J. (1987). The social rules that children use in their interpersonal relations. In J. Meacham (Ed.), *Interpersonal relations: Family, peers, friends.* New York: Karger.

Tesson, G., Lewko, J. H., & Bigelow, B. J. (1990). Adolescent social rule usage in family, peer and adult relationships. In P. A. Adler & P. Adler (Eds.), *Sociological studies of child development* (Vol. 3). Greenwich, CT: JAI Press.

Tesson, G., & Youniss, J. (1995). Microsociology and psychological development: A sociological interpretation of Piaget's theory. In A. A. Ambert (Ed.), *Sociological studies of children* (Vol. 7). Greenwich, CT: JAI Press.

Tisak, M. S. (1986). Children's conceptions of parental authority. *Child Development, 57,* 166–176.

Turiel, E. (1978). The development of concepts of social structure: Social convention. In J. G. Glick & K. A. Clarke-Stewart (Eds.), *The development of social understanding.* New York: Gardner Press.

Urbain, E. S., & Kendall, P. C. (1980). Review of social-cognitive problem-solving interventions with children. *Psychological Bulletin, 88,* 109–143.

Voyat, G. (1978). Cognitive and social development: A new perspective. In J. G. Glick & A. Clarke-Stewart (Eds.), *The development of social understanding.* New York: Gardner Press.

Vygotsky, L. S. (1962). *Thought and language.* Eugenia Hanfmann and Gertrude Vakar (Eds.). Cambridge: M.I.T. Press. (Original work published 1934)

Vygotsky, L. S. (1978). *Mind in society: The development of higher psychological processes.* Cambridge: Harvard University Press.

Waldrop, M. F., & Halverson, C. F. (1975). Intensive and extensive peer behavior: Longitudinal and cross-sectional analyses. *Child Development, 46,* 19–26.

Weber, M. (1968). *Economy and society.* New York: Bebminster Press.

Weiner, B., & Handel, S. J. (1985). A cognition–emotion–action sequence: Anticipated emotional consequences of causal attributions and reported communication strategy. *Developmental Psychology, 21,* 102–107.

Weiss, R. S. (1974). The provisions of social relationships. In Z. Rubin (Ed.), *Doing unto others.* Englewood Cliffs, NJ: Prentice-Hall.

Weisz, J. R. (1980). Autonomy, control, and other reasons why "Mom is the greatest": A content analysis of children's Mother's Day letters. *Child Development, 51,* 801–807.

Wentzel, K. R. (1991). Relations between social competence and academic achievement in early adolescence. *Child Development, 62,* 1066–1078.

Weston, D. R., & Turiel, E. (1980). Act–rule relations: Children's concepts of social rules. *Developmental Psychology, 16,* 417–424.

Wohlwill, J. F. (1973). *The study of behavioral development.* New York: Academic Press.

Wozniak, R. H. (1993). Co-constructive metatheory for psychology: Implications for an analysis of families as specific social contexts for development. In R. H. Wozniak & K. W. Fischer (Eds.), *Development in context: Acting and thinking in specific environments.* Hillsdale, NJ: Erlbaum.

Wozniak, R. H., & Fischer, K. W. (1993). Development in context: An introduction. In R. H. Wozniak & K. W. Fischer (Eds.), *Development in context: Acting and thinking in specific environments.* Hillsdale, NJ: Erlbaum.

Youniss, J. (1978). The nature of social development: A conceptual discussion of cognition. In H. McGurk (Ed.), *Issues in childhood social development.* London: Methuen.

Youniss, J. (1980). *Parents and peers in social development.* Chicago: University of Chicago Press.

Youniss, J., & Smollar, J. (1985). *Adolescent relations with mothers, fathers, and friends.* Chicago: University of Chicago Press.

Youniss, J., & Volpe, J. (1978). A relational analysis of children's friendships. In W. Damon (Ed.), *Social cognition.* San Francisco: Jossey-Bass.

Zajonc, R. B., & Markus, G. B. (1975). Birth order and intellectual development. *Psychological Review, 82,* 74–88.

Zarabatany, L., Hartmann, D. P., & Rankin, D. B. (1990). The psychological functions of preadolescent peer activities. *Child Development, 61,* 1067–1080.

Author Index

Subject Index